Building a Citizens' Partnership in Democratic Governance

Building a Citizens' Partnership in Democratic Governance

The Delhi Bhagidari Process
through Large-group Dynamics

George Koreth
Kiron Wadhera

SAGE   www.sagepublications.com
Los Angeles • London • New Delhi • Singapore • Washington DC

First published in 2013 by

SAGE Publications India Pvt Ltd
B1/I-1 Mohan Cooperative Industrial Area
Mathura Road, New Delhi 110 044, India
www.sagepub.in

SAGE Publications Inc
2455 Teller Road
Thousand Oaks, California 91320, USA

SAGE Publications Ltd
1 Oliver's Yard, 55 City Road
London EC1Y 1SP, United Kingdom

SAGE Publications Asia-Pacific Pte Ltd
33 Pekin Street
#02-01 Far East Square
Singapore 048763

Published by Vivek Mehra for SAGE Publications India Pvt Ltd, Phototypeset in 10/12 Berkeley by RECTO Graphics, Delhi, and printed at Saurabh Printer Pvt. Ltd.

Library of Congress Cataloging-in-Publication Data

Koreth, George, 1941–
    Building a citizens' partnership in democratic governance: the Delhi Bhagidari process through large-group dynamics/George Koreth, Kiron Wadhera.
        pages cm
    Includes bibliographical references and index.
    1. Municipal government—India—Delhi—Citizen participation. 2. Political participation—India—Delhi. 3. Democracy—India—Delhi. 4. Public administration—India—Delhi—Citizen participation. 5. Civil service—India—New Delhi I. Wadhera, Kiron. II. Title.
JS7065.D4K67   323'.042095456—dc23   2013   2013011295

ISBN: 978-81-321-1137-5 (HB)

The SAGE Team: Rudra Narayan, Shreya Chakraborti, Anju Saxena and Rajinder Kaur

This book is dedicated to the citizens of Delhi and to all the democracies around the world where citizens want to move into active partnership in governance, beyond merely voting periodically.

It is also dedicated to Barbara Bunker, Billie Alban, and Marvin Weisbord, pioneers in "multistakeholder large-group dynamics," who helped "discover common ground" among divergent and opposing interests.

Without the reliable processes and designs developed by them, this book describing the project of a citywide change in democratic governance would not have been possible.

Contents

List of Illustrations

Tables

Figures

Box

List of Appendices

List of Abbreviations

ACORD	Asian Centre for Organisation Research and Development
ACR	Annual Confidential Report
ADAG	Anil Dhirubhai Ambani Group
ASSOCHAM	Associated Chambers of Commerce and Industry
BRPL	BSES Rajdhani Power Limited
BRT	Bus Rapid Transit
BYPL	BSES Yamuna Power Limited
CAS	Conditional Access System
CCS	Citizen-centric Services
CEO	Chief Executive Officer
CFL	Compact Fluorescent Lamp
CGWB	Central Ground Water Board
CII	Confederation of Indian Industries
CM	Chief Minister
CMO	Chief Minister's Office
CNG	Compressed Natural Gas
CPWD	Central Public Works Department
CRO	Customer Relations Officer
CS	Chief Secretary
CSR	Corporate Social Responsibility
DC	Deputy Commissioner
DDA	Delhi Development Authority
DERC	Delhi Electricity Regulatory Commission
Discoms	Distribution Companies (for electricity)
DJB	Delhi Jal Board
DoEF	Department of Environment and Forests
DP	Delhi Police
DSS	Door Step Services
DTC	Delhi Transport Corporation
DVB	Delhi Vidyut Board

EDP	Electronic Data Processing
ENT	Ear, Nose, and Throat
ETP	Effluent Treatment Plant
F & S	Food & Supplies
FDI	Foreign Direct Investment
FGDs	Focus Group Discussions
FICCI	Federation of Indian Chambers of Commerce & Industry
GIA	Grant-in-Aid
GIS	Geographical Information System
HoD	Head of Department
HT	High Tension
HVDS	High Voltage Distribution System
IAS	Indian Administrative Service
ID	Identification
IEC	Information, Education, Communication
Info-Pack	Information Package
IT	Information Technology
IGL	Indraprastha Gas Limited
KM	Kilometer
LCD	Liquid Crystal Display
LGIP	Large-group Interactive Process
Max-Mix	Maximum-Mix (of stakeholders)
MCD	Municipal Corporation of Delhi
MGD	Million Gallons Per Day
MIS	Management Information System
MLAs	Members of the Legislative Assembly
MoU	Memorandum of Understanding
MPs	Members of Parliament
MTAs	Market and Traders Associations
MTs	Metric Tons
MW	Megawatt
NCR	National Capital Region
NCT	National Capital Territory (of Delhi)
NDMC	New Delhi Municipal Council
NDPL	North Delhi Power Limited
NGOs	non-governmental organizations
NOC	No Objection Certificate
NTL	National Training Labs
PA	Public Address
PDS	Public Distribution System (Food Rations)
PGC	Public Grievances Commission

PHDCCI	Punjab, Haryana, Delhi Chamber of Commerce and Industry
PIL	Public Interest Litigation
PNG	Piped Natural Gas
PPP	public–private partnership
PR	Public Relations
PVC	Polyvinyl Chloride
ROCE	Return on Capital Employed
RT	radio taxi
RTI	Right to Information
RWAs	Residents' Welfare Associations
SCAs	Senior Citizens' Associations
SEA	South East Asia
SLA	Service Level Agreements
SMS	Short Message Service
SPM	Suspended Particulate Matter
SPV	Special Purpose Vehicle
ST	Support Team
STP	Sewage Treatment Plant
T&D	Transmission and Distribution
TOI	Times of India
TPDDL	Tata Power Delhi Distribution Company
TRANSCO	Transmission Company
UGR	Underground Reservoirs
VAT	Value Added Tax
VKS	Vidyalaya Kalyan Samiti
UN	United Nations

Foreword: The Genesis of "Bhagidari"[1]

It was in the winter of 1998 when Delhi wore the exuberance of December weather and the new year was just a fortnight away. Ms Sheila Dikshit, who had taken over as the chief minister (CM) of Delhi just a week ago, called me in for a discussion. I had just assumed charge as her principal secretary.

Handing me the Election Manifesto, on the basis of which she had campaigned, Ms Dikshit said she wanted to plan her five years in office. Five years? Why not more? The dominant thought was that to aim for more would be to try and escape history. No party had been voted to power for the second term in Delhi. Of course, Ms Dikshit did believe in setting long-term goals, but she wanted quick short-term results. She also wanted to function with transparency and openness.

In making her intent clear, Ms Dikshit had created a friendly space, a space without discord. We spoke of two CMs; one of Madhya Pradesh and one of Andhra Pradesh who could win a second term in office. Was there anything common in their success? Was there a strategy that could make the template? Both of them worked directly with the people; one with the idea of Panchayati Raj and the other through information technology. Both these tools were geared toward the unification of aspirations of the people.

While many administrative points worthy of discussion were thrown up, we picked up two major umbrella factors: (i) the importance of capturing the people's imagination and (ii) ensuring people's participation in all schemes of the government and therefore in governance itself.

The second point appeared very important to Ms Dikshit. She was very keen and emphatic that she wanted peoples' active participation in

---

[1] "Bhagidari" in Hindi means partnership and refers to citizens' partnership with the government.

all her programs. The first aspect would find space for itself within the second at most times.

The idea, though desirable, posed a great challenge because peoples' participation is read as given in the process of election and through elected representatives. And then there is a procedure followed for any scheme to be launched. Generally, schemes in government are drawn up based on the felt need of the people as perceived by the ministers or senior officials, and sometimes after discussion with a few more elected representatives in the field. The need turns into a public reality after a series of steps through which concurrence of the concerned departments is obtained; the concurrence depends as much on the need of the scheme as on the availability of finance. Once all these clearances are in place, Cabinet approvals are sought and then the schemes are implemented. Though the need for planning at the grassroots level is often insisted upon for drawing up any scheme, it was observed more in breach than in actual practice. Peoples' participation is still a far cry.

Delhi's population was around 12 million in 1998, the year Ms Dikshit came to power. The question was how to involve all these people when they are not organized in recognizable bipartisan groups? Of course there were professional associations, groups, and bodies affiliated to political parties, but would they serve our purpose? Further, the population of Delhi was not and is still not homogenous. A culture where diverse goals are central to society presented a great challenge to any single strand of thought. People come from different states of India, income disparities are stark, living standards are widely different, people live in authorized and unauthorized colonies, rural areas and slums—the medley was mind boggling. Yet an answer had to be found.

In search of answers, I met many officials, thinkers, and people from different walks of life. In one discussion I had with the then Lt. Governor Shri Vijay Kapoor, another important question was raised. There was no provision in the Constitution for the direct participation of people in governance. It was only through elected representatives that people voiced themselves. How then will this idea be positioned?

Shri Vijay Kapoor also spoke the voice of caution. He said that the Delhi Development Authority (DDA) had recognized many Resident Welfare Associations (RWAs) in Delhi. They were not functioning to any measure of efficiency. So participation from the people though enthusiastic in spirit may be tardy in reality.

To me, this discussion was invaluable. Though I realized the Constitution did not make provision for people's participation in specific terms, there is also no provision in the Constitution barring people's participation or consultation with them. I also recorded that the RWAs would be my contact points. To invigorate them and to work through them as our windows into the society of Delhi could be a possibility.

The brainstorming continued. We held consultations and discussions with officials, professional bodies, public relations (PR) agencies, and many others in opinion building. The idea was new and so when presented was considered by many to be too idealistic. As is true for all ideas, this too had met with resistance ranging from total rejection to periodic flagging of spirits and conviction. I was used to this. Any large exercise is bound to go through these troughs and highs, and my experience when I had launched the "Education for All" program in Delhi, as Secretary Education in the year 1994, had equipped me to handle them.

The idea had one more sharp edge: was it a political stunt? An extended election-oriented act of tokenism? This cynicism made it all the more challenging to work across the board.

Both the factors above made some basic action points clear:

1. We target smaller and doable projects so that all the promises made are fulfilled. One failure would completely demolish the project. And one success, however small, would catch on like fire and galvanize it.
2. We address problems that are common, in some degree, to all people.
3. The first group we would work with would be smaller with no political identity.
4. We need to ensure the participation of my colleagues from different departments, addressing their misgivings and sometimes giving that extra push. Their willing participation was vital to the success of the program.
5. The deputy commissioner should be the pivotal point for implementing the program, coordinating with the people, departments, and elected representatives.

Against this background, it was decided that people's participation will be confined to identifying the major problems besetting them across the board in the first instance. Viewing the initial exercises as experiments, a further course of action could be charted out. The second major point was to identify a few RWAs as the points of contact and as the first group.

RWAs in authorized colonies and rural areas existed in different forms and they could be consulted for this exercise. Delhi having grown in all directions had led to a large number of diverse RWAs. How would one juxtapose a program aimed at individual participation with the amplification of numbers? How do we ensure the participation of all the RWAs? These were the questions that were yet to be answered.

Moving toward greater functional clarity, we engaged in dialogue with many thinking citizens of Delhi/India and others. One important suggestion came from Dr Jaya Indiresan and Professor P. V. Indiresan, educationists of repute. They suggested consulting Asian Centre for Organisation Research and Development (ACORD). Thus ACORD, a not-for-profit organization, which had done research in Large-group Interactive Process (LGIP) was called in. They, Professor George Koreth, the chairman of the board of governors, and Dr Kiron Wadhera, the CEO, spelt out the details of "Large-group Dynamics" through multiple stakeholders. It seemed to meet with most of our requirements.

After a few more discussions, ACORD was identified to provide solutions to the daunting task of involving peoples' participation in governance. Professor Koreth and Dr Kiron Wadhera explained to me the success story of Mexico where consultation was done by the mayor of the city with a large number of people on a football ground through LGIP. The idea could be replicated. Some customization to suit our needs could be made.

One of the first points ACORD emphasized was that people's participation begins with the first step. So they had to be involved for even planning the project from that moment onward.

The excitement was now palpable. More fence-sitters joined the program. The first step for us was to instruct the deputy commissioners to identify the RWAs for the initial phase of the program. The guidelines were simple: the RWAs should be active and non-political. But even while this progress was taking place an interesting task was yet to be addressed. What name should the project have?

While the Shakespearean question asking what is in a name could be asked when talking of individuals, for a mammoth program we did require a catchy and self-explanatory name: more in the manner of a title corresponding to something that could be discerned. Suhel Seth from the ad world suggested "Bhagidari," which means partnership in Hindi. It came to stay. In acquiring its very name, the project had drawn upon people's participation. Further, the logo had to be designed. College of Art, University of Delhi came up with the logo that has been used for the purpose.

Behind the public screen, there were more matters to be solved. There was no budget provision to meet the expenditure to conduct the program. So I contacted Confederation of Indian Industries (CII) and requested Shri Tarun Das, the then director general, about whether they would be interested in sponsoring the program since the CII, as an organization, was committed to promoting Corporate Social Responsibility (CSR). Shri Tarun Das responded positively to the idea and said he would have a word with his president and respond accordingly. The next day he had conveyed CII's readiness to sponsor the program and, thus, "Bhagidari" was launched.

The Program Is Launched

Twenty RWAs were selected as the first step. All the grassroots officials from the departments of Municipal Corporation of Delhi (MCD), police, education, civil supplies, Delhi Jal Board (DJB), and others were called to participate or interact with members of the RWAs. The program was to be held over three days; two full days and one half. We were doubtful if people in Delhi would be able to spend so much time but to our surprise all the 20 RWAs participated completely for all the days, actively and enthusiastically. Many of their representatives had taken leave to attend this function, we were told.

The response and the enthusiasm were infectious, and the ground for administrative vivacity where every citizen's autonomy was calling out had been set. The "Bhagidari" program had caught peoples' imagination. It was no longer a program of the government alone and yet it was only the first puff of the engine, and doubts and glitches still lingered.

Subsequent workshops worked to dispel reservations as well as cynicism and more participants were forthcoming. Market and traders associations and rural areas were enthusiastic and keen to participate as they felt that the program was taking shape and was truly benefiting people. One of the major benefits that people felt was accessibility; they could easily interact with local field officials and get their points of view through.

"Bhagidari" progressed effectively and efficiently to not just help the citizens find a voice but also help the government implement very complicated ideas. It held the edges of the two sides in place when discussions on issues like the privatization of power distribution or conversion to Compressed Natural Gas (CNG) fuel for public and private transport took place. The implementation of such ideas went through without a hitch since it followed consultation with the people.

Recognition came from both the people as well as those who watched. One such was the award by the United Nations (UN) in 2005 for the best practice being followed in governance (out of 215 global entries).

The "Bhagidari" program has come a long way, and I think one of the reasons why the progress caught on so fast was that it held a promise for restoring human dignity in the fast-growing capital of India to each and every participant. In continuation of this thought, there is still the large number of slum dwellers to be addressed. How should the program involve all of them? This question still awaits an answer. Being an actor in a public space tends to rust the sensitive and accountable nature of human character: this caution and truth have to be kept in mind by the RWAs for they become crucial for the success of the "Bhagidari" program. They should be clean, hold elections periodically, and actively follow up on their role of fulfilling their commitments given to the government.

If there is participation in governance it means the responsibility to bring in results is shared. Now for the future of the program and the immense possibilities it can unleash, the responsibility has to be shared by the people as much as by the government.

S. Regunathan
Principal Secretary to the CM (1998–2004)
Chief Secretary, Delhi (2004–2006)

Preface

In the 21st century, citizens around the world are raising their voices, demanding democracy where it has not yet been implemented. In countries like India, the largest democracy in the world, citizens are constantly demanding transparency, accountability, and responsiveness from their governments. The method used by and large consists of various forms of protests and activism, considered to be an integral part of democratic processes. While these methods make a major contribution in putting the right pressures on those who govern as well as in highlighting the deficiencies in governance, they rarely succeed in building a consensus between the citizens and the government. This happens largely because the demands and protests are in "adversarial" mode, with "offence" and "defence" from both sides, leading to anger, mistrust, frustration, and bad feelings on the part of citizens as well as the governments.

Toward the end of 1999, the recently elected CM, Ms Sheila Dikshit, of the city-state of Delhi (population: 12+ million at that time), and her principal secretary, Mr S. Regunathan, (senior civil service officer of the Indian Administrative Service [IAS]) were in an intensive discussion with the authors (who comprise the Senior Team of ACORD). The CM opened the meeting, saying:

> Let me come straight to the key point. We have developed a clear vision for governance in Delhi, which will be our guiding-star. We want to build a genuine partnership between the citizens of Delhi and government. While this vision, or even mission, is clear, we are searching for a set of methods or processes, which have been tested and proven anywhere in the world, which can help us achieve and build our partnership with citizens. Mr Regunathan, who is leading this mission, has been meeting and discussing this matter with several consulting organizations; he has briefed me that both of you from ACORD have some years of experience in such methodologies.

The authors then briefed the CM on the following key points:

1. A city represents a large number of stakeholders, with a history of past relationships.
2. Each stakeholder would be characterized by their "stakeholder interests," which they would strive to protect.
3. Hence, in the dynamics of stakeholder attitude and relations, apart from some "convergent" interests, the situation would contain
   (a) "divergent interests" and
   (b) "opposing interests."

The authors also briefed the CM that until 1985–1986, globally no effective methodology or process was available to handle "opposing interests"; even "divergent interests" presented great difficulties and could not be easily reconciled.

The search for processes to help discover common ground, led in 1985–1986 to the development and testing of a model of large-group dynamics with multistakeholders by Barbara Alban and Billie Bunker in the US. In the next 10 years, several principles and processes of multistakeholder large-group dynamics were tested, validated, and proven effective; it was also established that these processes could successfully be used cross-culturally in different parts of the world for discovery of common ground, for achieving a "paradigm-shift" toward consensus and collaboration on common-ground areas to begin with, and gradually in other areas of differences also.

The CM mentioned that she found these points interesting. At this point, the authors made a 12-minute presentation on the processes and steps involved in organizing large-group workshops with multistakeholders (including citizens associations, several government departments, civic service agencies, etc., across the city of Delhi).

The CM asked whether this large-group dynamics method had been used anywhere for "citywide change." The authors stated that it had not been used for covering a whole city, but

(a) In the case of Mexico City, it had been used successfully for the Municipal Corporation with 120,000 employees and citizens associations.
(b) In the case of Minnesota, it had been used for one government department (Public Health) and citizens' associations.

The CM then gave a decision, saying: "Let us start with three to four large pilot workshops; then let us review the feedback, and make a long-term decision if the impact and reactions are good."

This, briefly, is the essence of the initial discussion, which launched a 10+ year process of building and sustaining "citizens' partnership with government" across the city of Delhi, utilizing multistakeholder large-group dynamics, as the key process and framework.

Before concluding the discussion, Ms Sheila Dikshit asked: "What is the accepted parameter globally, of the effectiveness of this process?" The authors briefed her that the key measurable parameter would be the number of residential area-level projects taken up by citizens' associations, and actually implemented on the ground, in partnership with relevant government departments. In addition, the "soft" qualitative parameters could cover improvements in attitudes, communication style, and relationships between officers and citizens.

Further, these workshops could provide a forum where citizens could be consulted on any proposed new government initiatives.

Since the year 2000, the Government of Delhi under the chief ministership of Ms Sheila Dikshit has successfully sustained a different model of "democracy at work" in the city-state of Delhi in close collaboration with various other stakeholders such as citizens' associations, NGOs, government departments, and civic service agencies, etc. This has led to better communication and understanding between the citizens and the government with perceptibly higher level of trust, confidence, and feel-good factor by and large. This "citizen-government partnership" has been built by the Government of Delhi in consultation with ACORD through the process of "large-group dynamics," in which the authors have played the lead role for the design and facilitation.

This book documents the key points and principles of this process, and their application over the last 10 years.

Chapter 1 introduces the readers to the theory and practice of group dynamics, highlighting the principles and processes of large-group dynamics. This chapter also explains the large-group interactive process as a practical mechanism and its use in the city-state of Delhi.

Chapter 2 highlights the way in which the Government of Delhi built a citywide citizen's partnership in governance through large-group dynamics over 10–12 years. It highlights some of the issues, policies, projects, and schemes which were taken up by the Government of Delhi through the large-group dynamics process with considerable success.

Chapter 3 helps the readers understand the methodology adopted in the large-group interactive process in detail, with specific roles, responsibilities, and the steps required in the implementation of this process. The chapter works as a guideline for any other government or organization interested in utilizing this methodology for bringing about a positive change based upon discovering common ground and consensus-building.

Chapter 4 describes the views and perceptions of citizens of Delhi on the state of affairs vis-à-vis basic services like power, water, transport, and environment, and the challenges that the state faced in the years 2000 and 2001.

Chapter 5 provides an example of how one of the public service organizations like DJB (managing water systems and sewage systems) used the large-group dynamics process primarily with its staff and representatives of external stakeholders (consumers) to improve the services of DJB to the people.

Chapter 6 describes another process called "Future Search" (also based on multistakeholder large-group dynamics) used by the Delhi government to prepare a road map for the city over the next five years. The chapter gives details on the issues on which the multistakeholder participants both from the government and the civil society (95 of them) worked together over three days to discover common ground and developed consensus on the areas on which the city-state of Delhi needs to focus its attention in the future.

Chapter 7 takes the readers to the outcome and impact of the work done by the government and the citizens together, to improve the state of governance and people's perceptions in Delhi. The chapter also provides information on some of the ground-level projects implemented in Delhi by the citizens associations (RWAs and Market and Traders Associations [MTAs]) jointly with the government departments and power companies.

Chapter 8 describes the special initiative taken by the three power distribution companies in Delhi to have a clear and open communication with consumers/citizens' associations, using the large-group interactive dynamics process, and their ability to clear many misunderstandings and misconceptions about power.

In Chapter 9, the authors have made an attempt to describe the leadership style of the CM of Delhi, Ms Sheila Dikshit, who has been the prime mover in initiating and sustaining this vision of democracy through "citizens' partnership" and the methodology for better governance over the last 12 years.

In Chapter 10, we have shared our thoughts and views of the possible evolution of "citizens' partnership with government" in Delhi, in the future.

Chapter 11 lists citizens' views and the views of the civil service officials on "how to make citizen's partnership in governance more effective."

Hopefully the Government of Delhi will have a serious look at it to take the Bhagidari process forward in the future, based upon citizens' views and suggestions.

Chapter 12 provides a glimpse of the lessons learned as per the authors' experience and perceptions over a decade, so that it can be used effectively by anyone wanting to adopt this process in the future.

Chapter 13 describes the essential prerequisites and elements for sustaining the citizens' partnership in governance through the multi-stakeholder large-group dynamics process (since no other process can discover common ground out of divergent and opposing interests).

Chapter 14 provides insight on how this successful initiative can be replicated in any other state, anywhere in the world, in the context of "urban democracy."

The authors truly hope that this model of taking Indian, urban democracy to the next step will be seriously considered by other state governments not only in India, but also around the world, for a higher degree of citizens' partnership in governance. As a model, and a set of processes, multistakeholder large-group dynamics will be a proven, reliable center-piece for discovering common ground among competing interests and deepening democratic participation of citizens in day-to-day matters of governance.

Acknowledgments

We wish to express our gratitude to various organizations and individuals who have provided us with their valuable assistance in the process of writing this book.

We are grateful to the Government of the National Capital Territory of Delhi, specifically the Office of the Chief Minister, for providing us relevant information and data required for the book.

We thank the CM of Delhi, Ms Sheila Dikshit, for agreeing to be interviewed by us several times, on her mission to evolve democracy to a deeper level, through searching for processes to build a citizens' partnership with government.

We thank all the RWAs and MTAs who willingly came forward to share their views, perceptions, and details about the projects that they had implemented under the Bhagidari process over the last one decade.

We thank the chief secretary, principal secretaries, all the secretaries, heads of all departments, heads of all municipal bodies, civic agencies, Delhi Police, the divisional commissioner, and the nine deputy commissioners, as well as all the Delhi government officers who participated in one or more large-group dynamics multistakeholder workshops (from 2000 to 2010).

We are thankful to DJB and the power distribution companies—BSES Rajdhani Power Limited, BSES Yamuna Power Limited, and Tata Power Delhi Distribution Limited—for letting us use their information and data generated during the Large-group Interactive Workshops that were conducted for them with their consumers and citizen groups.

We are thankful to Vandana Sareen and Arun Kumar for assisting us with gathering data from the RWAs and MTAs. We are also thankful to Ravinder Kumar and Rajesh Kumar Rana for word-processing and typing and retyping several drafts of this book.

It would not have been possible to complete this book without the help of Jyotsna Majumdar and Uma Malhotra. We are thankful to them.

We are most grateful to S. Regunathan, IAS (Retd), for agreeing to write the foreword for this book.

1
Theory and Practice of Group Dynamics

It is well known that human groups (organizations, communities, and even families) often unknowingly want two opposite things at the same time, that is, change, as well as maintaining the status quo. The latter is desired for its stability, familiarity, and maintenance of what is known; the former is desired for finding a way to overcome the deficiencies and problems of the status quo. Sometimes societies achieve change through drastic processes like civil war, revolution, or social breakdown. However, since World War II, there has been a widespread interest in planned change with intensive research pursued at the US and European universities as well as by consultants in organization development. By the 1960s, one of the strongly emerging multidisciplinary subjects was "participatory change," combining insights from social psychology, applied sociology, psychology, survey research, and group therapy. There were also many studies on resistance to change and methods to reduce resistance through various group processes.

In the 1970s (in the US and Europe), research and practice into large system change identified the role of multiple stakeholders in helping or hindering change processes. It was discovered that while multiple stakeholders differed on many dimensions (social, educational, economic, religious, cultural, political, and so on), the emergence of stakeholders' interests turned out to be central. Most stakeholders were willing to change on other dimensions, but not on their basic or fundamental interest.

The core issues in rapid and sustainable change (in any sector, subject, or issue), through multistakeholder participatory processes, are twofold:

1. The proven necessity of getting all the stakeholders under the same roof—most change interventions focus on some of the stakeholders and not all, and hence do not sustain or succeed.

2. The moment multiple stakeholders are involved, two phenomena arise immediately, in terms of "stakeholder interests":
   (a) There will be inevitable "differing interests" amongst some of the stakeholders.
   (b) There will also be fairly predictably some "opposing interests" surfacing among stakeholders.

Although research and practice globally has been conducted in "group dynamics" since 1946, the problem of resolving opposing or divergent interests, and "discovering common ground" for consensus-based solutions and actions, was not solved till 1985. The breakthrough was achieved by two women consultants, Billie Alban and Barbara Bunker, who essentially combined "small-group dynamics" with "large-group dynamics," and worked with approximately 350 participants for three days, representing all internal and external stakeholders under the same roof, in a pilot strategy-change project with the Ford Motor Company in the USA. The field of "multistakeholder, large-group dynamics" has grown and expanded globally in the last 25 years, to become the most effective set of processes, for discovering common ground and building sustainable multistakeholder partnership and collaboration, despite divergent or opposing interests.

Very large systems, like huge industrial corporations (which are highly structured), and cities/towns (with characteristics of both formal organizations, as well as of organic communities) are both known to have properties of inertia and resistance to change.

Between 1945 and 1985, most of the processes and techniques utilized by social scientists and organizational consultants around the world to facilitate community, or organization change, have been based mostly on small-group dynamics. However, it has proved extremely difficult to achieve or sustain "system-wide" change in large systems through small groups, due to the following technical limitations of small-group dynamics:

1. As the term implies, small-group dynamics works with small groups of 20 to 30 people at a time—hence to cover a sufficient percentage of a large organization or city would take many years, thus losing the required momentum for change to be implemented.

2. The well-known fade-out effect sets in very quickly after each small group disperses and its members go back to their respective positions, since there is no support group large enough with critical mass for sustaining the effort to change.

3. The small groups are not large enough to include all relevant multiple stakeholders: both internal and external. In fact, the small-group method could not even include representation from all decision-making and decision-implementing levels of an organization. The small-group dynamics method failed to facilitate system-wide change, simply because it could not include all stakeholders, and therefore could not represent a genuine microcosm of the whole system.

4. As a result of (3) above, the small groups involved in the change attempts could not develop a mandate for change, or take any meaningful decisions for change, since they lacked key players and requisite authority. Even when all important decision-makers were involved in a small-group dynamics process, they were isolated from say workmen, unions, customers, clients, and citizens. Hence, there was no real participation by crucial actors and no "common ground" emerged in which all stakeholders had a common stake for improving or changing anything.

Despite the above limitations, much research and applied work was done from the 1930s to the 1970s using small-group dynamics, typically by organizations like the National Training Labs (NTL) Institute (Bethel, Maine, USA) and Tavistock Institute (UK). Small-group principles and practices were found very useful in areas like team building, interpersonal relations, catharsis of feelings and emotions, and communication. It took shape in the "human-relations school" of administration and management, as "sensitivity training" and "T-group labs" for personal growth. But it fell far short of expected results in areas of system wide change for large organizations or community-change projects.

However, social scientists and organization specialists continued the search for principles, methods, and concepts which could take forward the progress in the field of "large system change," by building on group dynamics, especially by studying the properties and characteristics of large-group dynamics. In the 1980s, pioneering work by Katherine Dannemiller, Marvin Weisbord, Billie Bunker, Barbara Alban, Ronald Lippitt, and others led to some very promising breakthroughs in working with large groups of 300–400 people, by including key stakeholders, at several levels, and bringing in the customers, suppliers, community leaders, and citizens into the process, in intensive and participatory dialogue. The focus was on developing multilevel, multistakeholder ownership of change, and discovering common ground (beneath the differences in background and interests), where all have a common stake for achieving change.

The processes and techniques for working productively with large-group dynamics did not exclude small-group dynamics, but actually incorporated and utilized small groups as the key component unit of the large-group process. Some of the key operating principles for achieving (i) widespread ownership of change and (ii) participative, collaborative, solution finding for joint action are:

1. As far as practically possible, get the whole system into the room—that is, get all levels and functions (including the very top) and representatives of all key multiple stakeholders into participative, large-group workshops.
2. Do not skip steps or compromise on the principles/processes.
3. Build ownership through involvement into each step.
4. Consultants and facilitators should only facilitate the processes, while the client system focuses on content, issues, and goals.
5. Carefully compose the small table groups (which are the building block of the large group)—utilize the principle of Maximum-Mix ("max-mix") of stakeholders in terms of levels and functions, in composing table groups (with no direct boss and subordinate at the same table). Only round tables are used, so that there is no head of the table or boss.
6. Scrupulously maintain anonymity and confidentiality when sharing and communicating perceptions, problems, and solutions (for example, do not report who said what during the discussions)—this is absolutely vital, since (i) this alone will ensure that everyone really speaks up in the table groups, without distorting facts; and (ii) this will facilitate dialogue, bonding, and taking ownership of the problems as well as implementation of agreed solutions.
7. Facilitators carefully design clear, simple process to act as a guiding software for table groups (since large numbers are involved, and micromanagement is not possible)—in fact, the software should enable every table group to become self-managing, problem-solving, collaborating teams, without intervention by the facilitators (except on rare occasions when some clarification is needed).
8. The basic principle that "feedback loops" need to be completed or closed should be carefully followed—several mechanisms

need to be used for sharing the output, suggestions, solutions, and strategies of all table groups after each session (for example, using mobile mikes for reporting out agreed causes, solutions, or perceptions; charts for displaying all outputs of all table groups; sufficient time for moving around and reading the display of outputs of all groups; quick typing, photocopying, and distribution of all outputs to all tables). In other words, everyone is important, and every participant needs to be able to know what others are thinking, feeling, analyzing, and recommending. The whole process works through transparency and feedback, without revealing any names or even table numbers in written feedback. Every participant should know what the whole room (or whole system) is thinking, and what common points are emerging. This is how, gradually, the discovery of common ground takes place, session after session, based on feedback.

This continuous closing of the feedback loop keeps everyone in the picture, and in the process intimately, and helps create one mind, and one heart. This energizes the large group as well as all the small table groups and creates a critical mass, with a mandate, and a momentum for implementing change. This helps generate the often surprising discovery of common ground, common interests, common problems, common solutions, and a common ownership of the change process.

9. The LGIP as a workshop must span at least two-and-a-half days (if not three), with two nights in between. This is based on interesting findings from sleep research that during sleep, the day's discussions and experiences in the small and large group are processed by the participants' "subconscious" minds. Only after such subconscious processing for two successive nights, does the phenomenon of "paradigm shift" (or change in mind-set and attitude) take place in 80 percent to 90 percent of the participants, at the experiential level. This experiential, paradigm shift provides the commitment and energy for large numbers of participants to create a momentum for achieving change, and overcoming obstacles to change. This finding of two nights' sleep and three days of large-group dynamics processes seems critical for successful implementation of change projects post the workshops—doing it for two days with only one night of sleep in between seems to drastically reduce the post-workshop change, as well as the motivation to sustain the energy for collaboration or change.

10. As a practical mechanism, to enable the participants to implement agreed solutions and strategies, action teams need to be set

up on the second or third day of the workshop, with an agreed time frame for implementing the agreed solutions. Alternatively, the table groups themselves could be constituted as action teams (based on zonal or area requirements, especially in community—change or city-change projects). These action teams are given a public mandate, both by the large group itself as well as the senior leadership group to go ahead and implement the most workable solutions emerging from the LGIPs. As resource material, all action teams are provided with all the solutions and strategies that emerge, as well as all the creative suggestions produced as output by all the table groups. The totality of all the brainstorming outputs are experienced and openly described as the property of the whole community, to which all individuals have contributed by listening, participating, and generating several agreed solutions.

11. Subsequent to the Large-group Interactive Workshop, the leadership group (or the "Design Team") is constituted into a steering group to provide help, assistance, and support to all the action teams, by removing roadblocks, speaking to the right people for smoothening the implementation, and so on. The steering group can also develop, along the way, some institutional mechanisms for sustaining the change momentum like "nodal change agents," champions of change, review and monitoring meetings on a fortnightly or monthly basis, and devolution and decentralization mechanisms, and so on to take the process forward on an action-learning basis. Newsletters, progress reports, recognition for successes, and sharing of learning are all mechanisms to sustain momentum, enlarge support bases, and encourage networking and collaboration, for achieving and sustaining change.

12. The LGIP is a facilitative process that combines strategy, action, and change, based on a strong consensus and sense of ownership created through large-group dynamics. It is clearly not a training program or seminar or conference. The process uses both small-group dynamics and large-group dynamics to tap the existing ideas, solutions, and suggestions from multiple stakeholders. Small-group work is used prior to, and also within, the Large-group Interactive Workshop, viz., in the Top Team Workshop, Design Team Workshop, and Support Team Workshop, to lay the essential foundation and create widespread ownership for the change process.

13. As per the traditional consulting process, the consultants are expected to provide the solutions, and the implementing agency

reacts and/or responds to it by accepting or rejecting it. On the contrary the LGIP creates an opportunity for collaboration, and a platform whereby the multistakeholders get an opportunity to meet as a large group but dialogue in their small groups. In this process, the consultants create conditions for the multistakeholders to brainstorm amongst themselves, and arrive at a consensus on workable solutions to the issues/problems being addressed.

14. Designing the LGIP requires a deep understanding of large-group dynamics and small-group dynamics, and technical analysis of how groups, organizations, and communities function. Since the process works on the issues of critical importance to each stakeholder involved, it also calls for in-depth understanding of how different problem-analysis and problem-solving processes need to be handled, so that they become functional, acceptable, and lead to a consensus on workable solutions. Specialized consultants with long experience of large-group dynamics are needed to carefully design and conduct the large-group workshop.

15. The LGIP needs to be simplified through worksheets (that is, simple steps and guidelines) as it will need to be worked upon by the participants on their own in their table groups. It is absolutely essential that multistakeholder table groups function as "self-managing" teams without a leader or boss. It needs to be experiential and self-generating, so that the process is creative, yet self-disciplined. Participants need to experience: this is our project to improve things ourselves and the facilitators are only helping us to find our own solutions, build our own agreement, and implement our projects together. Consultants and facilitators focus on process; stakeholders focus on content, issues, and finding consensus-based solutions—this is the basic principle.

16. The fully tested and proven model of participatory change through large-group multistakeholder workshops is about 25 years old, successfully applied around the world (for example, Municipal Corporation of Mexico City; Public Health, Department of Minneapolis; Boeing; Ford; Steel Authority of India; Planning Commission of India; and so on).

17. ACORD, New Delhi, has tested the effectiveness of this model and adapted the processes to suit the sociocultural and historical factors in India, while maintaining fidelity to the principles of large-group dynamics.

18. The authors have extended the use of large-group dynamics in India beyond formal structured organizations to apply the model to citywide change efforts in democratic governance.

19. The Bhagidari project over the past 12 years in Delhi has built strong bonds between citizens associations in the form of RWAs in residential colonies/housing cooperative societies, MTAs, Senior Citizens Associations (SCAs) and government departments, municipalities, district administrations, colleges, schools, nongovernmental organizations (NGOs), eco-clubs, industrial associations, and so on. The Delhi government has been awarded internationally for this project designed and facilitated by Professor George Koreth and Dr Kiron Wadhera (of ACORD), by (i) the United Nations Public Service Award (2005—out of 215 entries globally) and (ii) the Commonwealth Association for Public Administration (the UK, in 2002) for transparency, accountability, and innovation in democratic governance (please see Appendices 1 and 2).

2

Experience of Delhi Metropolis: Building Citizens' Partnership with Government through Large-group Dynamics

The First Citywide Change Project

While participatory change involving multiple stakeholders has been successfully implemented and documented in small organizations, large organizations, and some local communities, there is no report of any such effort on a citywide scale. Delhi seems to be the first large metropolitan city (population: 16–17 million in 2011—see Figure 2.1) where such an effort has been made, from the year 2000 to 2010 (and continuing), which this book attempts to cover. The purpose was to build and sustain "citizens' partnership with government" (named Bhagidari, which means partnership in the Hindi language). The authors have been involved as design, process, and facilitation consultants (to the Delhi government and the Office of the Chief Minister for the multistakeholder large-group dynamics model, which was utilized for conducting more than 100 large-group interactive workshops over the period of 10+ years (see Appendix 3).

Figure 2.1:
Map of Delhi

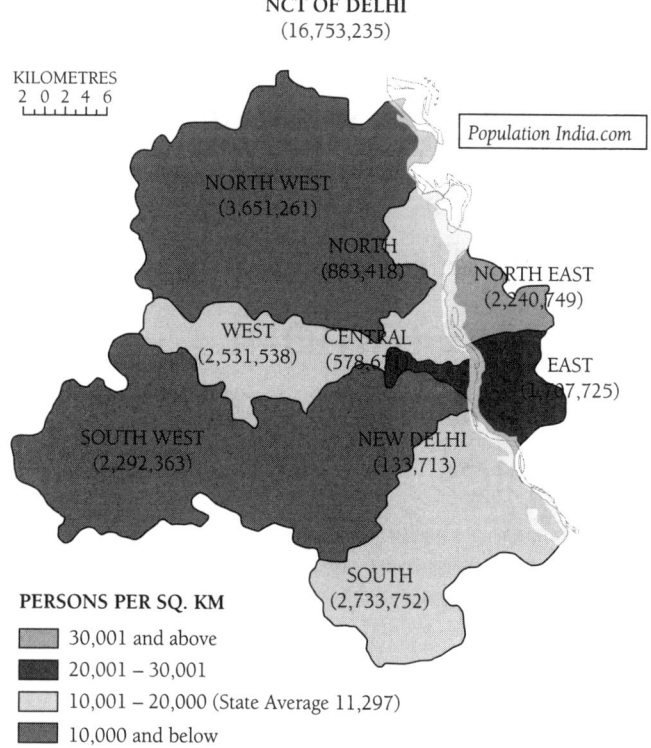

Source: www.populationindia.com
Note: Map as in year 2011.

These workshops based on the principles and processes of multistake-holder large-group dynamics were designed to be the anchor, foundation, and grid to hold the process together. As a process and grid, three components could be embedded into and carried by the large-group dynamics design template over the years:

1. The number and type of participating stakeholders
2. The issues and problems to be resolved, or the sectors to be addressed
3. New projects, policies, and schemes could also be incorporated in, and handled through the large-group dynamics processes

In this context, the principles of large-group dynamics constitute "process" and not "content"—the content in terms of the three points are suggested and brought into the process by the stakeholders and the leadership.

1. *Participating stakeholders*: For example, in terms of involving citizens from civil society (that is, nonofficials), the process began with 20 RWAs (RWAs from the authorized residential areas), and gradually expanded to cover more than 3,000 RWAs in 10 years, from both authorized and unauthorized residential colonies. Civil society was also represented by MTAs from over a 100 shopping areas.

   Subsequently, Senior Citizens Associations (SCAs) were also brought into the process, and later 1,000+ school eco-clubs. Industrial associations operating in 22 industrial estates were subsequently involved in the process. Finally, NGOs working in social welfare development and/or women's development were also included in the process. In each case, the introduction and involvement of a new stakeholder was related to the introduction into the process of issues or projects handled by the stakeholder concerned, or new programs and policies being considered by the leadership.

   In terms of government stakeholders, officers and technical staff of civic service agencies and departments of government handling water supply, sanitation and cleanliness, solid-waste management, sewage system function, street lighting, and safety and security of citizens, were initially involved in the process. Gradually, this was expanded to cover officers and staff of the Department of Education, Department of Health, Traffic Police, Food and Civil Supplies, Irrigation and Flood Control, Power, Environment and City Forests, Social Welfare, Women and Child Development Department, Value Added Tax Department, and all nine district administrations (revenue) covering the whole of Delhi, each headed by a deputy commissioner reporting to the overall divisional commissioner of Delhi.

2. *Issues and sectors*: Similarly, in terms of civic services addressed, initially, the civic services like water, power, sewage, street-lighting, and citizens' safety and security were taken up. Gradually, other services were added including traffic management, conditions of residential area roads, condition of community parks,

extent of tree cover, air pollution, noise pollution, condition of public transport, industrial areas' pollution, Yamuna river pollution (through MCD), government schools' performance and results, and many other social issues/women's issues/welfare issues.

3. *Policies, projects, and schemes:* In terms of policies, schemes, and projects, the following were introduced into the workshops from time to time in order to get the feedback of citizens' groups like a "mini-referendum":

(a) When air-pollution was deteriorating very badly and showing very high Suspended Particulate Matter (SPM), the idea of CNG for all public transport and phasing out the use of diesel in public transport, was introduced for discussion into the multistakeholder workshops, in which citizens represented more than 50 percent of the participants. At that time, 10 years ago, the private diesel bus operators' lobby was very powerful, and CNG was in short supply. The private bus operators lobby was using transport strikes to oppose the policy. However, the citizen partnership (Bhagidari) workshops gave strong feedback and support for the proposed policy of introducing CNG, on public health grounds. With the strong support of the citizens' partnership workshops for CNG, the government was able to, on grounds of public health, introduce and sustain CNG for all buses, autorickshaws, and taxis. The first two years were difficult, but citizen support was strong and sustained. Now, Delhi has the largest CNG-based, environment-friendly public transport system in the world, with much improved air-quality parameters between 2007 and 2010.

(b) In order to deal with 7,000 metric tons (MTs) of solid waste generated by the city every day, when the municipal commissioner wanted to test the acceptability of the idea of domestic segregation of waste, he introduced the proposal in the citizens' partnership workshops, and got it discussed in 26 large-group workshops. All of them were strongly in support of domestic segregation of waste (into biodegradable and nonbiodegradable). Based on the citizens' support, the Municipal Corporation introduced community bins for domestic waste, which were color-coded (green for biodegradable and blue for nonbiodegradable items like plastics, and so on). The project worked well for some time, but soon the technical design and quality of plastic used for the bins deteriorated quickly and broke down, thus leading to the failure of the project.

(c) When the Municipal Commissioner Mr Rakesh Mehta was mulling over the idea of simplifying residential/house property tax in Delhi by shifting to a simple criterion of the "area of the property" (which the owners could measure themselves), he suggested that the concept be discussed in several citizens' partnership workshops. As the citizens and officials discussed this concept, there was strong support for a simple self-assessment system based on unit area measurement. This enabled the Municipal Corporation to rapidly introduce this system, which not only removed a source of corruption by house-tax inspectors, but in a few years, subsequently, became an online system of paying property tax, based on self-assessment by citizens.

(d) When the central government was proposing the shift from the existing sales tax system to a value added tax (VAT), the concurrence of the states was needed before going ahead. Very soon, in most of the states, there was fierce opposition from millions of traders and shopkeepers as well as strikes and closures of markets. Delhi also saw a vociferous opposition to the introduction of VAT, not only by traders but also by the opposition party. A special workshop was designed and convened for the office bearers of the market and trade associations and the relevant officials. The merits and the demerits of the old sales tax scheme and the proposed VAT system were discussed in multistakeholder table groups. The discussions helped to dispel many of the misconceptions and myths which people generally held, and gradually the overall view which emerged was favorable to the introduction of VAT. Encouraged by this level of understanding and support, the Government of Delhi successfully introduced VAT as a system in the State.

(e) When there was wide public and media concern that the pass percentage of students in the Xth standard board exams was as low as 38.95 to 40.20 percent in the year 1999–2000 and 2000–2001 (edudel.nic.in/quick_report_2008/6-20.pdf), government schools were brought into this multistakeholder, large-group dynamics process.

For the first time ever, in a large-group dynamics workshop school principals, vice-principals, and teachers sat in small table groups with senior students, parents, eminent citizens, retired professionals, and presidents/vice-presidents of local community RWAs to find common, agreed solutions (to infrastructure and performance issues) and form Apex Committees (one for each school) called "Vidyalaya Kalyan Samitis" (VKS). These multistakeholder committees met regularly each month after the large-group dynamics workshop, and were provided a budget of ₹10,000 a month for setting the infrastructure quickly right, without waiting for departmental sanction (which often took six to eight months, or never). Later, this budget was increased to ₹100,000 a quarter, on seeing the good work done on school infrastructure through this fund.

After improving the infrastructure very quickly (this itself had a major positive impact in all the schools), the Apex Committees (VKS) in all the government schools began focusing its attention on performance improvement by teachers as well as students. Since the Apex Committees consisted of both "internal" and "external" stakeholders, for the first time the schools stopped functioning like "black boxes" (which were sealed, so that nobody could look in from the outside world). The Apex Committees began to look at data and discuss issues pertaining to the following:

- Attendance and punctuality of teachers
- Attendance and punctuality of students
- Classes taken
- Conduct of weekly tests
- Conduct of monthly tests
- Conduct of extra-curricular activities

News quickly spread around each school that the Apex Committees were analyzing the data pertaining to the above issues and many more. The informal feedback which spread each month began to have an effect and gradually the students' performance began to improve, first in the monthly tests, then in the annual exams. The most unexpected positive result, which occurred over a period of seven years, was the increase in the pass percentage of both standard Xth and XIIth public exams, which rose above 85 percent in both cases (almost double the previous average of around 40 percent). The most important changes were the following:

1. The multistakeholder large-group dynamics workshops involved principals, vice-principals, and teachers along with senior students, parents, retired professionals from the community, eminent

citizens from the community, and presidents/vice-presidents of the RWAs in the community around the school. This was the first time that principals and teachers were sitting together and having dialogue with students, parents, retired professionals, and so on (the concept of combining internal and external stakeholders in a dialogue is very critical in this context).

2. The Apex Committees were formed with multistakeholders, again both internal and external, meeting every month to discuss how to improve school infrastructure, functioning, and performance.

3. The Apex Committees were empowered with a monthly budget of ₹10,000 for infrastructure repair, which they were empowered to spend provided there was unanimity in the decision to spend, and the expenditure was meant only for infrastructure (later this budget was raised to ₹100,000 per quarter, after reviewing their excellent work).

4. The Apex Committees were empowered to look at and discuss all data about the schools, including attendance, monthly and quarterly test data, which opened up the school system; more importantly quite soon all the members of each school were aware that the Apex Committee had access to all data and information about the school functioning. While the Apex Committees had no power to discipline anybody, gradually, the opening up of the closed internal system led to the principals and vice-principals instituting their subsequent monthly meetings with the head teachers and senior teachers to discuss the same performance data. Gradually, the closed system began to open up and respond to the concerns of parents and the community (represented by retired professionals, eminent citizens, and RWA representatives).

5. In addition, the Department of Education also began to implement three things:
   (a) A widespread program of teachers' training
   (b) Computerized system of tracking school and class performance during the year in each quarter, without waiting for the end of the year
   (c) Providing the feedback from the above to each school and requesting the principals to discuss the data with head teachers and senior teachers, and providing a copy of the relevant data to each class teacher.

As described above, the education process and performance of nearly 1,000 schools were brought into the participatory-change process through (i) principles and processes of large-group dynamics multistakeholders, (ii) opening up the black box, and (iii) completing the "feedback loop."

The above measures together helped raise student performance in terms of pass percentage from an average of 40 percent to above 85 percent, in a span of six years (both for standard X and XII) across 900+ government schools.

Supportive Strategies of the Authors

The CM, after a discussion with the authors, accepted the following strategic suggestions to support the processes of building a citizens' partnership with government:

1. An annual exhibition of completed and ongoing projects (based on the choice and initiative of (i) citizens association and (ii) government departments) to which the general public and media were invited every year—the CM named it "Bhagidari Mela"
2. Awards and prizes for good quality projects completed, after verification on the ground (please see Appendix 4)
3. Starting and sustaining a monthly Bhagidari newsletter circulated to all citizens associations and departments to keep people informed of developments
4. Providing financial assistance to RWAs/MTAs for colony-level/ market-level projects—the CM named it "My Delhi I Care Fund"
5. A weekly FM radio infotainment program for half an hour in Delhi (and neighboring states) on different aspects of life and city development, involving citizens' participation in it every week
6. Providing Team Delhi Cards to each Bhagidar participating in the workshop

These additional processes helped to build a strong movement of "citizen's participation with the government" over a period of 10 years.

3

Understanding Large-group Dynamics as Applied to Building Citizens' Partnership with Government: The Methodology in Delhi

This chapter provides details of the methodology utilized in building and sustaining citizens' partnership with government, both in development and good governance. This involves a major paradigm shift and change of mind-sets, both on the part of citizens as well as officials. Grievance-handling meetings and communication meetings cannot bring about a paradigm shift; in fact, they reinforce existing stereotypes, roles, relationships, attitudes, and behavior. Conventional seminars, workshops, and conferences also are ineffective in achieving or sustaining paradigm shifts from dependency, power, and control to collaborative partnerships.

Therefore, in the 21st century, civil service administrators need to develop an understanding of experiential processes of participatory change facilitation, from the behavioral sciences, such as large-group dynamics and small-group dynamics.

Administrators will also need to understand and respect the scientific principles and processes involved in experiential change processes, and also form a good understanding and partnership with specialist consultants from the disciplines of large-group dynamics and small-group dynamics.

This chapter can also be used as a guide[1] and will, therefore, achieve the following:

1. Distil practical points from the scientific processes of large-group dynamics for facilitating a shift to a partnership paradigm between citizens and officials, through experiential processes.
2. Identify and clarify tasks, roles, and responsibilities of all the key players in the Bhagidari workshops to build and sustain citizens' partnership with officials, to jointly improve civic amenities and conditions in residential colonies, market areas, rural areas, industrial estates, government schools, and social development sectors.
3. Help newly transferred officers in all departments and revenue districts, to quickly understand the steps, roles and responsibilities of various stakeholders in the process of organizing Bhagidari workshops for citizens' partnership in governance. The guide is, therefore, designed as a reference material for all the officers, who may be involved in the citizens'-partnership-oriented Bhagidari workshops, so that they can plan as per the principles and steps of the LGIP.

The concept of Bhagidari was a very challenging and complex one, requiring special processes to act as catalysts of change from the entrenched passive-aggressive syndrome on the part of most of the citizens, and the authority–control–red-tape power position of the bureaucracy in general. The scientific principles and processes of large-group dynamics and small-group dynamics have proved to be effective enough to achieve step-by-step change, in a phased manner, over a period of 10+ years.

This chapter also helps the civil service understand this change-management process of citizens' partnership in good governance and provide help in clarifying the roles and responsibilities, sequencing the tasks and activities, and carefully preserving the fundamental scientific principles of change management. Besides this, the guide also fulfills the need of knowing how to smoothly coordinate between the different parts of the administrative systems and the multiple stakeholders, and it also gives answers to frequently asked questions.

With a focus on good governance across the world, several governments are looking at ways of creating and sustaining ownership of good governance in civil society beyond the political and bureaucratic authorities. This means reaching out to people, building partnership, and also empowering them.

Even in representative democracies, the traditional mode of interaction by citizens with government departments is basically one of seeking sanction or permission, and complaint/grievance handling sessions. Officials are seen as focused on control, regulation, and rules. In the process, a fair amount of alienation takes place between the two, with a high degree of dissatisfaction and frustration, especially among the people. This phenomenon is particularly more prevalent in the developing world; limitation of resources is another factor which reinforces the problem.

However, there are governments which are making special efforts to change this situation. The CM of Delhi nurtured a vision to create a citizens' partnership with government for the citizens of Delhi in an active working democracy. Thus, in the year 2000, the concept of Bhagidari (partnership) was evolved as a mission to be achieved. This concept needed reliable and scientific processes, to build dialogue, collaboration, and partnership between citizens and officials (in place of the previous, historical, adversarial, or manipulative relationship).

The LGIP which was selected in Delhi is a facilitative experiential process based on a strong consensus and sense of ownership created through the multidisciplinary subject of large-group dynamics. This change process involving both small-group[2] and large-group dynamics,[3] is based upon global research of over 60 years, based on the principles of discovering common ground, as well as the last 25 years practical experience of real-time strategic change. Common ground refers to those aspects where potential consensus exists, submerged within a group, but is discovered and surfaced through this group-dynamics process.

Understanding the Paradigm Shift: Principles and Processes of Experiential Change-facilitation through Group Dynamics

Globally, the practical experience and research backing for group dynamics spans 65 years (1945–2010), covering small-group dynamics for the whole period and 25 years for large-group dynamics (1985–2010). Both the practical experiences and the behavioral science research have established the fundamental fact that the change processes which work well are experiential in nature, and not conceptual or didactic. Second, carefully designed group processes involving all key stakeholders are needed to facilitate the discovery of a common ground and the creation of a win-win partnership, in order to help the identification and implementation of agreed solutions jointly by citizens and officials (or other participating stakeholders).

The main proven vehicle of catalyzing change in mind-sets, attitudes, and behavior, is the three-day Large-group Dynamics Workshop. It is completely participative and experiential, involving multiple stakeholders in discovering common ground, common interests, common problems, and consensus-based solutions which they feel motivated to implement jointly. The workshops need to be of three days' duration, because during the two nights sleep in between, the day's experiences are further processed subconsciously during sleep, and lead to the paradigm shift only on the third day. Reducing the Large-group Dynamics Workshop to two days, or one day, prevents the paradigm shift in mindset, attitude, and motivation from taking place. The design and conduct of the workshop must follow the scientific principles of small-group dynamics and large-group dynamics as established by the behavioral sciences, and the consultants need to have proven theoretical and practical experience—without this, there is a real risk of a breakdown in the process, leading to disorder and chaos.

Thus, the large-group dynamics processes make the Bhagidari workshop unique—it is not a conventional seminar, conference, mass-meeting, training course, or a grievance-handling session. These familiar, conventional models can add knowledge and information, but cannot bring about a paradigm shift toward cooperative behavior among stakeholders with different interests, since they are not experiential, but are only informational, and they are not designed to discover common ground.

The large-group dynamics model provides opportunities for bonding among all the stakeholders.

The Large-group Dynamics Workshop, for building and sustaining citizens' partnership with officials, needs careful planning, and prior participative consultative steps which include:

1. Consultative meeting by consultants with the top leadership: CM, chief secretary (CS), head of the nodal departments participating in the workshop, secretary to the CM, and so on
2. Orientation meetings with participating stakeholders (officials of participating departments and separately with citizens organizations), held by secretary to the CM and head of the Bhagidari Cell in the Chief Minister's Office (CMO), along with the group-dynamics consultants

3. Design Team Workshop conducted by the consultants with a cross section of the participants of the forthcoming large-group dynamics Bhagidari workshop

4. Support Team Workshop conducted by the consultants to handle the hall management, and camp-office work for the Bhagidari workshop

Each of these steps prepares the ground for a discussion of the focus areas, issues, problems, and concerns of the stakeholders, as well as experiencing the fact that this process is very different (especially the Design Team Workshop). In addition, the table-group composition has to be done very carefully, following principles of max-mix and area-based role-relationships among the participating stakeholders. The consultants also have to design specialized working sheets to guide the 250–300 participants to work cooperatively and develop consensus-based solutions, which they can implement cooperatively after the workshop. A certain percentage of table groups (ranging from 20 percent to 50 percent) will be able to successfully implement small and medium local projects after the workshop, through cooperation between citizens organizations (RWAs, MTAs) and officials of civic agencies/departments. Thus, the large-group dynamics process is neither a management model, nor an administrative model, but a heuristic, catalytic model of social dynamics. Specialist consultants are needed to design and conduct all the processes carefully, without violating any of the proven scientific principles of large-group dynamics.

Main Steps of the LGIP

Table 3.1 provides the seven steps followed during the LGIP, for each of the Large-group Dynamics Workshops.

Roles and Responsibilities: At a Glance Summary

In this section (Table 3.2), the roles and responsibilities of the different stakeholders are briefly described and clarified with regard to the following:

1. Orientation meetings
2. Design Team Workshop

3. Support Team Workshop
4. Main workshop (LGIP)
5. After the workshop

Table 3.1
Steps in Large-group Workshops

S. No.	Main Steps	Time Required between Each Step	Responsibility of Different Stakeholders
Step I	Meeting with the CM and CS	–	–
Step II	Meeting with the nodal department heads	1 to 7 days (gap between Meeting with the CM and CS and meeting with the nodal department heads)	The Bhagidari Cell informs the heads of the relevant departments about the meetings
Step III	Orientation of the participating stakeholders	7 to 15 days (gap between meeting with the nodal department heads and orientation of the participating stakeholders)	The Bhagidari Cell has to identify the participants from the departments and the citizens, that is, RWAs, MTAs, NGOs, and so on
Step IV	Design Team Workshop	2 to 10 days (gap between orientation of the participating stakeholders and Design Team Workshop)	• Consultants workout the structure of the Design Team Workshop • Bhagidari Cell makes all the preparations for the Design Team Workshop
Step V	Planning and arrangement for the Large-group Workshop	10–30 days (gap between planning and arrangement for the workshop and the first day of the Large-group Workshop) a) Minimum 10 days in case of repeat workshop b) Minimum 21 days in case of fresh initiative	• Consultants prepare the detailed sessions plan and working sheets for Large-group Workshop • Bhagidari Cell prepares the info-pack, ID cards, and does the planning for the Logistics and the registration process for the Large-group Workshop

Table 3.1 continued

Table 3.1 continued

S. No.	Main Steps	Time Required between Each Step	Responsibility of Different Stakeholders
Step VI	Support Team Workshop	10–15 days (gap between Support Team and Design Team Workshop)	• Consultants prepare the Support Team Ground Rules and Support Team instruction sheets for Large-group Workshop • Bhagidari Cell selects and prepares a list of members for the Support Team (camp-office)
Step VII	Large-group Workshop	1 day only (gap between Support Team Workshop and Large-group Workshop)	The hall arrangements, setting up the tables, Public Address (PA) systems, camp office and back office, putting the material together and so on are done a day prior to the main workshop

Source: Author.

The Design Team Workshop

Based on the principles of stakeholders involvement and ownership of the outcome which are fundamental to the LGIP, a Design Team is set up to work on the first draft of the design of the forthcoming large-group workshop involving 200 to 500 participants for 2.5 to 3 days under one roof. This is a critical step in this process and should not be sidestepped for any reason whatsoever.

A number of 25 to 30 representatives of all the stakeholders who will be affected by the decisions made on the issues, and who would be participating in the LGIP, constitute the Design Team. To put it in a nutshell, the Design Team is so composed that the team itself represents a microcosm of the macro-group that will participate at the Large-group Interactive Workshop. The ideal size of the Design Team varies between 25 to 30 participants, depending on the number of stakeholder groups to be involved in the large-group process (but it can sometimes go up to 40–45 participants).

Table 3.2
Roles and Responsibilities: At a Glance Summary

Stakeholder	Orientation Meeting	Design Team Workshop	Support Team Workshop	Main Workshop (LGIP)	After the Workshop
Bhagidari Cell	• To prepare, compare and finalize the list of Bhagidars (RWAs/MTAs) of the selected districts, with the deputy commissioner (DC) offices (for the workshop) • To carefully compose the table groups so that officials from various departments are seated at the same table as the RWA/MTA representatives from the same areas • To send out invitation letters to the heads of departments (HoDs). (In case of a fresh initiative, a HoDs meeting is organized with relevant departments and consultants under the chairmanship of the CS) • To provide logistic support (venue, stationery, and refreshment)	• Telephonic follow-up with the DC offices and the volunteers to confirm participation • To provide logistic support (venue, stationery and refreshment)	• To coordinate with the DC offices, government departments, and consultants regarding the main workshop details. (For example, hall arrangements, table rrangements, and composition, Back office support, material required and so on. • To check the venue arrangement and attend the Support Team training	• To coordinate with the Nodal department in keeping the info-pack ready for the workshop (as required and agreed upon by Design Team members) • To Prepare the Suggested Talking Points for the CM opening speech • Coordination with the Nodal Department for the participants ID cards • To compile and distribute the participants Queries to HoDs	• To feed the Commitments/ Projects generated in the workshop into the Computer System • To prepare Department-wise List of Commitments/ Projects

| Bhagidari Cell | • To brief about the Bhagidari scheme and introduce the consultants (at the beginning of the orientation meeting)
• To prepare the list of volunteers for the Design Team Workshop (toward the end of the orientation meeting)
• To prepare the Bhagidari Newsletter with details of projects undertaken by RWAs/MTAs in partnership with the relevant government departments—print and circulate copies to all stakeholders from time to time
• To organize the Bhagidari Mela as an exhibition of projects completed or ongoing, by RWAs/MTAs in partnership with appropriate departments—also to invite the general public and the media to see what citizens are achieving in partnership with the government. The Bhagidari Cell also organizes the committee that evaluates the projects, and then organizes the annual awards ceremony. | • Maintain regular contact with DC offices for coordination and administrative follow-up
• Introduction of the consultants and the work done so far under the Bhagidari scheme (at the beginning of the Design Team Workshop). The senior officials of the Bhagidari Cell perform this activity | • To prepare the answers of the queries directed toward the CM and the Bhagidari Cell
• To prepare additional relevant points which the CM wants to share with the participants
• To prepare the Suggested Talking Points for the CM's closing speech
• To send the participants queries to the respective departments (HODs) | • To send out letters to the departments giving out details of all the commitments made by their representatives (department-wise)
• To send out letter of thanks and a copy of their commitments made, to each and every participant
• To register complaints/grievances if appropriate action is not being taken on the commitments or any other issue related to Bhagidari and take appropriate action |

Table 3.2 continued

Table 3.2 continued

Stakeholder	Orientation Meeting	Design Team Workshop	Support Team Workshop	Main Workshop (LGIP)	After the Workshop
DC's offices (of the Nine Revenue Districts)	• To compare and finalize the list of partners (RWAs/MTAs) of the selected districts, with the Bhagidari Cell (for each workshop) • To send out invitation letters to the RWAs/MTAs of the selected areas/zones • Maintain telephonic follow-up with the Bhagidari Cell on the above • Maintain telephonic follow-up with RWAs/MTAs and confirm participation	• Telephonic follow-up with the volunteers to confirm their participation (in the Design Team Workshop) • To provide logistic support (for the Design Team Workshop)	• To recheck the complete logistic support required for the main workshop (for example, hall arrangement, material required, tentage and detailing of Resource Management [Support] Team members for the main workshop) • To attend the Support Team training along with Bhagidari Cell and consultants	• To provide logistic support (venue, tentage, catering, stationery, backdrop, advertisements, banners, and so on) • To coordinate and work as a Support Team member along with the Bhagidari Cell and the consultants. (For back office, Electronic Data Processing (EDP), and other resource management support)	• To coordinate and monitor the relevant departments and the RWAs/MTAs for the developmental work as committed in the action plans • Each DC (of the nine revenue districts) to hold the regular periodic review meeting (monthly or quarterly) with the RWAs/MTAs in the district and the departmental officers, and send the report to the Bhagidari Cell

| Consultants (specialized in Large-group Dynamics) | • Brief introduction about the organization and the process followed in the Bhagidari workshops | • To procure the list of participants of the Design Team Workshop from the Bhagidari Cell
• To prepare the list of materials required in the Design Team Workshop and send it to the Bhagidari Cell
• To prepare the design, schedule, and presentation of the large-group dynamics process for the Design Team Workshop.
• To conduct and facilitate the Design Workshop as per the schedule (2 day) | • To give training to the Support Team (hall management and Resource Management Team members) on their roles and responsibilities during the workshop
• To guide and delegate work accordingly | • Preparation of working sheets, program schedule, and so on)
• To design and conduct the whole 3 day workshop
• To utilize the process of large-group dynamics to facilitate each session of the workshop, so that the process goes smoothly, and any difficulty that may develop is resolved early | • To prepare the Workshop Report and submit it in a week's time
• To maintain close touch with the Bhagidari Cell after the workshops, to understand various development closely and make suggestions if required, to smoothen the processes, keeping in mind always fidelity to the principles and processes of large-group dynamics |

Table 3.2 continued

Table 3.2 continued

Stakeholder	Orientation Meeting	Design Team Workshop	Support Team Workshop	Main Workshop (LGIP)	After the Workshop
RWAs/MTAs	• To send out the request to the Bhagidari Cell for participation in the Bhagidari workshop and process • To help mobilize the participants • To attend the orientation meeting and understand about the Bhagidari workshop	• To volunteer and participate in the Design Team Workshop conducted by the consultants (along with a cross-section of officials from participating departments)		• To mobilize the participants and attend all three days of the workshop • To participate fully in the whole process of the workshop, in the allotted table groups, along with officials of the participating departments	• To collaborate in the developmental work as committed in the action plans during the workshop, in coordination with the respective departments • To remain in touch with the nodal officer of the relative departments appointed for the Bhagidari Scheme, with regard to the commitment made at the workshop • To share the progress/success, and raise the issues in the monthly review meeting at the DC offices • To write to the Bhagidari Cell in case of success or of any complaint, with a copy to the DC offices

Source: Author.

The Design Team serves the following purposes:

1. A feeling of ownership develops among the Design Team members, since they are representatives of the actual stakeholders and they are being involved in understanding the LGIP, as well as choosing/advising/recommending a first design for the same.

    In case of the Bhagidari workshops, various stakeholders are involved. The first Bhagidari workshop had only five stakeholders —MCD, Delhi Vidyut Board (DVB), DJB, (Department of Environment and Forests) DoEF, and RWAs. However, the stakeholders increased in the successive Bhagidari workshops. New Delhi Municipal Council (NDMC) was also included in the second workshop along with the earlier five stakeholders. The third Bhagidari workshop focused on the market and commercial area issues which were related to Market and Trader Associations, and not RWAs. The Delhi Development Authority (DDA) and the Delhi Police joined in the 3rd workshop. The fourth Bhagidari workshop once again focused on the issues related to RWAs.

2. Since all stakeholder representatives are present, all view points are considered before putting together the initial basic design. In the context of the Bhagidari workshop, issues such as law and order, electricity, water, sanitation, and so on were taken up and, therefore, representatives of all these departments are members of the Design Team, along with representatives of the RWAs or MTAs (in case of Market and Trade Associations).

3. The Design Team Workshop (minimum two days, maximum three days depending on the issues and participant availability) opens up the communication channels among the different stakeholders, and enhances the energy and enthusiasm of all the groups. Most of the participants go back and speak to their own colleagues about how the Large group Interactive Workshop will be very different from anything they have experienced before; they also share their confidence level about the possibility of change, since they now understand the power of the new, participative processes.

4. The Large-group Interactive Workshop also provides a wide spectrum of data, facts, and figures to inform and update the participants. Members of the Design Team take the responsibility of gathering that data, and preparing an Info-pack for the participants. The Info-pack is a collection of administrative, technical, and financial data, documents, papers, excerpts from journals, reports, and so on, which are relevant for the participants of the

workshop. In the context of the Bhagidari workshop, the information in the info-pack typically revolved around electricity, water, sanitation, and so on. The fundamental principle involved here is: All participants must start from the same broad database, and then add/exchange further information, to build-up the common data.

The consultants/facilitators work with the Design Team for two to three days in the Design Team Workshop. The Design Team takes up the agenda developed by Top Team, and works out the program outline and the methodology of the Large-group Interactive Workshop. In a nutshell, the design team draws a sketch of the three-day Large-group Workshop. From the Design Team (with at least 20–25 people) a small 6–8 member core Design Team is formed, by calling for volunteers. A coordinator leads the core Design Team. The core Design Team represents all the stakeholders and they take the responsibility of preparing the Info-pack, as well as carrying out additional functions as described in the next page.

The role of the Design Team extends beyond their workshop, right up to Large-group Interactive Workshop. During the Large-group Dynamics Workshop, the members of Design Team are full time participants. It is essential to communicate to the larger group that the ownership of the change process is not only with the organizers and facilitators. Therefore, on each day, the core Design Team members have a visible role in addition to being a regular participant.

In the context of the Bhagidari workshops, the core Design Team members have the following role to play, besides being a full-time participant.

Day 1

- In each workshop, one of the members of the Design Team, at the opening, presents the theme and purpose (as formulated by the Design Team during the Design Team Workshop held earlier).
- At the end of the day, the core Design Team collects all the feedback sheets from the participants, to analyze and collate the same and presents it before the entire large group on the next day (first thing in the morning).

Day 2

- One of the members of the Design Team presents the summary of the feedback collated the previous day.

- Similarly, at the end of the second day also, the core Design Team collects the entire feedback sheet from the participants to collate the same and present it before the entire group on the next day.

Day 3

- One of the members of the Design Team presents the summary of the feedback collated the previous day.
- Toward the end of the workshop, the CM presents the Team Delhi card to two core Design Team members, who are chosen at random, to represent the whole Design Team.

The role of the Design Team is, therefore, integral to the LGIP. It is a very important principle that the facilitators do not design the process alone (for example, without the members of the Design Team, or without a Design Workshop).

Without the involvement of the Design Team members

1. the sense of ownership will be confined only to the organizers and facilitators;
2. confidence in the ability to change will not develop; and
3. the change—project—will be seen as someone else's project, and not our project (this will lead to typical resistance developing).

Thus, the Design Team Workshop is absolutely a vital part of the change process, and to be done every time, to carry the ownership to all levels down the line, to the field levels.

Support Team

The Support Team (which is also called a Resource Team) is a critical success factor for the workshop.

Since the focus of the Large-group Interactive Workshops is on here-and-now problem identification and consensus on solutions, it is also called Real-time Strategic Change. The participants are not expected to move around during the working sessions to fetch stationery or materials, and so on. The fact that the number of participants is large, and a basic order is required in the room, it further necessitates the need for a Support Team.

Forming a Support Team is an important step in this process. The members with a variety of specific skills need to be selected very carefully.

This Support Team takes the responsibility for planning ahead for each session in terms of the deliveries of any instructions, information, communication sheets, work sheets, as well as recovery of the output from each table group—session-wise. Hence, the Support Team is constantly on its feet. It starts work at least two hours before the workshop begins; and closes two hours after the workshop ends for the day.

The Support Team can be divided into four subgroups:

1. Hall Management Support Team: This team primarily caters to all the table groups and participants with work sheets and other stationery and service requirements. Each Support Team member caters to four tables in the workshops for real-time deliveries/recoveries.

2. (a) Camp Office Support Team: This team primarily does the back-office job, that is, typing of the solutions, generated by the participants during the workshop and making requisite photocopies and sets to be quickly distributed as feedback to the participants. This is a critically important process, because it enables every single participant to know what all the table groups (of mixed stakeholders) are thinking and recommending after each work session on substantive issues.

   (b) Audiovisual/Technical Support Team: This team ensures that the sound system as well as the audiovisual systems, microphones, plus all other technical equipments required during the three-day workshop are in perfect condition. One of the team members takes the responsibility of video and photography of the three-day workshop.

   (c) Registration Team: This team is responsible for the registration of the participants. The members of this team ensure that the registration of the participants is completed smoothly and efficiently, so that the workshop can be started in time.

Both the teams work in close collaboration with each other to help the consultants in maintaining a smooth flow of the large-group dynamics process during three-day workshop. Both the teams work under the leadership of the Support Team coordinator.

The Role of the Support Team Members

The Support Team

- focuses on the process, but does not focus on the content

- follows the instructions of the consultants;
- stays neutral to the views or the subject of discussion;
- refrains from reacting to any comments of any individual from any table during the workshop venue; and
- has the ability to adapt to any changes that may be required in the program during the workshop.

Characteristics of the Support Team

Some important characteristics of Support Team are:

- Cool temper
- Ability to have good relationship with other members
- Ability to do multiple tasks
- Ability to adapt to any changes that may be required in the program during the workshop

Some of the Dos and Don'ts for the Support Team

Dos

- Work as a team
- Have an attitude of service and be ready to serve the participants water, stationery, and so on
- Be both physically and mentally present throughout the entire process

Don'ts

- Do not interrupt while participants are discussing or the consultants are giving instructions.
- Do not give opposite messages.
- Do not share own opinion during the work sessions.
- Do not create any tense situation in front of the participants.
- Do not respond to the questions asked by participants about the work sessions; if necessary, request the consultant to clarify any substantive query relating to the work to be done.

Role of Support Team Coordinator

The Support Team needs a coordinator who takes responsibility for following instructions, and prepares the team before each workshop. He ensures perfect service delivery during the workshop. He plays multiple roles and is the link person with all the teams, that is, Hall Management

Support Team, Camp Office Team, Design Team, and the consultants. He/she also coordinates with the coordinator, selected by the Delhi government for all the logistics arrangements. This person should have the following strengths:

- A cool head
- Ability to develop rapport with people
- An anticipatory mind-set and an excellent sense of timing
- Ability to get work done by the Support Team members
- Ability to lead and motivate the Support Team
- Ability to provide assistance to Support Team members in case of any emergency
- Ability to be well-respected by the Support Team members
- A good sense of humor and ability to appreciate people
- Tenacity to go through the three-days of hectic schedules and long hours

The coordinator of the Support Team needs to possess the following skills:

1. The Support Team coordinator should detail out every activity well in advance. He/she should be able to think of alternative solutions at the time of any unforeseen problem. Thus the ST coordinator should have flexibility combined with organizational skills.
2. He/she should have the ability to lead and motivate the Support Team, and should be able to continuously monitor the process, and to stay in close contact with the consultants.
3. The Support Team coordinator must have crisis management skills.
4. The coordinator should have the ability to develop excellent interpersonal relationship with people.
5. Giving Team Delhi ID Card to each participant.
6. The coordinator must respect and follow the decisions made by the consultants who are facilitating and designing the workshop.

The Space Required

The selection of the venue for the Large-group Workshop needs to be done very carefully. While selecting the venue, the availability of the following space should be carefully considered:

- Total space of the workshop hall (25 sq. ft. per person)
- Space for 8–10 service tables (size 4" × 2" each table) inside the hall for Support Teams
- Adequate size of the camp-office to set up required number of computers, printers, and so on
- Adequate number and size of the rooms, required for Support Team (for making sets and so on) as well as for the consultants
- Sufficient space for parking
- Adequate space for setting up the heavy duty photocopiers
- Adequate wall space and wall covering
- Adequate space for displaying the display boards
- Proper provision for the audiovisual/sound system setup
- Sufficient space for setting up the stage and podium
- Adequate area for the registration (space to set up 4–5 registration tables)
- Adequate space for lunch, tea and refreshment area
- Proper toilet facilities for men and women

Selection of the Consultants/Facilitators to Design and Facilitate the Large-group Workshop

The LGIP creates a opportunity for collaboration, and a platform whereby the multistakeholders get an opportunity to meet as a large group, but interact in their small groups. In this model, the consultants design suitable processes to enable the multistakeholders to discover common ground and arrive at a consensus on workable solutions to the issue/problem being addressed.

Designing the LGIP requires a deep understanding of large-group dynamics and small-group dynamics. Since the process works on the issues of critical importance to the stakeholders involved, it also calls for in-depth understanding of how problem analysis and problem solving processes need to be handled, so that they become functional, acceptable, and lead to a consensus on workable solutions.

In the above context, the selection of the consultants is very critical. The Consultants Team must have the following skills and competencies:

- In-depth experience of change-management processes
- Understanding of small-group dynamics and large-group dynamics, and maintain fidelity to their principles

- Ability to deal with large groups through the three days
- Ability to understand the issues in-depth, and design the workshop, processes
- Ability to simplify the guidelines and session work sheets
- Ability to communicate the issues in such a way that all participants can follow and understand them
- The consultants should have a good rapport with the large group of 250–300 participants (can go up to 800), plus ability to maintain process control
- They should be goal-directed, and maintain high fidelity to the principles of large-group dynamics
- Ability to understand human behavior and psychology
- Time management
- Good writing skills
- Should have a team/organization, trained and experienced in large-group dynamics

Frequently Asked Questions about the LGIP

What is LGIP?

The LGIP is the Large-group Interactive Process which creates an opportunity for collaboration and a platform whereby the multistakeholders get an opportunity to meet as a large multistakeholder group but dialogue in their small groups. In this model, the consultants design suitable processes to enable the multistakeholders to brainstorm amongst themselves, and arrive at a consensus on workable solutions to the issues/problems being addressed. This change-management process is not appropriate for a single stakeholder group.

Is LGIP like a training program or a seminar or a conference?

It is clearly not a training program or a seminar or a conference. The process uses both small-group dynamics and large-group dynamics to tap the existing ideas, solutions, and suggestions from multiple stakeholders. Small group work is used prior to the Large-group Interactive Workshop viz. in the Top Team Workshop, Design Team Workshop, and Support Team Workshop, to lay the essential foundation and create widespread ownership for the change process. Small-group dynamics is also used within the large group, by forming small multistakeholder table groups of eight to ten members each—the officials need to be working for the same area as the citizens.

How many issues can be taken up in a Large-group Workshop?

In a city organization/department, there are several issues of concern at any given point of time, which need change. It is neither possible nor advisable to initiate change on all these issues together. In the large-group dynamics model, globally the practice is to take a maximum of five to seven important issues only for initiating change. These issues should be those which emerge as a common concern during the confidential interviews, Top Team Workshop, and Design Team Workshop. If a stakeholder is not present, the issue pertaining to that stakeholder is not taken up.

In this process, why are the seven steps necessary?

The seven steps are necessary for the first time when you take up a new area, for example, when you take up an issue like VAT for the first time for the MTAs Workshop, or involve a new department for the first time, it is essential to meet CM/CS, relevant ministers, and the HODs so that there is clarity and common understanding of policy/goals and objective.

However, if more than one workshop is conducted in a series on the same issues/subjects/stakeholders, then all seven steps are not necessary each time.

But still five steps must be followed for every workshop. These are:

1. Meeting with the HOD of the concerned department and his/her senior team with the secretary to CM who is overall in charge of the Bhagidari workshop, with the purpose of assessing the need and focus of the workshop.
2. Orienting the participants of the workshop with the objectives and the process.
3. Design Team Workshop—to understand the perceptions and views of the different stakeholders on the design of the LGIP and the main issues to be covered.
4. Support Team Workshop—to form and train a team which co-ordinates among itself throughout the LGIP for the smooth functioning of the workshop.
5. Large-group Workshop—the main three-day workshop for identifying the problems of a specific area by consensus and jointly working on the implementable solutions.

Why do you need a Design Team Workshop every time?

The purpose of Design Team is to create ownership among the representatives of the stakeholders of the forthcoming workshop. These participants will represent all the participating stakeholders and work as ambassadors of the tables at which they are placed during the workshop, and help in dealing with various anxieties, problems, and so on of the other participants of the table. It also helps the consultants and the Bhagidari Cell in understanding the nature of the group for the forthcoming workshop as well as to see whether there is any fresh or strong issue which emerges and is distinct from the previous workshop. If so, that issue is taken up for the forthcoming workshop and the design and structure of the workshop is modified accordingly. The idea here is not to look only at the content, but also the process of involvement of the participants. Another important reason is formation of a Core Design Team of 8 to 10 members constituted of voluntary members for the forthcoming workshop, which performs specific tasks like the evaluation of feedback sheets on second and third day of the workshop.

Why cannot this workshop be done in a fewer number of days?

In the process of evolution of the LGIP, several attempts were made to reduce the number of days through various ways such as elongated hours, shortening of the contents, and so on. However, it was repeatedly established that the impact was not powerful enough, both on ownership and discovery of common ground.

It was established through research that two days of sleep made a major difference, since the subconscious mind continues to process the day's experiences and helps in achieving the paradigm shift in the minds of the participants. Another important reason for three days is the need for bonding among the participants in each table. Three days of open sharing, eating together, working together, singing together, and so on gives a face to a name, and develops bonds of collaboration even among the stakeholders with opposing interests. This happens because during the process of working in table groups on the specifically chosen problem, the focus is on discovering the agreed solutions. In addition, during the three days, every participant gets an opportunity to share their thoughts and to be heard on the table, without any individual dominating the scene.

Why cannot people individually ask questions from the floor in the three-day (LGIP) workshop?

Before understanding the answer to this question it is necessary to understand the basic principle and process of the LGIP. The basic principle and process include (i) equal opportunity of participation in table-group discussion to all, (ii) anonymity—it is not important who says but it is important what is said, (iii) consensus, and (iv) stay with the prepared agenda—no fresh issue can be taken at the last moment or on the spot (since preparatory work has not been done on that). The central focus is on dialogue and finding solutions, not complaint, grievance, or criticism.

Out of the 240–300 participants (or more) only a few will get an opportunity to ask questions (if allowed), thus giving an unequal platform to the others. The questioning model runs counter to the collaborative model, and soon leads to grievance and attack–defense, which reestablishes the adversarial model. Usually to meet the individual needs of a few participants (if the need comes up), they can put their queries or suggestions in writing and give it to the Support Team members; it will then reach the relevant persons. Alternately, a suggestion box can be placed in the hall on the third day of the Large-group Workshop for use by any participant.

An opportunity is provided to table groups to frame a question or two in writing, on the first day, after the presentations by the HoDs and the CM. These questions are given to the CM and HODs (depending on whom it is addressed to) who then come back to the workshop on the third day and respond to all the table-group questions. This is often the first time that citizens have had their queries answered in 48 hours, and that too by the CM, and department heads—this creates credibility that change is possible and is happening experientially.

Notes

1 In 2006, this kind of a guide was prepared by the authors as a reference guide for the internal use of the civil service officers of the Delhi Government, to help them in understanding and utilizing the scientific processes of multi-stakeholder large-group dynamics in building and sustaining citizen-centric administration and citizens' partnership with government.

2 Small-group dynamics deals with a maximum of 25–30 people generally (sometimes upto 50); this makes it possible to have one-to-one interaction by the facilitators.

3 Large-group dynamics deals with a minimum of 80 people (and can go upto 800 or more), and calls for a structure which eliminates the need for one-to-one facilitator interaction with participants. However, within the large group there are small table groups of 8–10 people. They function as small groups within the large group. Here they have direct one-to-one interaction. This group feeds its consensus back to the large group, and receives the same from the large group. This facilitates discovering of common ground.

This process has been tried and tested globally; for example, Minnesota Public Health Department and Mexico City Municipal Corporation used this process successfully to build partnerships with citizens and improve service levels.

4

Citizens' Views and Perceptions, and Challenges Facing Delhi

As preparatory work for Bhagidari workshops through the large-group dynamics process started, the authors, along with other team members of ACORD, began to first acquaint themselves with perceptions and views both of the citizens and the officials, along with the ground realities in Delhi at that time. To achieve this, intensive individual discussions were held with designated senior- and middle-level officials of civic agencies and departments concerned. Apart from the individual discussions, collective meetings were also held to understand their views and perceptions and the challenges experienced by them in the city-state of Delhi.

While it was easy to identify the officers who held legitimate role and authority of the concerned departments to share their views and perceptions, the citizens' situation was different. In such a large city with a population of 12 million (in the year 2000), the challenge facing the ACORD Team was the legitimacy that can be ascribed to the citizens' views. Not only that, it was also essential to ensure that the views of the citizens were not individuals' isolated opinions, but there was a representative character to them. At the time of starting in the year 2000, only 20 citizens associations were identified by Delhi government across the nine revenue zones in the entire city of Delhi, who had formed RWAs and had elected office-bearers. This was the first ever effort made by any government across the world (to the best of knowledge of the authors), where the large-group dynamics process was going to be introduced with multiple stakeholders and departments across the entire city, including several government departments/civic agencies along with citizens' associations for achieving citywide change in governance.

It was decided jointly by the consultants and the office of CM to first include the three major organizations (that is, MCD, DJB, and DVB) providing five major civic services to the citizens (water, drainage, sewage, garbage, and electric power) on a day-to-day basis. Since it was the very first effort and was being tried at a pilot level, the CMO decided to keep the number of participants manageable (about 200, including the representatives of RWAs as well as the three civic organizations).

It was also jointly decided to invite the elected office-bearers of the 20 RWAs, which were registered societies, so that the principle of legitimacy is clear and acceptable to all stakeholders. The registered society (under the Societies Act, 1860) with elected office-bearers becomes the accepted model for citizen's representing MTAs, senior citizens' associations, and industry associations; in the future their legitimacy to represent citizens authentically was never questioned by any stakeholder.

As per the principles and methodologies of the large-group dynamics process (please see Chapter 3), it is essential that each Large-group Dynamics Workshop is designed on the basis of the inputs of a representative group of 30–45 participants from the forthcoming Large-group Workshop. This is done by conducting a Design Team Workshop. After mutual discussion, it was decided that for a three-day Large-group Workshop, a two-day Design Team Workshop would be conducted separately for each workshop. Thus, each time, three to four weeks prior to the Large-group Workshop, a Design Team Workshop was conducted by ACORD to seek citizens' views, perceptions, concerns, and so on and to get a first-hand feel of the mind-set of the participants (RWAs and civic service organizations/government departments that were going to participate).

In the first two years, that is, 2000–2001 a total of nine three-day Large-group Workshops were conducted, preceded by a Design Team Workshop each time. In this process, several sessions were held to seek people's views and perceptions through one-to-one informal discussions, as well as small-group discussions about the situation in Delhi.

Given below is the broad picture that emerged in the year 2000–2001 about citizens' views and perceptions about the state of Delhi.

1. Overall there was an atmosphere of frustration, mistrust, hopelessness, and a belief that nothing can change in the present situation of the city. The general mood, both on the part of the citizens

and the officials was that of adversaries, grievances, grudges, accusations, and blame. The citizens generally felt there was total inaccessibility of the government departments and civic agencies, complete lack of transparency (they did not know what was happening inside those offices and in their files), and lack of accountability/answerability of the government to the people. There was widespread anger among the citizens against those who governed them as they felt that they had no voice or say in governance.

Similarly, the officers were much aggrieved. They, by and large, felt that the citizens were unreasonable and too demanding. They did not want to meet the aggressive citizens or have many dealings with them, preferring file work to meetings. The feelings of both the sides—of the citizens and the government officials—were negative and highly emotive. There was a glaring trust deficit between the citizens and the officials. Each tried to control or manipulate the other.

The ACORD Team considered it necessary to ensure that the views and perceptions expressed by the people were accurate. Hence ACORD office checked the ground realities. It was clear that the views and perceptions of the citizens and the challenges shared by the officials were fairly accurate when compared with the actual situation. For instance, there was no forum available for the citizens and the officials (i) to express their views, perceptions, problems, or listen to and understand their perceptions, and (ii) to meet each other to share their thoughts, feelings, concerns, expectations, roles, needs, limitations, and so on. All that the citizens could do was to take their grievances on a date and hour prefixed (by the government officers) for the public interaction with the officers. Usually the time was limited to one to two hours—too short for the large number of complainants. Some time the same person had to go repeatedly to the same office with the same complaint for a variety of reasons, for example, his or her turn did not come, or the officer was on leave, and so on. The only possibility was for the citizens to reach the grievance meeting on the date and hour allocated for the public interaction. In this extremely limited time, there were hundreds of citizens waiting to be heard with their long list of complaints, grievances, problems, and so on. The officers on the other hand were under the pressure of piles of files, overburdened, and overwhelmed with the demands of the citizens, and often found it beyond their capacity to satisfy them. These meetings stressed out both parties and often broke down into criticism and attack/defense mode of adversarial relations.

2. There was no way a citizen could know what was happening to their requests, applications, and grievances which were kept in the files and in confidence even though they were not classified items and were the issues of direct concern to the citizens.

It was rare for a citizen to know which officer was responsible for what, who were they supposed to approach for any problem, and what mechanism they could use to put the legitimate or required pressure on the officers to deliver what they were required to do. The situation was pervasive in all the departments and civic agencies at that time.

With regard to the services required in the day-to-day life of the citizens, the situation was clearly depressive as illustrated below:

(a) Power (Electricity): The power supply was very erratic in the year 2000 with long hours of breakdowns and load shedding. The theft of power was high and the overall Transmission and Distribution (T&D) loss was over 60 percent in Delhi. The infrastructure for power supply and maintenance was extremely poor and it was a herculean task to get a new power connection.

The meters were often defective and the electricity bills were erratic with high perception of rampant corruption in these areas. The maintenance of the transformers of the power houses of streetlights was negligible. Delhi had a huge power shortage and street demonstrations and protests were common around the city. The city was highly polluted with diesel-run generator sets both in the residential areas and the markets for long hours. It also caused heavy noise pollution and shopping was a nightmare, especially during the peak seasons of summer and winter. The markets were compulsorily closed by 7 p.m. One of the major reasons for this was power shortage. Due to voltage fluctuations, there were frequent bursting of electricity bulbs and breakdown of electrical appliances. Therefore, stabilizers were a must for all electrical appliances.

Due to poor quality low-tension wires (which carry current in the distribution system) high systemic losses and frequent breakdowns were caused. DVB used to lose power worth ₹1,200 crore every year due to power thefts. Over 60 percent of power bought by DVB did not yield any revenue because it was lost due to thefts.

Billing and fault repair: the best way of avoiding payment to DVB used to be to tamper with the meter. Meter-readers and linesmen were often partners in this crime. Nearly 15 lakh of the 2.2 million domestic meters were tampered with or worn out. Due to heavy T&D losses, DVB was in a very poor financial health.

The service to customers was nonexistent and payment of bills was a nightmare for most of the customers most of the time.

(b) Water: The water and sewage situation was very challenging. Generally, the water supply in the entire city was not reliable and most people had to wake up at odd hours to fill up their buckets.

Water wastage was very high. People were not cautious about conservation of water. Making a water bill payment and receiving a receipt for the same was a challenge.

In the year 2000, 577.5 million gallons per day (MGD) water was being supplied to over 12 million people.

(c) Transport: Delhi as a city of long distances highly relied on public transport in year 2000–2001, which was of a very poor quality at that time. For a population of over 12 million, only 1,932 buses were plying in 2000. There were long waits— Delhi transport department's buses were the major mode of transport except a few rickshaws and tongas in limited geographical areas. It was a common sight to see people waiting for a long time or several people hanging outside DTC bus doors, latching on to one part of the bus or the other (including the back of the bus, the ladder at the back of the buses, and on the roofs), thus, endangering their lives and throwing caution to the wind. It was also a common sight to see people running after moving buses to jump onto one, so that they didn't have to wait for long for the next bus.

(d) Environment: In the year 1997–1998, Delhi was a very brown city with a cover of dust, especially during summers, and clearly a concrete jungle. Only 26 sq. km (about three percent) of Delhi had green coverage. The area was highly polluted with citizens regularly complaining about respiratory and eye problems. There were very few parks in and around the residential colonies and the city.

In people's perception the performance of the MCD was pathetic. Huge piles of unremoved garbage were a common sight. Streets were not swept well. House tax was a matter of great harassment for people because the officials in the house-tax department often visited the households and arbitrarily demanded tax from them. People also avoided paying house taxes but even those who wanted to pay often faced harassment.

Challenges Facing the State

In the year 2000, most Delhites were unaware of the fact that Delhi was a city-state with a government of its own—one, because the Central government is situated in Delhi (the capital of the country), and second, prior to the elected government there was a Delhi Administration that managed the affairs of the city.

A major challenge for the newly formed government under the leadership of the CM Ms Sheila Dikshit was dealing with multiple authorities that had, and continue to have, several bodies of elected representatives:

1. The Central government represented by members of Parliament, elected every five years (seven of them represent Delhi)
2. Members of Legislative Assembly governing the city-state of Delhi (70)
3. MCD with 272 elected councillors (dealing with the various civic issues, such as garbage, sanitation, maintenance of parks and horticulture, roads, streetlights, house-tax, birth/death certificates, and so on)

The MCD, however, does not report to the Delhi government. It reports to the lieutenant governor of Delhi, who in turn reports to the Home Ministry (Government of India). In addition, it has two other bodies that deal with Lutyen's Delhi and certain parts of New Delhi, which are also elected bodies. The NDMC does not report to the Government of Delhi and has its own chairman who directly reports to the Central Government of India.

There is a Cantonment Board which deals with the matters of the Army within the cantonment area. The land in Delhi is mostly (95 percent) not under the control of the Government of Delhi. There is a

DDA, responsible for land and buildings, which does not report to the Government of Delhi but to the lieutenant governor.

The public works of Delhi are largely undertaken by the Central Public Works Department (CPWD) which also does not report to the Government of Delhi but to the Center. The elections of all the representative bodies are held at different times, although for terms of five years each time, for example, the last Delhi Government's election was held in 2008 and MCD's elections were held in 2007 and in 2012.

Delhi Police which is responsible for law and order, security, crime control, and traffic also does not report to the Government of Delhi but reports directly to the Ministry of Home Affairs of the Central Government through the lieutenant governor.

The multiplicity of authority (or the fractured authority) continues to be the biggest challenge facing the Government of Delhi in getting compliance and support for high quality governance with the involvement of citizens.

Not only does the MCD not come under the Government of Delhi State, but it also is often ruled by another political party. For instance, both in the election of 2007 and 2012, the main opposition party in the Parliament won the municipal election in Delhi. Another challenge that the Government of Delhi continues to face is the frequent transfer of officers to other union territories or states or to the Central Government, at times, without prior consultation with the Delhi Government. The shortage of officers is also often expressed as a major limiting factor by the Government of Delhi.

Another challenge facing the CM was the opposition from some of her own party colleagues and elected members from other parties. They expressed their opposition to the Bhagidari approach because they felt that the direct contact between the officers and the public was an encroachment of their role (of helping citizens solve their problems with the government departments). The CM on the other hand was inviting them to be a part of this process in good governance. Most of them were unable to see how this process of Bhagidari can provide them a platform for a better connect with citizens and an opportunity to provide a transparent, responsive, and accountable governance to them. However, there were a few people's representatives who understood this as the Bhagidari process progressed and supported it as well.

During several interactions with people and RWAs, ACORD realized that the citizens in Delhi were largely unaware of the situation. Most people hold the Delhi Government responsible for every action in Delhi and expect the government to straighten and fix things even though the Delhi government does not have the legal authority to do so (land, law and order, traffic management, crime control, drainage, sanitation and cleanliness, master plan for the city, and so on are outside the purview of the Delhi government).

Given this background, the newly elected CM of Delhi, Ms Sheila Dikshit, was genuinely concerned about the situation and was committed to changing it, and hence the Bhagidari process was started. She was aware of the fact that (i) between voting in elections once in several years, citizens really were not empowered to play an active, positive role in a day-to-day working democracy (in contrast to representative democracy); and (ii) an uneasy or even adversarial relationship and attitude normally existed between citizens and government officials/civic administration due to years/decades of poor civic service delivery, with citizens feeling weak and helpless/dependent, having to run from pillar to post like supplicants for civic services that are due to them.

She was clear that our working democracy needed to be improved on a day-to-day basis and citizens needed to be empowered and provided a partnership role in governance. As a part of a living partnership the CM wanted feedback and suggestions from citizens and was looking for a set of globally proven methods and participative processes whereby citizens and officials could work together, solve problems through partnership, and implement residential colony improvement projects through collaboration to improve the quality of life in all the residential areas of Delhi to start with.

The challenges faced by the state of Delhi under the leadership of CM Ms Sheila Dikshit were both on the technical side and the human side, with many problems in all the areas, which directly impact the quality of lives of citizens. An average citizen felt helpless so the challenge facing the government also included a shift in the people's perception and experiences of governance. The government was clear that it needed to build a partnership of hope and give positive experiences to the citizens.

The citizens' situation on electricity front, the public transport front, the water front, and the environment front called for pathbreaking innovative approaches and solutions. It is in light of this that the CM started to look for an approach and methodology which could build partnership and improve the situation within a reasonable period of time.

The consultants briefed the CM and her team that, given the past legacy, it would be natural for all or most stakeholders to experience doubt and skepticism as to whether a turnaround was possible. Briefing was provided that in all participatory change projects participants need time to experience and cocreate the change through multistakeholder dynamics and dialogue.

The situation gradually began to improve with the first two years of multistakeholder workshops based on large-group dynamics processes. The citizens started to experience the beginning of a change in their relationships with the officials. Details are given in the following chapters of how this grew into a citywide change process through building and sustaining a citizens' partnership with government in one decade (2000–2010), which is still a work in progress.

5

Large-group Dynamics for Water Supply: Internal Change Management for the Delhi Jal Board

This chapter provides an insight into the application of large-group dynamics to one organization, the DJB, that is, the Water Board. The mounting pressure of population in Delhi creates a rising gap between demand and supply of drinking water; the latter is an essential civic service provided by DJB. DJB faces the challenge not only of sourcing and distributing adequate water but also of ensuring that the water is safely potable. Given the fact that only about 55 percent of the city population has access to a safe toilet system and a technical sewage disposal system, most of which needs repair and replacement, the challenge is even greater since DJB handles both the systems (water supply and sewage disposal).

DJB had been an important stakeholder participating in the Bhagidari workshops conducted by the Government of Delhi. In these workshops the officials of DJB had been working with the various citizens' groups and departments of Delhi in three-day Bhagidari workshops to identify problems relating to water and sewage and find workable solutions amicably across the table. They had also been involved in jointly implementing some of the solutions at the colony level in collaboration with RWAs or independently.

As a result of this experience, it was decided by the chairperson of the Delhi Jal Board (CM of Delhi) and the then CEO of DJB, Shri P.K. Tripathi, to take the process of change management internally into the DJB as an organization, so that a much larger number of employees at all levels of the Jal Board can interact with selected and experienced RWAs. This way the Jal Board would be able to address several internal issues, which can go a long way in improving water service delivery to the citizens of the city.

In line with the principles, processes, and steps of large-group dynamics (the change management process), an internal change management workshop was designed and conducted by ACORD to create and sustain internal ownership of change at all levels of the DJB through a participative process.

Accordingly, the following eight steps were implemented in the internal Large-group Interactive Workshop for DJB:

Step I: Generating Feedback through One-on-one Interviews and Questionnaires

A cross section of 60 people including the CEO of DJB, all members of the Top Team, and representatives of HODs, officers, and staff of the Jal Board, as well as the critical stakeholders like workers, unions, and so on were interviewed in confidential one-on-one meetings. This helped ACORD to understand the range of perceptions both in terms of strengths/weaknesses and areas of potential improvement.

In addition, a written questionnaire was prepared on the above lines (which was filled by a cross section of 200 employees anonymously) for getting a first-hand understanding of the organization as seen by a cross section of the employees of the DJB at all levels.

Step II: Data Compilation

The above data was collated and compiled systematically by ACORD while maintaining confidentiality of the respondents' names/designations, who said what, and so on.

Step III: Top Team Workshop

The perceptions, information, and data gathered from Step I and Step II (as mentioned above) were shared with the Top Team of DJB and discussed thoroughly. A broad framework of change agenda was agreed for the forthcoming Large-group Workshop on the following points:

1. Improve customer satisfaction
2. Water quantity: augmentation, and supply improvement
3. Reduce water pollution (for health improvement)
4. Revenue increase
5. Cost reduction
6. Improvement of efficiency, productivity, transparency, integrity, and accountability

Step IV: Design Team Workshop

Based upon the above agenda for change, decided by the Top Team, ACORD conducted a two-day Design Team Workshop for a group consisting of one member from the Top Team and 17 participants from a cross section, representing all departments and all levels of DJB. During the Design Team Workshop, the agenda developed by the Top Team was taken up and the program outline and broad methodology of the pilot LGIP for DJB was designed.

During the Design Team Workshop, the theme and purpose of the pilot LGIP was unanimously decided as:

Theme: DJB—be every customer's delight
Purpose: Delhi Jal Board's slogan—to reach the flow of clean water to every household

The participants also gave useful suggestions and ideas on the closing and opening processes for the workshop as well as on the info-pack to be prepared for all participants. Responsibilities were taken by the participants for preparing the info-pack. The members also took responsibility for logistic arrangements for the three-day workshop as well as for inviting an external success story presentation (Bangalore Water Supply and Sewage Board: Performance Improvement).

Step V: Preparation of the Detailed Program Based upon the Inputs Taken from Various Groups

The ACORD Team prepared the final design as well as the detailed worksheets (software) and a minute-to-minute program for the three-day workshop based on the change in agenda points agreed during the Top Team and Design Team Workshops.

Step VI: Support Team Workshop— Two Days

In a Large-group Interactive Workshop which calls for intensive work in table groups on different subjects, session by session, the Support Team plays a very critical role. They were trained for their roles, responsibilities, communication system, and so on for the forthcoming three-day workshop. The Hall Support Team provides real-time supplies and support to participants during the workshop. The Back Office Support Team was trained for reproducing the outputs (including agreed solutions) of the table groups for distribution to all the nearly 300 participants during the workshop.

Step VII: Pre-workshop Meeting with Top Team and Core Design Team

A day before the workshop, a meeting was held with the Top Team to understand and address their last-minute concerns and to agree on the roles to be played by them during the three-day workshop.

Similarly, the Core Design Team members were also met with to clarify their roles outside the work sessions during the three-day workshop (that is, collating feedback at the end of the day and presenting it to the large group the next day).

The selected Core Design Team member was also briefed on the presentation to be made by him during the opening session of the workshop.

Step VIII: Internal Change Management Workshop

The DJB Internal Change Management Workshop was conducted with 287 participants in 30 table groups. Each of the 30 tables had eight to nine persons representing all departments, functions, and levels (including the CEO, members, and HODs full-time) from within DJB and one or two representative from among the consumers (domestic, institutional, small, and large) as per the principles of Max-Mix.

The total of 287 persons participating in the Large-group Dynamics Workshop included DJB employees working at different levels (upto Beldars) as well as various other stakeholders as follows (Table 5.1):

Table 5.1
Participating Stakeholders in DJB Workshop

Stakeholders	Total No.
DJB (Supervisors up to CEO)	225
RWAs	38
Industrial Associations	2
Apartment Cooperative Society	1
NGO	1
Central Jail (Tihar)	1
Hospitals	2
Irrigation and Flood Department	2
MCD	3
PWD	4
Delhi Metro Rail Corporation	2
State Bank of India	1
Delhi Police	3
DDA	1
Schools	1
Total	**287**

Source: ACORD Report titled *Delhi Jal Board Internal Bhagidari for Change Management* (2004).

Thus, the participants in this DJB Workshop were the CEO and nearly all the board members as well as HODs and representatives of all departments and all levels down to Beldar, plus a cross section of customers/users of its services. The process was as it is in the Large-group Interactive Workshop (please see Chapters 2 and 3 for details), which ensures, as per the cycle given in Figure 5.1, that there is participation and involvement of every group member.

Figure 5.1
The Consensus-building Process

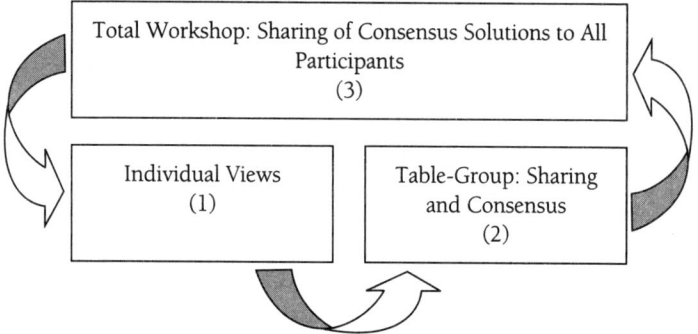

Source: ACORD Report titled "Delhi Jal Board Internal Bhagidari For Change Management" (2004).

During the last session on Day 3, the DJB participants were regrouped into their functional groups as following:

- Finance and Administration Group
- Revenue and Enforcement Group
- Water Supply Group
- Sewage System Group
- Water Quality Control Group
- Meter Inspection and Reading Group
- Water Consumer Groups (RWAs, Institutions, Bulk Customers)

All the solutions generated by the entire group for bringing about improvement in results in the change goals were provided to all participants as well as to the DJB Top Team for analysis and implementation.

In the workshop, various recommendations and commitments were also made by DJB functional groups as well as other stakeholders in the six areas around which workshop sessions were designed and conducted.

The CM of Delhi (as chairperson of DJB) made a keynote address as well as some special announcements during her presentation to fine-tune the communication, monitoring, and interpretation at the field level to improve service delivery to citizens.

Perceptions of Participants Who Attended the DJB Internal Bhagidari for Change Management (January 29–31, 2004)

1. Strengths of the Internal Bhagidari Workshop:
    (a) Internal Bhagidari workshop was a good effort and a wonderful job for building partnership between Jal Board and various internal stakeholders.
    (b) The problem areas of the organization were identified through this workshop.
    (c) Internal weaknesses of the departments/divisions could be identified through this workshop.
    (d) This workshop was very helpful in improving service delivery.
    (e) The workshop facilitated in developing better understanding with the consumers.
    (f) It sensitized the officials toward the community's needs and their frustration.
    (g) The officials started seeing the community as partners rather than adversaries.
2. Impact of the *action plans* made during the workshop:
    (a) Due to the action plans made during the workshops, we are able to sort out various problems of RWAs at different levels.
    (b) Now there is better coordination and mutual faith among Bhagidars.
    (c) Plans were implemented with a little bit of modification to make them workable and achieved a good impact.
3. Outcomes of the workshop:
    (a) Authorization of RWAs to receive payment of its member's water bills (on behalf of DJB) by check has been found successful.
    (b) We have won the trust of the RWAs. We are easily accessible and approachable to them and whatever we promised has been delivered in terms of service delivery on behalf of DJB.

    (c) Various projects of replacement of water lines were undertaken in consultation with RWAs.

    (d) Placing drop boxes for check collection for water bills at offices of RWAs.

    (e) Delivery of bills to senior citizens at their door step and opening of additional Senior Citizen Bill Collection Centre.

    (f) Organizing camps for spot-sanction of water and sewer connections.

    (g) Increase in water-bill collection centers through more banks/post offices and more counters.

    (h) For prompt receipt of complaints, introduction of free toll number and SMS facility.

    (i) The proposals of RWAs were implemented at the earliest possible time.

    (j) Regular interaction with RWAs leads to suggestions and improvement in management systems.

    (k) The workshop motivated the officers to meet the needs of the community.

    (l) The workshop motivated the community also to work in partnership with the officials.

    (m) The efficiency of the officials increased.

4. Effect of Bhagidari workshop and the commitment of decision-makers:

    (a) It varies from individual to individual; to some it gets set in some workshop and to some it doesn't make much difference, still, it is a good movement in the overall interest of the consumers and the service providers.

    (b) Some of the RWAs consider Bhagidari meeting as grievances redressal meeting. There is some lack of initiatives on the part of some RWAs.

    (c) Sometimes due to constraint of funds and budget availability, the department is not able to carry out the works as demanded by RWAs in time.

5. Way forward through Bhagidari:

    (a) The biggest achievement of the internal Bhagidari workshop at present seems to be that the consumer feels that the management and the staff are accessible/approachable and, with a little follow-up, things are happening. Now the way forward is to consolidate the trust generated, and bring in more reforms and efficiency in service delivery.

    (b) RWAs should now bring all the cases of leakages of water, unauthorized water connections, misuse of water, construction of buildings by using unauthorized DJB water; illegal sale of water in jars, bottles, and so on.

(c) The major success of any democracy depends upon the empowerment of its citizens through basic rights. The Bhagidari involves citizens to be more aware and alert about their basic rights and to inculcate in them the spirit of being dutiful in the interest of their desired environment.

(d) More such workshops should be held.

(e) Such workshops should also be held at zonal levels.

Some Feedback from the Consumers on the Improvement in the Performance of the DJB over the Last 10 Years

- Huge improvement in water distribution network and rehabilitation of sewer lines
- Improvement in drainage system
- Increase in underground water reservoirs and renovation of water bodies
- Water conservation through rain water harvesting in government offices and public places
- Increased tap water from 645 MGD to 850 MGD
- Better supply of clean and pure water
- Online payment of water bills
- Provision of rain water harvesting system in hospitals and large new buildings
- Introduction of solar water geyser
- Upgradation of sewage disposal system
- Sonia Vihar Water Treatment Plant has made a great difference to water supply
- Better control on theft of water

Subsequent Achievements of DJB

At the time of this multistakeholder Large-group Workshop, DJB was producing around 655 MGD of treated potable water. During the next five years, DJB focused on augmenting and increasing water supply and succeeded in achieving 850 MGD by 2010–2011 through tapping alternative sources and water conservation measures.

In addition to improving equitable water distribution to different parts of Delhi, 34 new underground reservoirs (UGRs) have also been built and commissioned by 2011. A Water Master Plan 2031 has been prepared with the help of the Japan International Cooperation Agency to provide infrastructure for water supply to the expected population increase in Delhi by 2031.

6

The Future Search Workshop: Creating the Preferred Future of Delhi: 2010

After five years of effort in working with citizens' groups (RWA, MTA, SCA [Senior Citizens Associations]) and government departments, the CM felt that the process needs to focus on the city of Delhi as a whole in terms of its future.

It is natural and more appropriate for the RWAs and MTAs to focus on the residential areas and on the market areas, respectively, for their project selection and implementation so that their quality of life could be improved. The RWAs and MTAs also naturally focused on the present needs, especially in terms of solving certain issues or problems. However, at this juncture it was necessary to also focus on the future, in addition to solving current problems.

What would be common, however, are two factors:

1. Involving multiple stakeholders
2. Discovery of common ground, amidst the welter of competing interests and interest groups in a large capital city like Delhi/New Delhi

In 2006, to focus on creating a better future for Delhi, the Delhi government agreed to organize a Future Search Workshop (henceforth, Future Search) to focus on The Preferred Future of Delhi: 2010. The workshop was designed and conducted by ACORD.

A Future Search is one of the few processes that builds up owner-ship to change the future and helps the participants discover common ground among multiple stakeholders, who often have different inter-ests and even opposing interests. As the name Future Search implies, this version of large-group dynamics focuses on a future 5–10 year time horizon to create a preferred future; in contrast, the LGIP utilized for Bhagidari focused on finding solutions by consensus to current issues and problems (as described in other chapters of this book).

The group of 95 full-time participants in the Future Search included the CM, and a cross section of ministers, Members of the Legislative Assembly (MLAs), and Members of Parliament (MPs) representing Delhi, civil service officers from Delhi and the Center, officers from NDMC and MCD, NGOs, RWAs, MTAs, Chambers of Commerce and Industry, students from universities and schools, eminent citizens, retired senior bureaucrats, and corporate executives. Approximately, half the group had citizens and the other half consisted of elected representatives and civil service officers.

A Future Search is neither a conference, nor a seminar, nor a training program, but an experiential, interactive process based on small-group dynamics and large-group dynamics; it requires full-time participation for 16 to 18 hours, spread over three days (afternoon half day, full day, and morning half day, with two nights' sleep in between).

The full-time participation and involvement of the CM herself com-municated the genuine seriousness of the Future Search, and helped to involve more than 95 percent of the participants in full-time work on The Preferred Future of Delhi: 2010.

As per the principles of Future Search, there were no lectures, pres-entations, or speeches.

As summarized by Weisbord and Janoff:

> For decades it was assumed that the best way to bring a large group together was in the presence of expert speakers or "panelists" who would answer peoples' questions. The belief that 'someone else has the knowledge we need' is deep in us. So is the belief that "if others tell us what to do we can do it". Future search turns those assumptions around.

- Instead of speeches or presentations, there are working sessions among a wide range of stakeholders who have information, a rel-evant role, and interest in the sector or outcome, regardless of their status.
- People make different choices when they discuss matters with other stakeholders, than they would make while working alone, or in a single-stakeholder group.

- People have the skills and motivation to do much more than they are doing now, but each person has a piece of the reality, and needs dialogue with all the stakeholders to get the whole picture.
- Future Search first develops a consensus on the future that we want, and are prepared to take ownership for, and only then develops projects or action plans.

As Russell Ackoff puts it succinctly: "First future; then plan."

The facilitators from ACORD (who had been trained in this process by Weisbord and Janoff) guided a series of interactive processes and focused on the workshop objective: Delhi 2010.

All participants worked as peers in three types of groups:

1. Mixed-stakeholder groups
2. Single-stakeholders groups
3. Total large group altogether (hence, the ideal group size is 60–70 people, with an outer limit of 100 in our experience, since eye contact with all members is very important)

The output of a Future Search is the discovery of common ground and taking ownership (in this instance of The Preferred Future of Delhi: 2010) through the agreed projects that emerge by consensus on the final day.

The first list of projects to build the future of Delhi was the following, as developed by eight subgroups of mixed stakeholders.

Group A

1. Full statehood and removal of multiplicity of authorities
2. Public transport strengthening:
   (a) Multimodal transport
   (b) Adequate multilevel parking at markets/residential colonies/ societies
3. Roads—new technology options for roads and pavements:
   (a) Bypass roads around Delhi
   (b) New links (elevated included)
   (c) Elevated roads/flyovers
   (d) Underpasses
4. Transparency and accountability:
   (a) RTI–e-governance–institutionalized accountability
   (b) Fixing accountability

5. Remove encroachments:
    (a) Clear laws and provisions
    (b) Effective implementation
6. Yamuna cleaning and development
7. Power:
    (a) Uninterrupted power supply
    (b) Stop theft
    (c) Conservation
    (d) Improved management
8. Water Supply:
    (a) Better management
    (b) Conservation
    (c) Equitable distribution
    (d) Stop theft
9. Housing for the marginalized in situ, wherever possible
10. Set up a water commission and a land commission
11. More voice to civil society and people's participation
12. MCD split into smaller units (for example, efficient NDMC)
13. Holding areas for migrant laborers
14. Garbage-less Delhi
15. Better sewage system for all
16. Health and education for all
17. New Projects:
    (a) Karol Bagh
    (b) Walled City
    (c) South Extension
    (d) Villages/rural Delhi

Group B

1. Development of satellite towns under National Capital Region (NCR) to decongest Delhi
2. Full statehood for Delhi
3. Reorganization of urban local bodies
4. Clean Yamuna
5. 24 × 7 water supply through water conservation and better management
6. Replacement of slums by affordable and quality habitation
7. Uninterrupted power supply with energy conservation

8. Regularization of unauthorized colonies
9. Better roads with better aesthetics with pedestrian pathways and bicycle lanes
10. Underground multilevel parking
11. Women's security
12. Transparency and accountability to remove corruption in all the departments
13. To have new technologies and public–private partnership (PPP) for sanitation and solid-waste management
14. Well developed sewage and drainage system
15. Completion of 1,000 megawatt Bawana Power Generation Plant
16. Ownership rights to resettlement colonies
17. Finalization and implementation of Master Plan 2021

Group C

Yamuna

1. Sewage Treatment Plants (STPs) at mouths of large drains
2. Riverfront development and beautification by 2010
3. Shifting of slums from riverfronts
4. Constitute a Special Purpose Vehicle (SPV) for implementing the above

Land

1. Remove all encroachments from all public land
2. Computerized land-record system
3. GIS-linked property registration and titling system

Transport

1. Set up authority for Delhi Metro Rail, road transport, and parking
2. Bypass express way (like the Peripherique around Paris)
3. Decongestion tax and policy on private vehicles

Redevelopment

1. Commercial areas like Karol Bagh/South Extension/Sarojini Nagar
2. Heritage areas such as Chandni Chowk

Group D

1. Clean Yamuna
2. Restructure MCD
3. Multimodal public transport
4. Remove multiplicity of authorities
5. Regularization of unauthorized colonies
6. Improvement of roads
7. Management of solid-waste sites—also identify new sites
8. Uninterrupted power supply
9. Sanitation and waste segregation
10. Social security schemes and women's security/safety
11. Water conservation/water bodies' rejuvenation
12. Social audit of all projects
13. Multilevel parking
14. Redevelopment of CP

Group E

Transportation Infrastructure (by 2010)

1. Multimodal transport project:
   (a) Monorail—three corridors, 48 km
   (b) High-capacity bus system—seven corridors, 100+ km
   (c) Establish interchange points
   (d) Augmentation of road space
      • Eight laning of Ring Road
      • Elevated roads
   (e) Augmentation of DTC fleet
      • 300 low-floor CNG buses
      • 700 regular CNG buses
      • 500 low-floor CNG mini buses
      • 800 diesel buses
   (f) Augmentation of radio taxis (RTs)—20,000 new RTs
   (g) Conversion of black and yellow taxis into RTs—15,000
   (h) Increase and restructuring of three-wheeler autorikshaws
   (i) Introduction of electrically operated autorikshaws

Transportation Services (1–2 years)

1. Origin–destination study for more responsive supply
2. Route rationalization of bus services (including link services to the Metro)
3. Formulation of mini-bus policy
4. Restructuring of non-DTC bus operations
5. Pedestrianization of Chandni Chowk and Connaught Place
6. Restructuring of cycle rickshaw operations and optimum augmentation of other modes of transport
7. Development of "park and ride" facilities

Cleaning of Yamuna

1. Relocation of all residential units on the banks of the river and all major drains
2. Micro-STPs to treat colony sewage and recycle treated water for local use (public parks/horticulture/toilets, cover all DDA and Housing societies/colonies)
3. Effluent Treatment Plants (ETPs) for all remaining industrial estates and ensuring that they are operated
4. Macro-STPs on all drain-heads falling into Yamuna
5. Continuous cleaning/desilting/channelizing of river through mechanized processes

Slums (Magnitude—2,800 locations, 35 lakh people)

1. Make enabling policy/regulatory/legal framework for FDI-based PPP for insitu replacements of slums by affordable and quality habitation
2. Implementation of policy
3. Actual fieldwork
4. Specific projects for education/health/water/electricity/drainage and sanitation/transport facilities
5. Simultaneous implementation in areas taken up under above policy

Group F

Projects

1. Apex and sectoral action group for PPP
2. Power (Memorandum of Understanding [MOU] signed by the state with Punjab Haryana & Delhi Chambers of Commerce & Industry (PHDCCI)—PPP for generation, conservation, distribution, and theft control
3. Service industry—development of convention centers, hotels, malls, hospitals, schools, marriage halls, service apartments, and IT parks
4. Water (MOU to be signed with CII)—conservation and dissemination of knowledge
5. Health—by PPP with local bodies, privatized medical waste management can be taken on
6. Education—review of policies and feedback to government for optimization, augmentation, and quality
7. Waste management (MOU can be signed with FICCI)
8. Associated Chambers of Commerce and Industry (ASSOCHAM) willing for collaboration on pollution control (air and noise quality)
9. Affordable houses—corporates will construct multistoried low-cost housing in notified industrial areas
10. Review of existing administrative rules and regulations; suggest changes with a view to bring transparency and reduce corruption—led by PHDCCI
11. Development of satellite towns (NCR), setting up of facilities and Chambers of Commerce and Industry to work with other states around Delhi on this
12. Transport—Chambers can take care of privatized bus systems, also privatization of DTC
13. Request for splitting of MCD—for better and focused services
14. Chambers can act as partners in putting in place a disaster management program for the city

Group G

1. Training electricians to check internal wiring through BSES and NDPL
2. Senior citizens/women's helpline made more effective
3. To remove encroachments/illegal construction with authorities
4. Identification of senior citizens living alone
5. Educate people on water harvesting and undertake projects
6. Fight corruption by forming citizens' pressure groups
7. Improve condition of parks/roads/sewage system with assistance of local authority
8. Garbage segregation and composting
9. Adoption of parks by citizens' groups
10. Putting up and manning security gates in colonies
11. Public Interest Litigation (PIL) against encroachments
12. School grounds to be provided with sports facilities and civil defense

Group H

Professionalization of Government Organizations

1. Training of trainers—leadership and management training for all levels and all stakeholders
2. Develop mechanisms for government organizations and NGO partnerships

Optimum Utilization of Health Facilities

1. Specialized training
2. Health Management Information System (MIS)
3. Low-cost quality health care model
4. Health care delivery to the vulnerable groups
5. Cost effectiveness analysis of existing government health facilities
6. Develop government organizations and NGO network for planning implementation and monitoring of health care facilities

Social Security for Vulnerable Groups

1. Assisting institutional development of existing facilities
2. Assisting creation of new facilities
3. Develop government organization/NGO network for planning, implementation, and monitoring

Security for Women

1. By providing special training of self-defense to girls at school level
2. Distributing Knock Out Chili-Pepper Spray on regular intervals to women through its door-to-door campaign
3. Awareness of laws made for women in society
4. Availability of helpline numbers
5. Formation of anti-eve teasing cells
6. Creating gender sensitization
7. Training in trauma care

Education

1. Facilitate development of more vocational courses
2. "Training for trainers" for need-based teacher training for diverse groups
3. Create communities/groups, following the concept of "Each One Teach One"
4. Develop government organizations and NGO network for planning, implementation, and monitoring
5. Distance education programs for various job-related subjects
6. Publication of educational material
7. Leadership training for students
8. Creating clean and adequate toilets through PPP
9. Need for teachers' evaluation

Transport (Commercial and Public)

1. Creation of awareness on issues relating to environment and safety both for general public and schools
2. Differently abled–friendly transport infrastructure

Common Ground

By analyzing the agreed, consensus-based, projects of all the eight groups, the common ground projects on which all stakeholders agreed emerged very clearly; they are listed below. In terms of the future-search process, these common ground projects are considered high priority and consensus projects, which have received the mandate of all stakeholders. Most of the citizen stakeholders offered their voluntary time and effort to work on any of these or other projects (of the eight groups) that the Government of Delhi wished to set up task forces for.

Common Ground Themes that Emerged during the Future Search Workshop as Identified by the Whole Future Search Group

- Clean Yamuna
- Conservation of water
- Full statehood for Delhi
- Replacement of slums with affordable and quality habitation
- Development of satellite towns in NCR to decongest Delhi
- Reorganization of urban local bodies
- Underground and multilevel parking
- Multimodal public transport
- 24 × 7 water supply with water conservation and better water management
- Appropriate disposal of hospital waste
- Increased and optimal utilization of health care facilities
- Opportunities for service sector
- Better roads
- Well developed sewage and drainage system
- Women's security
- Uninterrupted power supply
- Water commission
- Land commission
- Garbage disposal sites
- Augmenting/strengthening of Police and accountability of Police (law and order)
- Social security of senior citizens and accessibility for the differently abled

Progress Made

By June 2012, the main projects on which substantial progress had been made were the following:

- Reliable power supply with 99 percent uptime
- Trifurcation of the Municipal Corporation and municipal elections completed
- New low-floor and air-conditioned buses
- Feasibility study of monorail system (for multimodal transport)
- Interceptor Project to clean 80 percent of the Yamuna River pollution initiated
- Three pilot projects for 24 × 7 water supply initiated
- Seventy-five flyovers built across Delhi to smoothen traffic flow
- Multilevel parking projects under construction—some completed
- Low-cost housing under construction—some allotments already done
- Better and wider roads, better street lighting, and modern signages
- Women's welfare schemes (operational)
- Signal-free Ring Road (largely operational)
- Metro rail service expanded to 186 km
- New specialty hospitals set up

The main impact was that the Future Search process (with the CM participating throughout) energized and unified the political executives and the senior bureaucrats to step up the pace of rapid infrastructure development in Delhi on a mission mode. The Future Search was very much a part of the Bhagidari process and involved RWAs, MTAs, SCAs, civic societies, college students, professionals, bureaucrats, ministers, and the CM herself as a full-time participant, as well as in her leadership role.

7

Outcome, Impact, and Change in People's Perceptions of Governance and Development

In a number of democratic countries, there are concerns that the role of citizens are limited to: (*i*) voting once in a few years, (*ii*) paying taxes, and (*iii*) obeying rules. In India, the city-state of Delhi under the leadership of the CM Ms Sheila Dikshit took up the challenge of developing a new relationship and an active partnership between the citizens and the government institutions. The purpose was to achieve a paradigm shift in the minds of both the citizens and the government officials from seeing citizens merely as subjects and voters (who periodically cast their ballot) to a citizen-centric governance, thus putting citizens as active stakeholders in their own right and empowering them at the heart of the day-to-day working democratic process.

This chapter is based on the data and feedback gathered through the formal workshops, interviews, and focus-group discussions, both from the citizens' associations and the government officials over a period of 10 years, as well as the observations of the authors who have been working as consultants to this process for over a decade now.

Since the year 2000, the city of Delhi has changed visibly in several areas such as infrastructure, environment, transportation, power, education, the social sector, and so on. Obviously, many of these changes have occurred because of the specific policies of the government (which pumped in resources for over a decade into infrastructure development). After the rapid developments of the decade 2000–2010, the city of Delhi leads on several dimensions (http://delhi.gov.in/wps/wcm/connect/DoIT _Planning/Planning/our+services/budget+of+delhi), such as:

1. Delhi's per capita income is ₹175,812 per annum, which is approximately three times that of India's per capita income (National Per Capita Income is ₹60,972 per annum—year 2011).
2. Delhi's economic growth rate is 11.3 percent as against the national economic growth of 6.5 percent—year 2011.
3. Delhi has been named as the most competitive city in India for its demonstrated ability to attract capital, business, talent, and tourists by the Economist Intelligence Unit (this worldwide study was commissioned in 2012).
4. Delhi has taken major e-governance initiatives including Service Level Agreements (SLAs) for 97 public services with time-bound delivery commitment (failing which the officer concerned has to pay a fee to the citizens). This also includes Jeevan Citizen-centric Services (CCSs), which makes it possible for people to pay their bills (for water, electricity, and so on) online in their neighborhood itself, thus reducing footfall in the service delivery organizations as well as the time and cost of commuting, transportation, and waiting.
5. In the social sector, Delhi is one of the first cities in the country to be Polio free in the year 2010.
6. Welfare schemes introduced like pensions to poor women (widow, deserted, senior citizen, and so on) and to the physically or mentally challenged have impacted poverty reduction.
7. Delhi today has a large health infrastructure (though still not adequate) both public and private, including specialty hospitals which draw patients not only from India, but also South Asia, West Asia, Southeast Asia, and Africa.
8. A free (or highly subsidized) mid day meal is provided to the destitute (and poor).

A clearly visible improvement in the infrastructure and transportation, and the timely completion of a large number of projects, specifically metro network (some segments even achieved completion before time) has successfully created a positive perception about the Delhi government's performance in the minds of the people. In India, where project delays, postponements, and so on are the norm, such a performance stands out indeed. The credibility that the Delhi government has achieved for itself by timely completion of visible projects, which directly impacts upon the day-to-day life of citizens (such as power, transportation, roads, flyovers), has built confidence and trust in the minds of the citizens about the sincerity of the government to deliver results. Citizens have experienced a turn around in several areas which were a matter of concern to them in the first three to four years of the Bhagidari process. As given in the comparative Table 7.1, issues which were of concern to the citizens later got converted into improvements as reported by participants.

Table 7.1
Improvement in the Major Areas through the Bhagidari Process

Major Issues during 2000–2004	Significant Improvement during 2005–2009
DJB (Water)	**DJB (Water)**
• Water bill collection and payment • Optimum distribution of water • Rain water harvesting • New water connection • Water conservation • Maintenance of sewage system	• Replacement of old water pipelines • Collection and payment of water bills • Improvement in water supply in colonies • Change of old sewer lines • Rain water harvesting
DVB (Electricity and Power)	**Discoms (Electricity and Power)**
• Maintenance/upkeep of street lights • Old meter replacement • Checking of unauthorized electricity connections • Installation of new meter • Maintenance of power supply/breakdown/restoration • Conservation of energy	• Improvement in power supply • Street light poles fitted with sodium light • New electronic meters • Provision of electricity in parks • Erection of electricity poles in the colonies • Change of old electricity wires • Energy conservation • Billing center of discoms near the colonies

Source: Working report, *Bhagidari: The Citizen–Government Partnership*, Phase I–V; study sponsored by the Administrative Reforms Department, Ministry of Personnel, Pension & Public Grievances, Government of India.

Environment

During the Bhagidari workshops, the citizens repeatedly complained about the environmental pollution in Delhi, and they repeatedly requested for enhancement of green cover, community parks, trees, and so on. In response to these repeated demands, the Government of Delhi set up Delhi Parks and Gardens Society (DPGS) to monitor and coordinate the management of all the parks and gardens in NCT Delhi, under various civic agencies. The society was registered in August 2008 (under the Societies Registration Act, 1860) headed by lieutenant governor. The CS chairs the Governing Council, and secretary of Environment and Forests is the president of the Executive Committee. The CEO of the society is the member secretary of the governing body, the Governing Council and the Executive Committee of the society. All the civic agencies are members of the society being represented by their director, horticulture. The society provides funds to RWAs/other registered societies, who have to sign an MoU for proper utilization of funds. The society uses funds from the Government of Delhi as well as MP/MLA funds, and so on.

This initiative plus the overall focus given by the CM on increasing the green cover has made a visible impact in the environment of Delhi through the increased green cover. As given below (comparative Table 7.2), the green cover in Delhi in 1997–1998 was 26 sq. km, which increased to 299 sq. km in 2008–2009 (Box 7.1). The detailed list of the projects supported by DPGS is enclosed in Appendix 5.

Table 7.2
Green Cover in Delhi

Green Cover in 1997–1998		Green Cover in 2008–2009	
Area	*Percentage*	*Area*	*Percentage*
26 sq. km	3	299 sq. km	20

Source: Forest Survey of India. 2009. *India State of Forest Report 2009*. Ministry of Environment & Forests, Government of India (cited in Delhi Parks and Gardens Society, Government of NCT of Delhi).

Box 7.1 A Million Tree Campaign, 2011

As per the latest Forest Survey of India Report 2011, the green cover of Delhi has increased to about 296.20 sq. km in 2009 from 26 sq. km in 1997. After having achieved unprecedented success in increasing the green cover, efforts have been sustained to plant more and more trees on vacant lands through the active involvement of greening agencies and community participation. This also includes free distribution of saplings to schools, RWAs, NGOs, and other citizen groups through the Forest Department's nurseries, petrol pumps, CNG stations, mother dairy booths, and so on, and financial assistance to RWAs for maintenance of parks and gardens.

In 2009, Delhi received the Indira Priyadarshini Vriksha Mitra Award from the Ministry of Environment and Forests, Government of India, for increasing and maintaining the green cover of Delhi.

Today, Delhi has nearly 20,000 small/medium/big parks and gardens, 40 city forests, 5 ridge areas, 2 biodiversity parks, and other green belts.

Under the City Plants a Million Tree Campaign, 2011 conducted during the monsoon, a total of 14.5 lakh saplings have been planted by various departments/agencies/organizations. In 2012, a similar campaign during the monsoon was also conducted.

The Forest Department is striving to increase the forest and tree cover in Delhi to 310 sq. km by the end of 2012, with the partnership of citizen groups (Figure 7.1). Parks and gardens in Delhi are being maintained and developed through DPGS, an autonomous body under the Department of Environment, which also provides financial assistance to RWAs/NGOs for maintaining parks/gardens. So far, 1,205 parks are being maintained by 253 RWAs through grant-in-aid from DPGS, which amounts to Rupees 3.34 crores (one crore is 10 million).

Figure 7.1
City Plants a Million Trees Campaign 2012–2013

Source: http://www.delhi.gov.in/wps/wcm/connect/environment/
Environment/Home/Campaign

School Education

As detailed in Chapter 2, the field of school education also went through a major transformation on several fronts, including the following:

1. Doubling of the pass percentage in 900+ government schools in both the secondary and senior secondary final exams
2. All-round improvement in the school infrastructure
3. Intensive teachers training
4. Computerized tracking of school, class, and subject performance data
5. Curriculum design and content improvement

As compared to public perception of government schools in 2000, by 2010 they were seen as out-performing or equaling the private schools in terms of exam results.

It can be safely said that, in over a decade, both the standard of living and quality of life of citizens have positively impacted Delhi through the Bhagidari process and movement. While all this could probably be achieved even in the traditional way of top-down governance through strong policy programs and their effective implementation on the ground, the process of Bhagidari has successfully created an inclusive experience and flavor to this growth and development in the minds of a large number of citizens through the multistakeholders' Large-group Dynamics Workshops, which build dialogue, two-way feedback, and bonding while discovering common ground through common interests in water, power, health, education, and other civic services.

During the Bhagidari workshops, when citizens and officers jointly identify problems and their solutions, the CM personally takes a briefing and reads their points at the workshop venue itself. This first hand information is used by her to immediately communicate with the people with regard to the points of their concern, along with her decisions on dealing with them appropriately. Although it is not possible for the government to respond to all the problems, concerns, and suggestions made during the interactive processes, yet the fact that a noticeable percentage of them are taken up and dealt with positively motivates the citizens to stay associated with the Bhagidari process actively and continuously.

The Bhagidari workshops provide an opportunity to the government (through the participating departments) to directly share with the citizens their plans and projects, and inform them about the actions they are undertaking to improve service delivery to the citizens. This creates in the minds of the citizens a feeling of openness and transparency on the part of the government. They rarely fail to point out any lapse in the delivery on promises made by the government, thus keeping an informal pressure on the departments to perform. The senior-level officials are usually present in the sessions where the citizens get the answers to their well thought-out and considered questions (given to officers in writing by the participants). The official responses to the questions are well pre-pared since they are given after a gap of 24 to 48 hours (depending upon the duration of the workshop). This once again helps raising the credibility of the government and the entire Bhagidari process, and also keeps the official machinery responsive. Participants often bring along with them several suggestions and complaints not directly related with the issues being covered in the workshops. They are separately gathered and responded to by the concerned departments in writing within a few days. This too raises the credibility of the Bhagidari process in the minds of the citizens.

The citizens have not remained only passive consumers/users of the services provided by the government. Through the Bhagidari process, they have continued to work closely with the government departments and have undertaken several projects within their residential or market areas to improve the quality of life at the residential and market areas. The decision on the first such specific ground-level project is often taken by the RWAs/MTAs during the three-day Bhagidari workshop itself in consultation with the relevant department or agency official sharing the table with them. Once this rapport is built between the citizens and the officials through a Bhagidari workshop, a continuous interaction follows and more projects are undertaken over the years. Some of the citizens have worked with several departments and implemented six to ten pro-jects in their colonies/markets for improvement, during the decade from 2001 to 2011.

The largest project so far has been implemented by the Dilshad Colony RWA of laying sewer systems in the colony (in 2003). The idea of this project was developed during one of the Bhagidari workshops. Dilshad Colony in east Delhi was developed by a private developer who had not provided adequate sewer systems or storm water drains, lead-ing to health hazards and hardships to the residents. The residents of the colony, participating in a three-day Bhagidari workshop, discussed this problem with the DJB officials present on their table throughout. It was agreed between DJB and the colony that if the colony raises some funds for this project on "no profit no loss" basis, DJB will do the need-ful. The residents raised an amount of ₹1.24 crores. Consequently, DJB laid 7,944 m of sewer lines in an area of 1.53 sq. km of the colony on both sides of houses, with a provision of treatment of 5.2 cusec waste water in Kundli sewage treatment plant. This colony later constructed an Underground Reservoir (UGR) for water, again in collaboration with DJB. The total cost of the project was ₹80 lakhs, out of which ₹31 lakhs was contributed by the residents. The UGR has a capacity of 1.5 lakhs gallon. This colony has also undertaken other projects such as bringing in water from river Ganga for the colony and the establishment of a senior citizen center.

Similarly, the joint forum in Vasundhara Enclave was able to develop a community hall after winning approval of a grant-in-aid of ₹2,500,000 from Government of Delhi. The colony has also undertaken other projects such as getting supply of Ganga water and covering open drains by DJB. Listing of various projects implemented by RWAs/MTAs is given in Appendix 6.

Another colony (RWA, New Krishna Nagar) has actively participated in growing medicinal plants and flowers, improving the security in the colony with the Police Department, and improving the sanitation in the colony. These are illustrative examples.

In the year 2007, six review workshops were conducted with all the RWAs/MTAs who had previously participated in the Bhagidari workshops as well as the government departments. The purpose was to review the success and gaps of Bhagidari process at the colony level and the further improvement required. All those Bhagidars who had participated since 2000 were invited for one-day reviews in these district-wise Bhagidari workshops. The participants shared the projects implemented successfully by them in their colonies and markets under various categories across all the nine revenue districts in Delhi in partnership with the concerned departments (Table 7.3 provides details). The projects were chosen by the RWAs/MTAs as per their own priority, and they worked closely with the relevant department officials to complete the projects on the ground.

The above data is also depicted below in a bar chart form (Figure 7.2) for easy visualization.

At the workshop, each round-table group consists of the civic society members from the RWAs/MTAs and the officials of the departments, civic bodies, and service organizations (such as DJB, discoms, and so on) whose operational territory is the same area as of the civic society representative with whom they are sitting on the table. Obviously, this situation and platform breaks several communication barriers between the two.

The nameless, faceless government officials in India (normally, the government officials are known by their designations only) and citizens now get a name and a face for each other. A distant impersonal role-relationship gets converted into face-to-face and personal interaction-based relationship. The first names, residential addresses, mobile phone numbers, and so on are exchanged over a period of three (or two) days between officials and citizens when they work together on problems and

Table 7.3

Number of Projects Implemented by RWAs and MTAs in Partnership with Government, Departments up to 2007 in Delhi

S. No.	Type of the Projects	Name of the Revenue Districts							Total
		South-West and New Delhi	South	North-West	East	West and North	Central and North-East		
1	Water supply system	53	33	52	71	80	88		377
2	Sewage	33	22	33	30	43	53		214
3	Drainage	20	13	19	26	43	46		167
4	Sanitation/garbage cleaning	35	24	24	40	56	66		245
5	Bill collection and payment: water/electricity/ House Tax, and so on	22	16	19	43	43	41		184
6	Electricity	16	22	32	41	49	58		218
7	Parks	32	16	41	41	34	37		201
8	Tree cover/greenery	20	9	12	28	19	33		121
9	Senior citizens	14	6	11	20	27	32		110
10	Safety and security	28	8	24	24	39	35		158
11	Encroachment removal	4	2	13	8	26	26		79

Table 7.3 continued

Table 7.3 continued

S. No.	Type of the Projects	South-West and New Delhi	South	North-West	East	West and North	Central and North-East	Total
				Name of the Revenue Districts				
12	Rain-water harvesting	4	12	3	3	6	5	33
13	Colony roads	29	27	31	41	53	60	241
14	Back lanes	1	8	7	10	8	12	46
15	Environment	4	0	4	9	9	10	36
16	Pollution reduction/removal	4	2	2	7	12	6	33
17	Mosquitoes/flies reduction	19	7	15	19	20	27	107
18	Street lighting	34	19	34	44	62	69	262
19	Water logging	5	3	5	12	11	12	48
20	Composting	0	5	0	4	2	0	11
21	Colony traffic/parking	3	1	2	5	10	4	25
22	Conservation: water/electricity	2	1	2	2	4	4	15
23	Any other	50	46	37	51	61	62	307
	Grand Total	**432**	**302**	**422**	**579**	**717**	**786**	**3,238**

Source: Data collected from those RWAs/MTAs who participated in the six district-wise Bhagidari Review Workshops in 2007.

Figure 7.2

Type of Projects Implemented by RWAs and MTAs in Partnership with Government Departments up to 2007 in Delhi

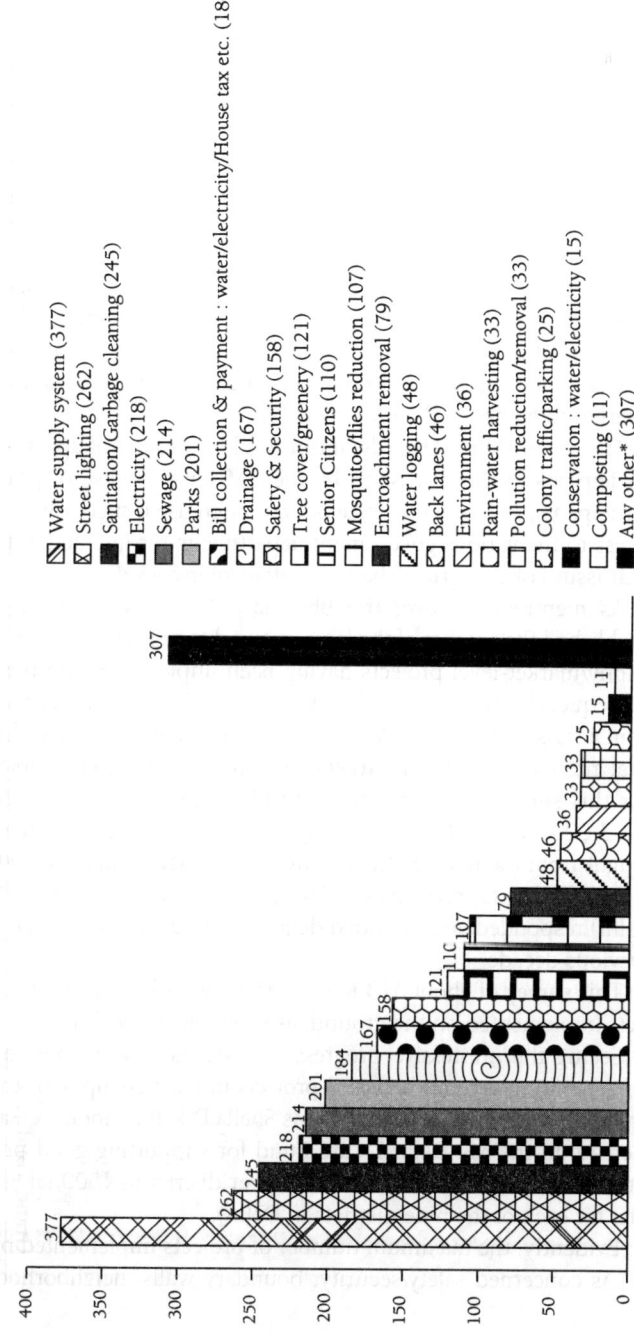

Water supply system (377)
Street lighting (262)
Sanitation/Garbage cleaning (245)
Electricity (218)
Sewage (214)
Parks (201)
Bill collection & payment : water/electricity/House tax etc. (184)
Drainage (167)
Safety & Security (158)
Tree cover/greenery (121)
Senior Citizens (110)
Mosquitoe/flies reduction (107)
Encroachment removal (79)
Water logging (48)
Back lanes (46)
Environment (36)
Rain-water harvesting (33)
Pollution reduction/removal (33)
Colony traffic/parking (25)
Conservation : water/electricity (15)
Composting (11)
Any other* (307)

Source: Data collected from those RWAs/MTAs who participated in the six district-wise Bhagidari Review Workshops in 2007.

their solutions, eat together, laugh together, and even sing together (the specifically composed songs for the Bhagidari process). As per the methodology adopted in the workshop, both are able to listen to each others' views, develop a consensus, and agree upon a doable project to be implemented on the ground.

The process itself builds a hope in the minds of the participating citizens as well as motivates the officials to perform. About half of the projects agreed at the end of the three-day workshop do move forward beyond the discussions to be implemented on the ground. The officers often visit the residential colonies and market areas and the meetings are held over there, cups of tea and coffee are shared together at the colony-level, a relationship builds, and the work progresses. Both stakeholders (citizens and officials) go through an action-learning process in working together to complete the project on the ground.

The Team Delhi ID cards, introduced as a token of appreciation for participants in the workshop by the CM, give a sense of pride to the participants, specially the citizens, who often use it successfully to get an access to the various government departments for interaction regarding their issues of concern at the residential/colony-level.

As mentioned above, the Bhagidari Review Workshops in 2007 established the success of the large-group dynamics process with 3,000+ colony/market-level projects having been implemented on the ground. Subsequently, in the year 2010, ACORD conducted a survey with RWAs from across all the nine revenue districts of Delhi to further identify the total number of colony/market-level projects that were implemented. For this survey first a list of 1,029 RWAs/MTAs was prepared out of the 3,000+ RWAs/MTAs through random sampling. Information was sought from them about the colony-level projects implemented. A total of 513 RWAs (approximately 16 percent of the total RWAs/MTAs in Delhi) responded and provided details of projects completed during the previous decade.

This survey of about 513 RWAs/MTAs provided a total of 4,928 projects implemented on the ground, as shown in Table 7.4.

Seeing the impressive progress by citizens' associations in actually implementing several thousand projects in partnership with the appropriate departments, in 2012, CM Ms Sheila Dikshit announced a ten-fold increase in the My Delhi I Care Fund for supporting good projects by citizens associations (from ₹50 lakhs per district to ₹500 lakhs per district for each of the nine districts in Delhi).

Evidently, the maximum number of projects implemented by RWAs/MTAs concerned safety/security, boundary walls, neighborhood watch

Table 7.4

Type of Bhagidari Projects Implemented by RWAs in Different Revenue Districts

	No. of RWAs Responded	2001–2010									
S.No.	Projects/Districts	East N = 35	West N = 111	North N = 10	South N = 92	Center N = 64	North-East N = 110	South-West N = 34	North-West N = 42	New Delhi N = 15	Total N = 513*
1.1	Safety and security	18	83	9	83	37	64	18	35	15	362
1.2	Boundary wall	15	66	6	70	25	38	22	31	11	284
1.3	Neighborhood gate	26	70	7	80	40	44	24	25	10	326
1.4	Neighborhood watch in the colony	34	92	7	83	50	82	32	33	7	420
	Total (1.1 to 1.4)	**93**	**311**	**29**	**316**	**152**	**228**	**96**	**124**	**43**	**1392**
2.1.	Energy saving/conservation of power	15	89	7	70	30	81	3	37	8	340
2.2	Power supply/breakdowns/load-shedding	32	105	9	83	58	98	33	42	13	473
	Total (2.1 to 2.2)	**47**	**194**	**16**	**153**	**88**	**179**	**36**	**79**	**21**	**813**

Table 7.4 continued

Table 7.4 continued

S.No.	Projects/Districts	No. of RWAs Responded	2001–2010								
		East N = 35	West N = 111	North N = 10	South N = 92	Center N = 64	North-East N = 110	South-West N = 34	North-West N = 42	New Delhi N = 15	Total N = 513*
3.1	Maintenance and upgrading of sewage system	21	72	9	75	36	50	15	32	10	320
3.2	Maintenance of drainage system/prevention of flooding	21	74	5	70	33	44	16	34	12	309
	Total (3.1 to 3.2)	**42**	**146**	**14**	**145**	**69**	**94**	**31**	**66**	**22**	**629**
4	Sanitation/cleanliness in the colony	20	81	8	77	41	77	21	38	12	375
5	Maintenance of roads in the colony	21	78	9	77	34	64	15	38	11	347
6	Water bills/power bills payment in the market	32	62	7	77	31	66	30	23	11	339
7.1	Recreation center	9	24	3	25	17	21	5	12	6	122

7.2	Community center	10	49	5	38	25	37	13	16	4	197
	Total (7.1 to 7.2)	**19**	**73**	**8**	**63**	**42**	**58**	**18**	**28**	**10**	**319**
8	Maintenance of parks/greenery in the colonies	17	67	7	68	25	52	11	33	13	293
9	Colony traffic	14	44	2	13	24	63	18	5	9	192
10	Water conservation and rain water harvesting	2	23	4	37	26	22	8	7	10	139
11	Public library or reading room	7	14	2	18	17	16	8	5	3	90
	Grand Total	314	1,093	106	1,044	549	919	292	446	165	**4,928****

Source: This survey was conducted by the authors for the information of the Bhagidari Cell, Delhi government in 2010.

Notes:

* The N = 513 in this table represents about one sixth of the RWAs and MTAs who have participated in Bhagidari process (including federations) till 2010.

** This figure of 4,928 projects successfully implemented by 513 RWAs/MTAs is 65 percent more than those listed by the RWAs/MTAs in 2007.

• In 2007, 1,534 RWAs/MTAs reported having implemented 3,238 projects on the ground in their residential/market areas (please see Table 7.3).

N = 513

in the colony, and so on followed by power supply, breakdowns, energy saving, and conservation of power.

In terms of the district-wise distribution of projects, the maximum number of projects was implemented by the west and the south, followed by the north-east. However, given the fact that the central district was a much smaller district, the number is impressive, as shown in Figure 7.3.

Figure 7.3
Number of Projects Implemented by RWAs/MTAs District-wise

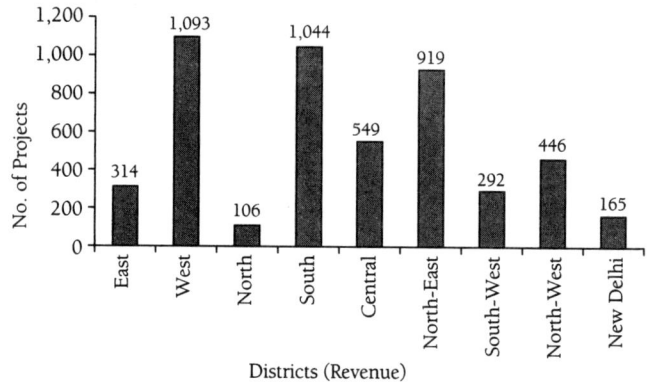

Source: Rapid Survey Report titled *Achievements of Bhagidari: Citizens' Partnership in Governance* by ACORD, submitted to Delhi government (2010).
Note: N = 513

In this survey both the data on the actual field-level projects, conducted by RWAs/MTAs as well as their views and perceptions about the Bhagidari process were taken. A high percentage of citizens' associations attributed the success of their projects to the Bhagidari process (as given in Table 7.5).

The highlights of the appreciation given by the citizens to Bhagidari were about:

- Getting a platform to sit with the officers/citizens and discuss matters
- Enhancement of information about the way the government works, its schemes, and the projects
- Improved communication with the government
- Motivation and self-confidence among the citizens and officers

There were dissenting voices as well, where people expressed their dissatisfaction with the government departments. However, those were

Table 7.5
Type of Projects Implemented and Success Attributed to Bhagidari Process

Type of Projects Implemented	Success Attributed to Bhagidari Process (in Percentage)
Safety and security	70.6
Neighborhood watch	81.9
Neighborhood gate	63.5
Boundary wall	55.4
Sanitation and cleanliness	73.1
Maintenance and upgrading of sewerage system	62.4
Maintenance of drainage system/prevention of flooding	60.2
Maintenance of roads	67.6
Power supply/breakdowns/load-shedding	92.2
Energy saving/power conservation	66.3
Water/power bills payment	66.1
Maintenance of parks and greenery	57.1
Community center	38.4
Traffic management within the colony	37.4
Recreation center	23.8
Public library/reading room	17.5

Source: Rapid Survey Report titled *Achievements of Bhagidari: Citizens' Partnership in Governance* by ACORD, submitted to Delhi government (2010).
Note: N = 513

mostly with regard to the projects to be implemented with the MCD or the DDA, which are not under the authority of the Delhi government yet. The other dissatisfaction was expressed about the slow responses by some government officials.

On the whole, the Government of Delhi, under the leadership of the CM Ms Sheila Dikshit, has successfully built the confidence of a large number of citizens' associations on the Bhagidari process, over the years, by valuing their inputs and making some of the government policy and program decisions based upon these inputs. For instance, when in 2000, people complained about the lack of transparency, she introduced the Right to Information Act—Delhi became one of the first states to introduce the Right to Information (RTI) Act in 2001. Subsequently, when the national RTI Act was introduced in 2005, the Delhi government invited all the RWAs and MTAs in a Bhagidari workshop to educate them about the benefits and the ways of utilizing each RTI Act in Delhi. Similarly, when people expressed their strong concerns against the introduction of the Conditional Access System (CAS) for household TV sets, even at a pilot level, during the first term of CM Ms Sheila Dikshit, she withdrew the scheme to respect their views.

There is a drastic change in the perception of people based upon their experience of the power, transportation, education, and infrastructure in Delhi. While supply and quality of water is appreciated by many, there are some disgruntled areas on this issue. This rapid survey was done during the peak summer season when the water supply across the country including the state of Delhi is inadequate.

As mentioned in Chapter 8, one of the major reforms done by the Delhi government has been in the power distribution sector after adoption of a PPP model between the Delhi government and private power companies to set up three discoms for distribution of power in Delhi. The idea of this power reform was regularly shared by the CM Ms Sheila Dikshit in the Bhagidari workshops prior to its adoption, during the year 2000–2001. She got a massive supportive mandate from the citizens to go ahead, and she did so. The situation by 2010 is almost in total contrast to what it was in the year 2000 with 99 percent uptime in the power supply by the discoms themselves (barring the Delhi Power Transmission Co. [Transco] or Grid short supply, and so on). The voltage fluctuations have been eliminated almost completely, thus protecting the electrical equipments from damage. There are hardly any generator sets in the market areas creating air and noise pollution. While Delhi continues to have a shortage of power, discoms purchase it at the available cost from anywhere in the country and supply it to the consumers. The discoms have also adopted the Bhagidari concept and are conducting multistakeholder workshops using the same methodology to communicate with consumers and build relationships with them.

During the various Bhagidari workshops conducted over the years, the improvement in the power situations is one of the highlights shared by many of the stakeholders. There was a drastic positive change in the processes of getting new meter connections, load enhancement, payment of bills, and attendance to various power-related complaints. Earlier, getting a new meter connection was a major challenge but by the year 2010 an average lead time for a new connection was seven days.

Generally, consumers are fairly satisfied with the power situation. However, there are some pockets where there is still poor power infrastructure mainly because of power theft and also because several of them are unauthorized colonies.

Since Delhi is largely dependent on the riparian states for water and there is a continuous population influx, water has been a major challenge. In the initial stages of Bhagidari, citizens' associations had several complaints, both about the availability and the quality of water in year 2000. The suggestions and inputs by citizens' associations during the Bhagidari interactive process were seriously considered by the Delhi government and responsive decisions were made to both augment the water and to improve the water supply. Over the years, the following actions (*Working Report 2011* by the Government of NCT of Delhi) have been taken:

- Water conservation and rain water harvesting
- Increase of water from recycling plants at Haiderpur, Wazirabad, and Bhagirathi and full commissioning of Nangloi Water Treatment Plant
- Commissioning of underground water reservoirs to rationalize water supply
- Installation of bulk meters in plant outlets and booster pumping stations to do water audit
- DJB laid sewerage systems in 120 urban villages and 34 rural villages in Delhi as well as in all 44 resettlement colonies, 528 regularized colonies, and 267 unauthorized colonies
- Project developed to lay interceptor sewers for the three largest drains
- Revamping of old sewage pumping station and sewage treatment plants
- Introduction of project management system for online management of physical and financial progress of water supply
- Authorization to Jeevan Centers and post offices to collect the water bill payments

(Please also see Chapter 5 for the DJB case study of internal change management through large-group dynamics.)

The Delhi government continues to make efforts to improve the situation in consultation and collaboration with citizen' associations through the Bhagidari process.

As of December 2010, the Government of Delhi continues to face the challenge of multiple authorities in the Bhagidari process and also the lack of understanding on the part of the people that major organizations such as the MCD, DDA, Delhi Police, and NDMC do not come under the authority of the Delhi government.

The overall impact of the Bhagidari concept and the large-group dynamics process has been very positive. Yet, there is a lot more to achieve over the coming years. The RWAs and MTAs are demanding a legal framework for citizens' partnership with government. However, it is beyond the jurisdiction of the Delhi government to do so. Yet, in an informal way, the system has already been institutionalized. The citizens have become accustomed to interacting closely with and being consulted by the government. It appears that no government in future can afford ignoring the citizens' associations or the process of citizens' partnership with government (see Table 7.6 for awards and citations).

Table 7.6
Awards and Citations

Year	Award	Recognition/Award-giving Agency
2001[a]	Bhagidari scheme recognized by the Government of India by sponsoring Bhagidari documentation and recommending for implementation to other state governments	Government of India
2002[a]	CAPAM International Innovations Award Programme 2002 (category: Innovations in Governance)	Commonwealth Agency for Public Administration and Management
2003[a]	Participated in the URBIS 2003 International Fair and Congress on Modern Techniques for Urban Management	Sao Paolo Municipal Government
2004[a]	Dubai International Award for Best Practices 2004 (category: Urban Governance: Citizen–Government Partnership and responsiveness in the Public Sector)	UN Habitat and Dubai Municipality
2005[a]	United Nations Public Service Award 2005 (Category 'Improving transparency, accountability, and responsiveness in the Public Service')	Division for Public Administration & Development Management of UN Economic and Social Affairs
2005[a]	International Innovations Exhibition 2005 held as part of the 6th Global Forum on Reinventing Government, Seoul, South Korea	Exhibition Secretariat, 6th Global Forum, Seoul, South Korea

Table 7.6 continued

Table 7.6 continued

Year	Award	Recognition/Award-giving Agency
2006[a]	CAPAM International Innovations Award Programme 2006 (Category Innovations in Governance) 1. Stree Shakti 2: Bhagidari Scheme	Commonwealth Agency for Public Administration and Management, London, UK
2006[b]	Smt. Sheila Dikshit awarded Golden Peacock Award for Women Leadership	Institute of Directors, India
2008[c]	Best e-Governed State of India Award was conferred on Delhi following a survey conducted by IDC India for Dataquest.	Dataquest
2009[d]	Indira Priyadarshini Vriksha Mitra Award for increasing and maintaining the green cover in Delhi.	Ministry of Environment and Forests, Government of India
2010[e]	Delhi bagged the 8th India Today State of States Conclave Award 2010 in the category of best small state.	India Today

Sources: The sources for different awards marked by a, b, c, and d and e are as follows:
[a] Bhagidari Report: *Eight Years of Success—Glimpses of Partnership Progress*, Bhagidari Cell, Government of NCT of Delhi.
[b] http://goldenpeacockawards.com/
[c] http://blogs.thehindu.com/delhi/?p=4674
[d] http://www.delhi.gov.in/wps/wcm/connect/environment/Enviroment/Home/Environmental+Issues/
[e] *2010 Working Report*, p. 35, Government of Delhi.

• ◆

8

Bhagidari Initiatives by Discoms

As mentioned earlier in Chapter 4, in the year 2000 a major woe of the citizens of Delhi was the power supply in Delhi in almost all aspects. In the first few years of the Bhagidari workshops, any feedback process adopted to seek views and perceptions of the citizens invariably highlighted power as a major problem. The power infrastructure was poor, there were long breakdowns and load-sheddings, frequent voltage fluctuations were a regular feature, and customer service was poor. It was extremely difficult to get a new connection (see Appendix 7). The revenue loss (including theft, transmission, and distribution losses) was very high (above 60 percent).

In this background, after seeking people's views and gaining full-hearted support for power-sector reforms, the CM of Delhi, Ms Sheila Dikshit, decided on the PPP model and set up three joint-venture companies with Tata Power and Reliance Group (Anil Dhirubhai Ambani Group [ADAG]) with 49:51 percent equity share between the Delhi Government and each of these companies for power distribution in Delhi. The power reform package included setting up a Delhi Power Generation Co. (Genco) and a Transco. While the New Delhi Municipal Council and Delhi Cantonment Board continued to distribute power in the New Delhi and cantonment area, respectively, the three new power distribution companies took over the responsibility of power distribution in the rest of the city as per the geographical areas delineated in their agreements. While Tata Power Delhi Distribution Ltd. (then known as NDPL) was given the north and north-west part of Delhi, the Reliance Group was allocated in central, west, south, and east Delhi for power distribution. Subsequently, Reliance Group (known as BSES) further subdivided itself into two groups:

1. BSES Rajdhani Power Ltd. (BRPL)
2. BSES Yamuna Power Ltd. (BYPL)

While BRPL distributes power in the south and west areas, BYPL distributes power in the central and east areas of Delhi. This joint venture under the PPP model created a merger-like situation. Several of the employees of the erstwhile Delhi Vidyut Board (DVB) now became employees of these new entities for power distribution. Thus, all the three power distribution companies had both the erstwhile DVB employees as well as employees of the two private companies.

The distribution companies became active participants in the Bhagidari process. Having found it useful, they decided to use this process directly between them and their customers. Tata Power first used this process for internal change management for organizational integration, and later on BSES for interaction between the company employees and the RWAs/MTAs. NDPL (Tata Power) titled these workshops as Srijan Workshops and BRPL and BYPL named them as Bijli Bhagidari Workshops.

Areas served by Tata Power Delhi Distribution Ltd. (formerly NDP) in Delhi: Shakti Nagar, Civil Lines, Model Town, Keshavpuram, Moti Nagar, Pitam Pura, Bawana, Narela, Shalimar Bagh, Badli, Mangol Puri, and Rohini.

Internal Change Management for Organizational Integration through Large-group Dynamics by Tata Power Delhi Distribution Ltd.

The management of the then NDPL under the leadership of its CEO, Shri Anil Kumar Sardana, was concerned about the fact that two different cultures were operational in the company (i) those of erstwhile DVB and (ii) those of the Tata Power Company employees. This was having an adverse impact in the atmosphere and team work in the company. After discussion with the authors, the management decided to adopt the Large-group Dynamic Process to improve this situation.

In the year 2005, NDPL organized two internal workshops in the month of June and October to ensure that a large number of employees from both entities could sit together and share ways and means of becoming one integrated organization. In preparation of these workshops, first ACORD had a meeting with senior officials of NDPL to plan for this process. This was followed by personal interviews with a cross section of all levels of employees.

The findings of the survey were presented to the Top Team of NDPL in a one-day Top Team Workshop attended by the CEO and Top Management Team of NDPL. In this workshop, the Top Team of NDPL identified the following six major change goals to be focused upon during the two Large-group Interactive Workshops of approximately 240 and 225 participants, respectively:

1. (a) NDPL as one integrated organization
   (b) NDPL as our organization
2. How to build one culture and one identity?
3. How to increase/improve effectiveness of communication at all levels in NDPL:
   (a) Building full trust
   (b) Developing fact-based communication
   (c) Reducing/eliminating rumor
4. How to build/evolve a performance-based and performance-recognition culture at all levels?
5. How to enhance employee engagement in productive work at all levels?
6. (a) How to enhance employee development and employee satisfaction?
   (b) How to integrate employee goals and organization goals?

After this, the standard steps of the process like Design Workshop and Support Team Workshop were conducted. A Core Design Team was formed out of the Design Team each time.

The Top Team fully participated in both the workshops of three days each. In some sessions, they sat on different tables with personnel from other levels and functions in the organization, and in some other sessions, they sat together as a group of the Top Team itself. Similarly, other participants also worked in mixed groups in some sessions and in their functional groups in others as per the design of the workshop.

After the standard steps of Design Team Workshop and Support Team Workshop, the Top Team was briefed one day before the workshop on the preparations done. At the end of each day of the workshop, a review meeting was held with the Top Team and appropriate decisions were taken for the following day. The workshops were received very well by the employees. They energized the group to work together. The fact that the entire Top Team sat throughout the three days, participating with all levels of employees, in itself was a morale booster. During the workshop, the employees got an opportunity to work together, both in their mixed group of different functions and levels of employees, as well as with their own functional group for different sessions.

Outcome of the Workshops

Apart from open sharing of views, perceptions, problems, and solutions in an unanimous manner and appreciation and expectation, six Action Teams were formed on each of the above mentioned change-goal areas. Each team consisted of 10–15 officials from across NDPL zones/departments. Some of them were volunteers and others were nominees—each Action Team had a mentor from the Top Team with the main responsibility to guide, remove road blocks, and smoothen the part for rapid implementation of the committed action plans to achieve the change-goals and performance improvement parameters.

Srijan and Bijli Bhagidari workshops

Areas served by BRPL in Delhi: Alaknanda, Khanpur, Saket, Vasant Kunj, Nehru Place, Nizamuddin, Sarita Vihar, R.K. Puram, Hauz Khas, Janak Puri, Najafgarh, Jaffarpur, Nangloi, Mundka, Punjabi Bagh, Tagore Garden, Vikas Puri, Palam Vihar, and Dwarka.

Areas served by BYPL in Delhi: Chandni Chowk, Darya Ganj, Paharganj, Shandar Road, Patel Nagar, Karkardooma, GT Road, Krishna Nagar, Laxmi Nagar, Mayur Vihar I & II, Mayur Vihar III, Yamuna Vihar, Karawal Nagar, and Nand Nagri.

The employees of the three power distribution companies have been regularly participating as stakeholders in all the Bhagidari workshops organized for civic issues. In these workshops, they have been interacting with the RWAs and exchanging views, perceptions, and information with them for the benefit of both. Apart from this, the Top Team of these companies have been sharing information with the participants on their plans, schemes, policies, achievements, and so on for a few minutes in each of those workshops. However, since the Bhagidari workshops for citywide change takes up issues of several civic organizations, the power distribution companies like other organizations get only some of the time of the workshop on issues of direct concerns. While this is useful for both the companies and the citizens, it does not provide them enough time to deal with all the issues of their concerns.

Therefore, all the three distribution companies have been using the LGIP Process designed and facilitated by the authors and their colleagues under the leadership of:

- Shri Sunil Wadhwa, managing director of TPDDL
- Shri Gopal Saxena, CEO of BRPL
- Shri Ramesh Narayanan, CEO of BYPL

These workshops are of one or two days' duration. The major objectives of these workshops are to help both the companies and the citizens to communicate openly with each other and develop a clear understanding of each other's problems, expectations, roles, and limitations, so that the power distribution in the city continues to be highly efficient.

Over the years, this communication has assumed greater importance in the background of drastic shift in the policies, procedures, systems, infrastructure, and so on adopted by the joint venture initiative between the government and the power distribution companies under the PPP model. While on the one hand, the actual service delivery has continued to improve over a period of time as per the citizens' feedback (Appendix 8), they did not necessarily understand this changed structure and model. Therefore, the companies used the Srijan and Bijli Bhagidari workshops to communicate with them on these and other issues of regular services. Not only were the positive and negative perceptions of the citizens along with those of the employees who were sitting together on the tables understood, the employees and the consumers identified problems and solutions for better performance. All the standard steps of large-group dynamics were followed in these workshops. Some of the issues worked upon during the workshops included:

- Plus and minus points of the distribution companies' performance
- Understanding of the fact that the distribution companies are 100 percent regulated under Delhi Electricity Regulatory Commission (DERC), which is an independent, statutory body, not under the Delhi government
- Helping people to understand the concept of capital employed and the 16 percent limit on the return on capital employed only—not 16 percent on revenue as commonly misunderstood
- Causes of power outage and how to reduce the power bills of consumers by the companies

- Solution to customer care issues and the actions required by the citizens
- Improvement in the power supply and services

These workshops are highly appreciated by the citizens since they deal with several of their concerns. The companies are also highly appreciative of the process that provides them an opportunity to understand the citizens' concerns and address them in their future policies and plans.

9

Political Leadership for Building Citizens' Partnership with Government

In the previous chapters we have described the processes followed for deepening urban day-to-day democracy under the banner of Bhagidari based on the new democratic vision and commitment of the CM Ms Sheila Dikshit through citizens' partnership. As mentioned earlier, in terms of the available data, Ms Sheila Dikshit is the only political leader in Asia, and probably in the world so far, consistently using multistakeholder Large-group Dynamics Processes involving both the citizens and the officials in a partnership to bring about citywide change for citizen-centric governance.

Right at the beginning of her first term, Ms Sheila Dikshit developed a vision of participatory democracy in the specific form of building citizens' partnership with government. Subsequently, she actively searched for what she called a proven set of processes to build and sustain such a partnership between divergent stakeholders. She even clarified that such proven processes could be from any part of the world as long as they could be successfully adapted for the culture and ground realities in India.

Out of several options she chose the Large-group Dynamic Process in which ACORD had experience and expertise in India. This indeed was a bold decision made by her in the early days of her very first term as the elected leader of the city-state of Delhi. Although based upon the discussion with the authors, the CM was eager to start this process for achieving citywide change in Delhi (the capital city of India), she was reasonably cautious that in the first year the process should be tried at a pilot level to see how it works and to get feedback from participating stakeholders.

Ms Dikshit had to face a fair amount of natural skepticism and even opposition to her decision, both from some of her political colleagues as well as from parts of the bureaucracy (even though her Principal Secretary Mr S. Regunathan was a prime mover in introducing the process for achieving the vision of citizens' partnership in democratic functioning). Her manner of dealing with both skepticism and opposition was non-confrontationist. Though she listened to their doubts and objections, yet it did not deter her from the decision to follow the process of large-group dynamics, and she continued to persuade her political colleagues to join in the larger vision of citizens' partnership in a democracy. Gradually, some of them did become supportive but others refrained or continued to oppose. She went ahead resolutely and confidently yet listening to all points of view.

Ms Dikshit saw this process as a great opportunity for her to get more varied feedback as an elected representative by building a rapport with very different stakeholders. In her own words, the Bhagidari process actually provides her with an "opportunity to 'connect' with people on a continuous basis" without impinging upon the duties and rights of the elected representatives.

Ms Dikshit was born in a nonpolitical, middle-class professional family of Punjab (Kapurthala)—this is quite rare in Indian politics. She grew up in Delhi and studied at prestigious educational institutes till her postgraduation from the University of Delhi. She married a bureaucrat who was the son of a senior political leader. Probably, it is this background that has given her a unique opportunity to see governance from all the three perspectives, that is, of an ordinary middle-class "citizen," a "bureaucrat," and a "politician." She seems to have developed a fairly good blend of these three perspectives in her leadership style. Well educated and well groomed, she comes across as a warm yet professional leader. In her dealing with citizens, Ms Sheila Dikshit positions herself as a leader beyond the party line. Consequently, most RWAs and MTAs (regardless of their personal preferences and loyalties toward different political parties) continue to actively engage with the Bhagidari process. For instance, while being approached by an RWA member who, after seeking her help, deliberately informed her about his political loyalties with an opposition party, she asserted that as a CM she was responsible for the welfare of all the citizens of Delhi regardless of their political preferences.

Ms Sheila Dikshit has also consistently shown respect for the principles and methodologies that need to be followed for successful implementation of large-group dynamics processes to achieve the citywide change, and also respected the expertise of the consultants trained in multistakeholder large-group dynamics. The processes require large-scale meticulous organization and hard work by government officials. Her sincere and genuine commitment to achieve results through the Bhagidari process is often not shared by some in government. Yet she has successfully managed to carry most people along for over a decade to ensure that it is implemented properly. Till the writing of this book (2012), over 100 Bhagidari workshops have been organized successfully by the Delhi government, designed and facilitated by ACORD for 200 to 800 participants based on multistakeholder large-group dynamics. In her endeavor to ensure that the officers were serious about their involvement in this process, her government got a clearance from the Ministry of Home Affairs (Government of India) to add performance evaluation in Bhagidari as a part of its annual confidential reports. Since her first term in the year 2000, the authors have closely interacted and worked with Ms Dikshit as the CM and seen her as genuinely democratic in her actions with the following demonstrated actions:

1. She encourages people to share feedback, ideas, and opinions so that she can make her decisions based on them.
2. The participating citizens have largely felt included, involved, and engaged with the government, both for sharing their concerns as well as for suggesting solutions jointly with officers.
3. She likes to include her political colleagues in the process and continues to invite them to join the Bhagidari process.
4. The officers working closely with her have often expressed their satisfaction with the fact that the CM encourages them to be creative and gives them the opportunity to try new ideas.
5. In the nearly 100-citizen official workshops, she is seen and experienced directly as genuinely empathetic and yet willing to state facts for the sake of clarity, and also to avoid misunderstanding of issues.

As she once stated, her major satisfaction in the Bhagidari process is the opportunity that it provides her to listen to the voices of the civil society. The fact that this process keeps her in touch with people's views, perceptions, and needs makes it possible for her to make several accurate decisions, policies, and programs based on the people's needs and feedback. An important fact here is that unlike a normal day-to-day interaction that the elected representatives have with the people, this process takes her and them beyond their geographical constituency. She has successfully utilized the process, method, and spirit of Bhagidari to relate and interact with people of all sections and strata of society in the city. Based on this direct feedback from stakeholders (both officials and the citizens), she has introduced programs and schemes affecting a wide range of people from all strata of society. This includes feeding the destitute through Aap ki Rasoi[1] or a subsidized mid day meal for them, welfare schemes, and financial support to the poor and introduction of CNG fuel in all public vehicles in Delhi to reduce the air pollution in the city. The Public Grievance Commission for the city was also set up by her in response to the citizens' feeling that the people's grievances were not being heard or resolved.

Another unique characteristic of Ms Sheila Dikshit is her ability to motivate the citizens as well as officers in joining her in her vision of making Delhi a world-class city. For instance, planting a million trees to increase the green cover in Delhi, promoting natural colors during the "Holi" festival, and reducing use of crackers under the campaign of "Say No to Crackers" during the festival of Diwali has reduced air pollution in the city in that festival season.

However, she regrets that she has not yet succeeded in improving the sanitation and waste management in Delhi through Bhagidari for a variety of factors (including the fact that the MCD, which handles this responsibility, is not under the jurisdiction of the Delhi government).

The CM's biggest regret is the multiplicity of authority (or the fractured authority) in Delhi, which continues to obstruct her endeavor to improve governance in Delhi. This includes major organizations which do not report to the Delhi government or its CM like the MCD, DDA, and Delhi Police who are responsible for 60–70 percent of work in Delhi but come under the Government of India, Ministry of Home Affairs. An average citizen, and even the media, is either ignorant or forgetful of this situation. This puts the Delhi government in an unenviable situation where the authority lies elsewhere but people hold them responsible for whatever goes wrong in Delhi, regardless of jurisdiction.

Yet, she has succeeded to some extent in bringing in Delhi Police who have worked with the RWAs/MTAs on projects and schemes like neighborhood watch, security gates, boundary walls of the colonies, market-level traffic management, and so on. Some departments and officers of MCD have also participated, but not significantly enough to make a major difference.

Ms Sheila Dikshit has encouraged the citizens to improve the quality of life at the colony and market levels through the Bhagidari project based on large-group dynamics. Through this process, colony-level projects have been jointly identified and implemented by the citizens' associations and the concerned departments (at the colony/market level). As mentioned in Chapter 8, in a Bhagidari Review Workshop during 2007 the number of projects implemented at the residential colony-level and market-level had already crossed 3,000 at that time, and subsequently increased further.

Her ability to respond to the reasonable suggestions and requests of the citizens also keeps them motivated to stay engaged in the Bhagidari process. For instance, My Delhi I Care Fund, introduced by the government in the year 2006, provides financial support of up to ₹5 lakhs to the RWAs/MTAs for colony-level projects (after due diligence by the DC of the concerned revenue district—the limit per district was ₹50 lakhs). Based on more than 5,000 successfully implemented projects, she has now raised this fund to ₹5 crores per district.

She is clearly a people's person and a charismatic leader. Most people find her warm, pleasant, and accessible yet professional. The authors have heard many citizens from different strata of society say that she reaches out to everyone and is a patient listener to all points of view. Citizens have often remarked that it is the Bhagidari process, which has brought her back to power twice consecutively (after the first election), since it is a two-way communication and bonding on a continuous basis.

On the whole, the CM Ms Sheila Dikshit comes across as a unique political leader with a clear vision and commitment:

1. To build and sustain citizens' partnership with government
2. To make Delhi the best city in the country, and one of the best in the world
3. To do this through reliable processes of multistakeholder large-group dynamics, which help in the discovery of a common ground

She has demonstrated this in action for more than 10 years through a mission to create a "day-to-day working-democracy" in partnership with citizens' associations, the civil service officers, the elected representatives, and the political executives. She also searched for reliable processes from the social sciences and behavioral sciences from around the world to help in discovery of common ground to successfully resolve divergent and opposing interests.

Note

1   Your kitchen.

10

The Possible Future Evolution of Citizens' Partnership with Government in Delhi

During the last decade (2000–2010), utilizing the principles and processes of multistakeholder large-group dynamics, the foundation process of building the citizens' partnership with government has been achieved. More than 90 large-group multistakeholder workshops have been designed and conducted by ACORD, New Delhi, based on group dynamics, involving:

- Over 2,500 RWAs including federations (run by citizens)
- Over 100 MTAs (run by citizens)
- Twenty-two Industrial Estates Associations (run by citizens)
- Over 900 schools
- Over 1,000 eco-clubs
- More than half the SCA
- Several government departments and Civic Service Agencies, including
    - The MCD
    - The NDMC
    - The DJB, handling water supply systems and sewage systems
    - The three discoms (Power Distribution Companies)
    - Delhi Police
    - Department of Education

- Department of Health
- Department of VAT
- Department of Environment and Forests
- Department of Irrigation and Flood Control
- Department of Power
- Department of Social Welfare
- Department of Women and Child Development
- Nine Deputy Commissioners' offices (each heading the district administration and revenue functions of the nine districts in Delhi)

Spread over this period of 10 years, the following momentum indicators provide a snapshot of key parameters of effectiveness:

1. Starting with 20 citizens' associations (in the form of RWAs) more than 3,000 RWAs have got formally formed in 12 years (by citizen groups in 3,000 residential areas or housing societies) and registered themselves with the Bhagidari Cell (in the CM's office) to request participation in the multistakeholder large-group dynamics workshops (called Bhagidari workshops) in Delhi. More RWAs are constantly getting formed (as registered societies under the Societies Act) and, at any given time, 400 to 500 RWAs are patiently waiting to participate in their first Bhagidari workshop along with officials working for civic services delivery in their residential areas. This itself indicates
   (a) the informal feedback citizens have given each other about the usefulness of these workshops;
   (b) the pull factor or attraction factor of this process.
2. During this decade, over 4,000 successfully implemented projects (up to 2010) have been reported and documented briefly by RWAs and MTAs (please see Chapter 7). These are ground-level projects for improving more than 25 types of civic services through partnership projects taken up by RWAs/MTAs in collaboration with one, two, or even three different departments or civic service agencies. After proper verification on the ground, these projects are documented (including photographs) and showcased in an annual Bhagidari exhibition to which the public and media are invited. The best projects (both of citizen groups, as well as the larger ones undertaken by departments) are given public recognition through annual awards and prizes. Some

RWAs have completed more than 10 projects successfully in 10 years and nearly 40 percent of them have completed two to three projects in this period. It is these completed projects taken up by the RWAs' initiative and implemented by RWAs and departments jointly that are a major parameter of effectiveness of the multi-stakeholder large-group dynamics process.

3. During review meetings, review workshops, and surveys, RWAs are also reporting that there is better cooperation and help from most departments in terms of acting on their complaints or requests for help with regard to solving some problem of their residential areas (this is different from partnering in a project initiated by the RWA or MTA reported in [2] above).

4. While the citizens' associations have got energized and have sustained their energy over the years to initiate and implement small and medium residential-area projects, the government also seems to have been energized to initiate and complete large cityscape changing urban projects. Comparing the Delhi of the year 2000 to that of 2010, the RWAs report many significant improvements in survey workshops. Chief among them are:

   • Building, running, and continuously expanding the new metro electric train service

   • Shifting the whole public transport system (including buses, autos, taxis) to CNG instead of diesel, thus lowering the air pollution significantly

   • Phasing out the old buses and bringing in new, low-floor buses (including air-conditioned buses)

   • In contrast with six to eight hours of power cuts across Delhi in 2000, especially in peak summer and winter, now there is an average of 98 percent uptime in electricity supply mainly due to the government's power reform program through the PPP model through three power distribution companies in Delhi, in which the Delhi government holds 49 percent equity and the private partner company holds 51 percent and also runs the operations, maintenance, and technology upgradations

   • More than 70 new flyovers to ease traffic congestion (Delhi has more cars than Mumbai, Kolkata, and Chennai combined, not counting all other forms of traffic)

   • Tree-cover increase from 27 sq. km in 1999 to over 300 sq. km in 2010

- The vast improvement in government school students' pass percentage (Standard X pass percentage from 40.20 percent in 2000–2001 to 99.23 percent in 2011–2012 [http://edu-del.nic.in/Result_Analysis/2012/ResultCBSE10th2012.pdf] and Standard XII pass-percentage from 70.20 percent in 2000–2001 to 87.72 percent in 2011–2012 [http://edudel.nic.in/Result_Analysis/2012/ResultCBSE12th2012.pdf])

In one of the review workshops, organized in 2012, half the table groups cited 30 or more improvements in Delhi achieved since the year 2000, while one table group listed 59 tangible positive developments in Delhi in the last 10 years (for detailed listing by the citizens, see Appendix 9).

Thus, the citizens' associations and the government have been mutually energizing and motivating each other through this unique partnership process based on large-group dynamics. This government also has built a lot of credibility and trust through its visible performance-orientation and achievement-orientation, under the leadership of the CM Ms Sheila Dikshit.

Some governments focus on infrastructure development and schemes, but neglect the continuous communication and bonding with citizens. Other governments focus on the soft-skill communication and welfare measures but neglect infrastructure development. In contrast, since the year 2000 the Delhi government has successfully sustained its efforts and achievements on all three fronts:

- Continuous communication, listening to feedback, partnering, and bonding with 2,000 to 3,000 citizens' associations
- Building up the welfare measures where needed, especially for the poor, the old, women, children, slum populations, the destitute, unauthorized colonies, and so on
- The fast pace of development, construction, and completion of several types of city infrastructure improving public transportation, power, water, air-pollution, hospitals and health services, bus-stops, street signages, street-lighting, and so on among others

What about the next 5 to 10 years? How can the democratic project of citizens' partnership with government evolve and grow beyond the phase of citizen-initiated projects (small and medium, at the residential-area level or market/shopping-area level), which are implemented in partnership with relevant departments?

In response to this question, three specific paths can be visualized.

The Citizens' Feedback Path

The 3,000+ citizens' associations can be given a regular formal feedback role, covering some of the civic services that are important to the people. To start with, a monthly feedback system can be designed to cover:

- Drinking water supply
- Drainage in residential areas
- Sewage system performance
- Street lighting
- Power supply
- Garbage cleaning

A monthly five-point rating scale can be utilized (where 1 = excellent and 5 = very poor). The 3,000+ RWAs/MTAs can be familiarized with the system in one-day workshops. An independent agency can be appointed to collect the monthly feedback (on the above six civic services), computerize the data, and make a simple A–B–C analysis, highlighting urgent/immediate action by the department/civic agency concerned about the areas getting a five or a four. One copy of the monthly analytic report would go to the concerned HoD/civic agency and one each to the CMO's and the CS's office.

This is based on the fact that

1. any system is only as good as the feedback it is seeking from its consumers on a systematic basis, and not on a complaint basis;
2. any system is only as good as the value it places on the feedback from consumers and the quick action it takes on consumer feedback.

The Government of Delhi (and hence each department or civic agency) has 3,000 potential points of possible regular feedback (feedback can later even be sought weekly, if necessary). This Citizen's Feedback System can be initially introduced as a pilot program since both citizens' associations, as well as departments/civic agencies need to go through an action-learning process to work together in partnership with different public service systems. In this way, gradually, both citizens associations and departments/civic agencies can get empowered to function at a high level of partnership and collaboration in (i) providing regular, reliable feedback; (ii) acting fast on the feedback provided; (iii) raising the overall systemic performance levels of several civic services; and (iv) building a culture of citizen-centric public administration, and placing "service delivery for all" at the center.

Involvement of Citizens' Associations in Participatory Planning

The next phase of evolution of citizen's partnership with the government (after the monthly or weekly feedback role works well for a year or two) could be to add a role: citizens' association could be involved in participatory planning for the city-state of Delhi.

As of December 2010, the city of Delhi was divided into 272 municipal wards. The 73rd constitutional amendment also envisaged the setting up of "ward committees" to devolve democratic functioning at the ground level in terms of urban democratic governance.

The citizens association (whether RWAs, MTAs, or SCAs could be invited to nominate a member or office-bearer each and along with the Ward Councillor form a Ward Planning Group in a formal sense.

The members of the Ward Planning Group can be trained in basic techniques of participatory planning (these have been quickly learned by rural and urban groups around the world over the past 20 years, including semi-literate groups).

Subsequent to their orientation and training, the members of the Ward Planning Groups can begin their work with basic surveys of the colonies in their ward, covering:

- Condition of drains (including blockages, breeding mosquitoes, and flies)
- Condition of water supply (including quantity, quality, and timings)
- Condition of street lighting
- Condition of garbage clearing and sanitation
- Condition of sewage system (including blockage and overflow)
- Condition of roads (including internal roads and back lanes) and footpaths/pavements
- Condition of air pollution

- Condition of traffic congestion, parking congestion, and so on
- Condition of electricity supply (including safety aspects, power theft, and so on)
- Condition of community parks, municipal gardens, tree cover, and so on
- Any other points agreed by the Ward Planning Group including the number and condition of schools and public health facilities

After the members of the Ward Planning Group complete their surveys, they meet under the chairmanship of the Ward Councillor to share and discuss their survey data and prepare a Ward Survey Report.

The Ward Councillor can then request relevant municipal officials (who handle ward planning) to meet the members of the Ward Planning Committee and make presentations on the principles and practices followed for ward planning in the past by the municipal body.

The Ward Planning Group then meets several times to prepare:

1. Priority needs of the ward
2. A Basic Ward Plan to meet the high priority needs of the ward

In this way citizen-based ward plans can be prepared for all the municipal wards in Delhi, and through the Ward Councillors forwarded to the commissioner (Municipal Corporation) as citizens' perceptions and priorities for Ward Planning to be utilized by the Planning Department of the Municipal Corporation.

A similar process of involving citizens' associations in participatory planning all the Delhi Assembly constituencies can also be considered for raising the level and involvement of citizens partnership with government. This section has focused on current or short-term planning, involving citizens associations in the process.

Involving Citizens' Associations in Delhi's Long-range Planning

To further upgrade and evolve citizens' partnership with government in Delhi, they can be involved as a partner in critical long-range planning for Delhi.

Delhi has many professionals (both retired and working) from a wide variety of service, technology, engineering, medicine, management, water, environment, economics, accounting, legal, and so on both from theoretical and applied disciplines.

By 2050 Delhi's population will double to 32–35 million and Delhi has no space to expand.

Water is likely to be the number one major crisis point, a short list of potential major crisis points could include:

- Water, including recharging of ground water and how to augment new sources of supply
- Housing, especially low-cost housing in the context of the expected growth of slums and unauthorized colonies
- Basic infrastructure such as drainage, sewage pipelines, STPs, water distribution lines, and so on
- Air-pollution, vehicular congestion, climate change, and global warming
- Public transport systems
- Public health systems
- Roads and road-systems
- Overcrowding and in-migration to Delhi from all states
- Use of the fixed area of 1,473 sq. km of space (Delhi, unlike other capital cities, cannot expand at all since it is hemmed in by other state boundaries)

For each of these aspects of Delhi's explosion growth and potential crisis points, a Long-range Planning Group can be set up consisting of half the members from eminent professional citizens (retired or working) and half from civil service officers.

While the members should be fully briefed on the short-term and medium-term plans which are already in place, their entire focus needs to be on creative long-term planning focusing on a 10-year to 25-year (or even 50-year) timeframe, and finding and pilot-testing solutions to manage Delhi's expected explosive growth and its predictable crisis points. Professionally qualified citizens and civil service officers who are constituted into Long-range Planning Groups can build valuable partnerships and resources in developing solutions to the major issues that can become major threats to Delhi's goal to build and sustain a clean, green, and world-class city. Long-range planning for anticipatory solutions is a neglected area (especially in the 25–50–100-year horizon) and technically qualified and experienced citizens can add much value in working closely with relevant qualified officials to build much needed resources for the future of Delhi.

Citizens' Report Cards on Government Performance

Citizens' associations (whether RWAs or MTAs) have been interacting closely (through their office-bearers) with most of the Civic Service Departments as well as with elected MLAs and councillors (of the Municipal Corporation). Similarly, the office-bearers of the citizens' associations have detailed interactions with civil service officers in various departments (whether for solving problem or providing necessary services to residential areas and market/shopping areas. Over the period of 10 years (2000 to 2010), the RWA/MTA elected office-bearers get to know who are helpful, who are hard working, who are honest, and who are effective in problem solving and service-delivery (both in the bureaucracy as well as in the political establishment).

This special knowledge that has accumulated over 5–10 years can be tapped and utilized through citizens' partnership to improve governance—through Citizens' Associations Performance Report Cards.

These Citizens Report Cards could be produced on a six-monthly basis and could initially cover:

1. Civic service departments and agencies handling:
    - City-cleaning and garbage disposal
    - Drainage
    - Drinking water supply
    - Sewage system functioning
    - Power supply and quality
    - Public hospitals
    - Government schools
    - MCD schools
    - Bus transport
    - Auto transport
    - Public distribution system for rations
    - Social welfare department
    - Citizen's safety and security
    - Traffic management
2. Performance of all the elected Ward Councillors of the MCD
3. Performance of all the elected MLAs
4. Performance of the ministers holding portfolio

The Centre for Public Affairs in Bengaluru (formerly Bangalore) has accumulated experience in developing and testing systems and processes for generating reliable Citizens Report Cards on government performance. They also have experience in training and educating citizens and citizens' associations in generating reliable and useful feedback for improving governance and civic service delivery. A government that could ask citizens' associations for regular, periodic Performance Report Cards (whether for departments, civic agencies, MLAs, councillors, or the cabinet), and which could utilize such reports and feedback for improving governance and service delivery levels, would represent the height of citizens' partnership in governance. Many details need to be worked out and pilot-testing done extensively but first a clear democratic vision needs to be developed that citizens are the source of power in a democracy as well as partners in improving governance.

The systems and measures suggested in this chapter can not only help in evolving and upgrading the level of citizens' partnership with government but also raise the quality of day-to-day "working democracy" and help to institutionalize the role of citizens' associations in good governance.

11

Feedback from Citizens' Associations and Civil Service Officials on Steps Needed to Improve the Effectiveness of Bhagidari

The basic principle running through the movement to build and sustain citizens' participation with government since the year 2000 has been the principle of stakeholder's continuous feedback—both negative and positive feedback. Ms Sheila Dikshit, the CM, has been personally present at every workshop listening patiently to much feedback, reading a lot of feedback, responding with openness to feedback, and thinking of ways to improve the quality of life for citizens, thus setting a live example for senior and mid-level civil service officers to shift gradually to a citizen-centric administrative model. The CM comes through sincerely when she thanks the citizens' associations and officials for their feedback and suggestions, and she also communicates how several concrete projects to improve the quality of life were inspired by the stakeholders' feedback on issues, problems, and minus points of life in Delhi. This she has done consistently in nearly 100 large-group workshops over more than 10 years, thus providing a live example of "seeking feedback, openness to feedback, and looking for ways to act on feedback." This key feature has provided the credibility and trust in the relationship between citizens and the government; she has often also admitted that some problems are not yet solved, especially larger "systemic" issues.

This tradition of seeking and sharing feedback from citizens' associations and officials (including frontline or ground-level officials) continues till now.

In June and July 2012, a series of eight large-group workshops for review, feedback, and consultation were held in a large stadium. One of the subjects on which feedback was sought was on: How to improve the effectiveness of the Bhagidari itself?

A wide range of feedback and suggestions have emerged from more than 1,500 citizens' associations and officers from key civic-service departments and DCs' offices across all nine district administrations of Delhi. The feedback and suggestions range from micro to macro and are given below in the original and authentic words of the citizens and officials. This feedback is being taken very seriously and is being analyzed by the nine DC offices and the Bhagidari Cell (in the office of the CM) to come up with a plan of action for improving the process and effectiveness of Bhagidari (the citizens' partnership with government in Delhi). As one reads through the points (even repeat points) one gets a direct feel and flavor of a working democracy in action from the citizens; most of these points were read out and shared (in the large-group workshops) over the public-address system, so that all participants could hear what other table groups were thinking and saying. If the authors (or anyone else) edit or summarize the points, it will lose the flavor of democracy at work—hence the points are retained in the words of the participants.

The top 8 to 12 points of the feedback and suggestions given during these workshops are provided below—the points given in Hindi have been translated into English for this book.

How to Improve the Effectiveness of the Bhagidari Feedback and Suggestions from Citizens' Associations and Officials

West District (June 26, 2012)

- Bhagidari meetings should be more frequent and held in smaller groups at least three to four times in a year.

- Greater participation and coordination between the citizens and the government is required.
- Time-bound response, progress, and reporting of all matters/issues suggested by members in Bhagidari workshops.
- There should be proper monitoring or transparency regarding the funds sanctioned/spent on My Delhi I Care Scheme.
- Regular follow-up action on the points made in the monthly Bhagidari meetings with the HoDs being made personally responsible.
- Democratization in RWA and quasi-judicial powers should be given.
- For carrying out any proposed development work in any colony, the councillor/MLA/MP should also be involved in discussion with the concerned RWA in advance/anticipation before approval and carrying out of the work.
- The RWAs/MTAs should be given due importance by the service providing departments like DJB, BSES, MCD, and so on and their representations should be considered on a different footing/priority.

North-West District (June 27, 2012)

- Regular interaction between the concerned authority and officers of the Bhagidari Cell with RWA should be arranged.
- Proper coordination between the Bhagidari Cell and local bodies along with RWAs.
- Most of the day-to-day problems are being faced by women, so participation of women should be increased.
- Public should be made aware of work done through Bhagidari.
- RWAs should be involved at the stage of planning of development projects in their areas.
- The contact numbers of various office-bearers and authorities involved with Bhagidari must be provided to all association members of Bhagidari.
- RWAs' consent should be taken by government officials regarding development work and other important issues.
- RWAs' complaints/suggestions should be taken up on priority basis.
- More and more RWAs and Senior Citizens Groups should be associated with Bhagidari.

East District (June 28, 2012)

- There should be a meeting within a month with RWAs at their locality.
- In order to make Bhagidari more effective, any request/grievance received from RWA/MTA must be looked into through some coordinator to redress it in a time-bound manner.
- New developments in the area should be brought to the knowledge of RWAs for more effectiveness/awareness.
- Transparency needed in the whole system. More funds should be available for RWAs to improve the basic service in the area.
- Action taken report should be prepared and sent to all RWAs of the jurisdiction. Wherever action has not been taken in any matter, the reason for not doing so should be communicated to the concerned RWAs.
- There should be coordination among the executives and RWA for development works.
- All concerned officers should be present from all respective departments at Bhagidari meetings and ATRs should be communicated to all Bhagidars within the specific periods.
- Quantum of funds allocated under the Bhagidari scheme should be earmarked for respective RWAs.
- My Delhi I Care Fund should be provided on RWAs' request for developing its areas small needs. Thanks should be given for increasing the fund.

North-East District (June 29, 2012)

- Bhagidari meetings with RWA office-bearers and members should be held once in a month in which solutions to all problems of the district can be found after consultation.
- Information about the government's development plans and public interest works should be given to the RWA from time to time.
- The planning for development works of each colony should be done in collaboration with RWA representatives.
- Government should pass orders to the department officials that they should coordinate with the citizens who are working under the Bhagidari scheme, so that government schemes reach people.
- The Bhagidari Cell of the Delhi government should give some rights to RWAs along with duties, so that the concerned departments increase their efficiency by respecting RWAs.
- The action taken report on the decisions taken in the monthly meeting should be circulated in detail in the next meeting. Then only the decision on the next issues should be taken.

- RWA should be given funds to get small-level works done quickly in the colony, such as repair of hand pump, dustbin, water tap, motor in the parks, and expenditure on RWA office.
- All department officials should coordinate with RWA members so that each and every RWA can relate the problems of its area to the department officials and find solutions to them.

South District (July 3, 2012)

- There should be effective coordination in solving the day-to-day problems between civic agencies and RWAs/residents.
- My Delhi I Care Fund should be distributed quickly (within a month), so that the scheme can be started early.
- The regular camps of Bhagidari are required in different colonies along with the responsible government officers so that collective or individual problems can be solved on the spot.
- Public awareness must be created at a large scale and transparency in an organization's working through frequent meetings with the members of RWAs and all government departments.
- Any development work must be sanctioned in consultation with the RWA and after completion of work No Objection Certificate (NOC) should be issued by RWA.
- Time-bound delivery of services and its notification by DC's office.
- The senior citizens and ladies should be given more chance to attend the Bhagidari.
- Bigger and better publicity of Bhagidari movement is required so as to reach the public more readily.
- The list of names, phone numbers, and designations of Bhagidari officers should be shared.
- The amount sanctioned for projects for any RWA should be utilized within a certain period. How much fund is utilized for the RWA should be reported regularly to the Bhagidari Cell.
- Schemes launched by Delhi government must be informed to RWAs from time to time in writing.

South-West District (July 4, 2012)

- Higher degree of cooperation as well as coordination by interacting more through Bhagidari workshop/meeting, video conferencing. Core committee meeting at district level.
- Transparency in utilization of funds in RWAs.
- Sensitization of RWAs about their roles and responsibilities.

- Involvement of senior citizens and housewives in development works/activities in the area.
- Bhagidari meetings should be held monthly and regularly with officers of all concerned government department and RWAs and SCAs in each colony.
- Transparency and time-bound factor must be considered in solving problems reported during the workshop period.
- Bhagidari should also interfere in law and order situation with police and beat officers' meet with RWAs to improve law and order to minimize crimes.
- In every development work RWAs must be involved and NOC of work completion must be issued by RWAs before making payment to concerned party.
- The general public to be made more aware about Bhagidari through different sources.
- There should be transparency in allocation of funds and should not be restricted to the hands of DCs/nodal officers.

North District (July 5, 2012)

- Any development in the area should be executed after taking into confidence the RWAs regarding the scope of work.
- Bhagidari meetings should be held on a monthly basis.
- The Bhagidari Cell should have a better coordination with the RWAs through which they will be able to know the problems faced by the RWAs.
- Bhagidari programs should be decentralized up to colony/area level. For more effectiveness feedback be taken up in the next meeting.
- Publicity about Bhagidari programs through display of hoardings/charts, handbills, as well as through visual media.
- The allocated funds from Bhagidari should be used for the development of the RWA and the fund's intimation and allocation should also be circulated to the RWAs.
- All suggestions received in the Bhagidari workshop should be noted very seriously and a time-bound frame should be made for implementation of the suggestions. Also the respective officers should be made responsible for the same.
- It should be mandatory for the concerned departments to attend the meetings and their timely reply/work. There should be disciplinary action taken if they do not adhere to this.

Central and New Delhi District (July 6, 2012)

- Bhagidari meeting of a zonal area should be held at least once every month along with officials and local councillors.
- Time-bound programs should be there for the work to be done.
- A monitoring mechanism for evaluation of progress achieved is needed.
- For effectiveness of Bhagidari, government officers should be held responsible for the implementation of decisions taken in Bhagidari meetings very strictly.
- Interdepartment cooperation needs to be strengthened and accountability be fixed.
- Coordination between the government and public should be neat and clean and it should be time-bound.
- Bhagidari should be a two-way communication with regular feedback and meetings.

The complete details of all the points of feedback and suggestions for further improving citizens' partnership with government are provided in Appendix 10, covering all eight district-level workshops (which included citizens' groups and officials of 13 departments/civic agencies from all nine revenue districts).

12

Lessons Learned from 10 Years' of Delhi's Bhagidari Project on Building Citizens' Partnership in Governance

Reviewing the experience of Bhagidari, and after holding Focus Group Discussions (FGDs) with department officers and many telephonic survey interviews (one-to-one) with office-bearers of RWAs, the main lessons learned so far are the following:

1. The commitment, vision, and mission (of developing citizens as partners in governance, and not as the ruled) of the political leadership are vital and critical. This vision and mission of a higher level of democratic governance through partnership is needed to initiate and sustain the movement—it is nothing less than a movement, a new paradigm of democracy. The people can sense if the leadership is not genuine or not sincere, or is just using a technique for some other ends, or just temporary without deep conviction. Credibility is the first principle learned on which this quiet revolution is based.

2. The second learning is that the citizens need to be organized into living communities or units—citizens cannot be involved as separate individuals, but as a part of organized society. The key

concept here is legitimacy of the citizen groups. Hence the formation of registered societies, structured and formed with proper memorandum of aims and objects, and rules and regulations with elected office-bearers was a vital learning (for residential colonies, housing complexes, market, and trade associations, senior citizens, rural area associations, industries' associations, and so on). Both legitimacy and clarity of organization are important learning in working systematically with citizens to build a partnership with the government for democratic governance, partner projects, and development of a better quality of life.

3. The third learning is that a careful and appropriate choice of processes and models need to be made when working with different stakeholders, since different stakeholders have (i) differing interests and (ii) opposing or divergent interests. These meetings where differing and opposing interest groups meet for discussions without an appropriate, proven process very often breakdown and degenerate into conflict zones of different kinds. Stakeholders who are frustrated, angry, apathetic, or in a defensive/offensive mode share their pent-up feelings in a predictable cathartic process. The processes utilized need to handle the catharsis safely.

   Hence the related learning is that, as global research and practice has established so far, there is only one model and set of processes called large-group dynamics (which incorporates and uses small-group dynamics) which can successfully build consensus, ownership, and which can discover common ground out of different and opposing stakeholders or interest-groups. Without this careful and correct choice of process and model, the best of efforts could have broken down and failed. The alternate approaches of training programs, seminars, conferences, grievance-meetings, and so on do not work when multiple stakeholders with different, divergent, and opposing interests are involved in trying to achieve consensus or partnership.

4. A special Project Team needs to be set up at a very high level (under a principal secretary reporting directly to the CM) so that a clear signal goes out to all levels and departments that this is a serious, important project (Appendix 11).

5. The fourth learning is that the choice of colony-level or housing-complex-level project to be taken up after the Bhagidari workshop is best left to the choice and priorities as felt and decided by the RWAs/MTAs in a genuine democratic process—rather than being suggested or persuaded from the leadership at the top.

This is because the large-group dynamics and small-group dynamics processes create and sustain a strong sense of ownership and motivation during the three-day Large-group Interactive Workshop, which sustains even after the workshop. Second, the citizens' association know their colonies and housing complexes in great detail and will also be more committed to the task of implementing the project along with relevant department officers with whom they have built a bonding process during the three-day workshop. Finally, it is simply more democratic to let citizens identify their own colony-level needs and priorities for action.

6. The fifth learning concerns the question: Why do some RWAs/MTAs succeed much more than others in getting residential-area projects implemented successfully than other RWAs/MTAs? Why do some RWAs/MTAs successfully get several projects completed on the ground including some large projects, while other RWAs/MTAs struggle to get even one implemented, or even fail to open their account in terms of execution of colony projects.

To try to find answers to this question and explore learning in this aspect, ACORD conducted a cross section of interviews telephonically with office-bearers of a range of RWAs/MTAs, as well as conducted face-to-face FGDs with a cross section of departmental/civic agency officers. Emerging from these discussions are three broad patterns of behavior mainly on the part of the RWAs/MTAs (because they initiate the projects).

1. The RWAs/MTAs who achieved several successful completed projects on the ground in their area (including some large projects) used soft-skills well, especially in terms of
   - building good relationship legitimately with departments/civic agencies;
   - using skills of persuasion, convincing, and communication;
   - being very persistent and not giving up when things got delayed but staying focused and maintaining communication well;
   - helping the departments/civic agencies at their colony/housing-complex end on the ground;
   - mobilizing their RWA/MTA members to pitch in and help with the project.

2. The RWAs/MTAs who put in efforts but did not succeed in getting the cooperation of relevant departments/civic agencies broadly exhibited the following patterns:

- Behaved in an aggressive and even autocratic manner with department/civic agency officials
- Assumed that being given a Bhagidari ID card gave them the right to walk into government offices, demand meetings, and speak in a rude or loud tone to officials

This behavior pattern of "control-power" or "coercive-power" behavior was based on an erroneous concept of empowerment, and predictably, did not lead to much success in building a partnership with officials, or getting their help with their projects.

3. The third pattern is where some RWAs/MTAs did not make much effort to begin with, and after an initial meeting with officials, assumed that now it was the officials' responsibility to take all necessary action to implement the project suggested. In discussions with them it emerged that they made an inner assumption that nothing much would change despite Bhagidari and, in line with this pessimistic prediction, remained too passive and inactive in their approach, thus fulfilling their belief-system that nothing much will change.

Thus, one can see three patterns of behavior in RWAs/MTAs:

- Confidence, optimistism, and use of soft skills to build a partnership and reach out to officials in departments/civic agencies, and seek their help effectively (help-seeking behavior) for implementing projects that they believed in—this appears to have led to the most success in project implementation.
- Aggressive, almost autocratic behavior, demanding action by officials, probably as a reaction to earlier felt frustration and helplessness, based on mistaken notions of empowerment—this appears to have led to few successes in terms of project implementation on the ground.
- Pessimistic, passive, weak attempts by citizens' associations, without much conviction or confidence, and giving up very easily (without persistence) when quick responses and results did not come. This pattern did not lead to achieving much success in terms of actual implementation of projects on the ground.

In terms of the broad overall success rate of projects implemented during the six Review Workshops held, more than 3,000 successful projects have been reported between 2000 and 2007—this works out to approximately one third (between 30–35 percent) of the projects attempted.

The main factor emerging here is the process of action-learning. When a project is first identified and taken up by the RWA or MTA, they have to be able to first convince the relevant department (or departments) to support and help in implementation. Sometimes they are successful in persuasion, and sometimes not. After this hurdle is crossed, even when the department works closely with the RWA or MTA, they may not be able to anticipate all the problems on the ground. For example, in attempting to reclaim community parks, which had been encroached and taken over by illegal elements, sometimes they succeeded in reclaiming the park land, and sometimes they failed. Here again, a certain percentage of projects could not be completed, despite the best efforts of the RWA/MTA and the concerned departments. This process is referred to as "action-learning." The biggest learning was that citizens' groups and civic officials learned how to solve problems on the ground, and successfully implement approximately one third of the projects taken up. The fact that most of them did not give up testifies to the motivational efforts of the Large-group Dynamics Processes.

13

Sustainability of Building Citizens' Partnership in Governance through the Multistakeholder Large-group Dynamics Process

The issue of "sustainability" of Bhagidari as citizens' partnership in governance is linked to the following factors:

1. The continued commitment of the political leadership to the mission of building and sustaining the democratic concept of citizens' partnership in governance in Delhi
2. The power and robustness of the central model and processes of multistakeholder large-group dynamics as a methodology to discover and sustain common ground out of the divergent interests and opposing interests of different stakeholders
3. The extent to which citizens' associations (that is, RWAs, MTAs, SCAs, and so on) feel empowered and encouraged to take up local (colony-level, market-level, housing-complex-level) projects for improving the quality of life, and also work collaboratively with departments and civic agencies in a win-win (rather than a grievance or complaint) mode

4. The willingness of officials of departments and civic agencies to shift from a regulated and controlled mind-set to a service-delivery and collaborative mind-set with citizens' associations

5. The willingness of elected representatives to support and encourage the empowerment of citizens' associations and view them as partners in the democratic process rather than as rivals

6. The role and functions of the team in the Bhagidari Cell (CM's office)

Leadership Commitment

The present leadership in the person of the CM has demonstrated and practiced full commitment for 12 years (2000–2012) to the vision and mission of empowering citizens as full partners in democratic governance. In this period of almost a decade 3,000+ citizens' associations (RWAs, MTAs, SCAs), NGOs, 1,900 schools, 47 Social Welfare Schemes, Delhi Police, MCD, NDMC, nine departments and nine DC (revenue) establishments have been involved in implementing projects selected by RWAs/MTAs/SCAs and also improving "civic-service-delivery."

The Right to Information Process as well as 1,900 government schools and 47 social welfare schemes have been brought under the ambit of Bhagidari. In addition, the responsibility for planning, organizing the Bhagidari workshops, and reviewing of the progress of Bhagidari has been devolved and delegated to the nine DC (revenue) offices, instead of being kept as centralized functions.

The leadership has conveyed with crystal clarity in many fora and workshops that the citizen's democratic role or function is not confined to voting and then remaining passive or powerless between elections.

As a partner in democratic governance, the citizens' associations have been empowered and encouraged by the leadership to take up colony-level and housing-complex-level projects, and the leadership has also encouraged the HoDs, department officers, and civic agency officials to help and assist the citizens' associations in getting their projects implemented on priority. In the officers' ACR or performance appraisal, their effectiveness in promoting citizens' partnership is one of the important parameters for assessing their performance. The My Delhi I Care Fund is another leadership initiative to support and strengthen the community needs under Bhagidari (for example, community centers, senior citizen's centers, reading-rooms and libraries, and so on.)

1. It is well recognized that the role of leadership is vital in empowering citizens and citizens' associations for partnering in democratic governance. Therefore, the issue of sustainability needs to squarely face the question: What happens to sustainability when a different government or different leader takes over? To find an answer to this one needs to ask a different question, that is, can a new government or new leaders afford to ignore or alienate 3,000+ citizens' associations (representing 15 lakh households or 50–60 lakh people), especially when they have successfully implemented 3,000+ colony-level projects in partnership with nine departments/civic agencies? The short answer is that a new government or leader cannot ignore or alienate such a critical mass of citizens, but needs to win their support for the future. Future leaders or governments may even think of further empowerment of citizens' associations, perhaps via the legislative route and/or funding support enhancement route. Hence, in summary, the sustainability factor of Bhagidari is definitely better than 50–50, and probably closer to 70–75 percent probability, in terms of the political leadership also needing the support of the people and the citizens' associations.

2. The power, reliability, and robustness of the multistakeholder group-dynamics model and process has been proven globally both in research as well as applied practice. Small-group dynamics (which is a component within large-group dynamics) has a long history of research and practice from 1940s till date in a variety of practical applications, especially in attitude change, motivation, and behavior. Large-group dynamics has been proven successful in multistakeholder situations as the only process which helps discover common ground from the welter of divergent interests and even opposing interests that different stakeholders hold normally. In the bibliography we have provided a list of publications covering research and practice, establishing the unique reliability of large-group dynamics to help discover common ground and create ownership for joint, collaborative goals. The large-group dynamics model and process has also proven itself to be culture free since it works well in many different cultures around the world.

3. The citizens' associations (RWAS, MTAs, SCAs), spread across all nine revenue districts of Delhi, have experienced success of working closely with the departments, civic agencies, and nine DC (revenue) offices in two ways:

(a) by successfully implementing over 3,000 colony-level/ housing-complex-level projects (selected by them) in partnership with various departments/civic agencies; and

(b) by getting various pending problems solved in their residential areas through working closely with the departments/ civic agencies.

Till now, success in actually implementing projects on the ground was very elusive. Till now, citizens were mainly in the role of powerless supplicants, running from pillar to post (as they often described it) to get problems solved or things done. Now, after nearly a decade of experiencing success through partnership, citizens' associations know what is democratic success and power to achieve things—this is a strong force for sustainability and cannot be ignored or brushed aside easily.

The track record of practical success through empowerment is very strong. With the massive success achieved on the ground through successful implementation of 3,000+ colony/housing complex projects, the citizens' associations have experienced success and power in a positive sense, that is, to get this done and to do things in partnership with departments/civic agencies. This bodes well for the sustainability of Bhagidari. The periodic Bhagidari Melas and awards also exhibit and showcase many of the achievements and projects implemented through citizens' partnership with government—the media also highlights the exhibits and achievements of citizens' associations and officials/ departments/civic agencies. In this way, the credibility and solid achievements of Bhagidari have been established, and citizens' experience of success has been proven with credibility.

4. Departments and civic agencies are generally known to take their cue from the leadership. The main hard data indicating the departments' or civic agencies' willingness to support and work with citizens' associations on colony projects is the over 3,000 colony projects successfully implemented on the ground. As mentioned earlier in point (1) above, it is reasonable to take the view that future governments or political leaders

(a) would not like to alienate or annoy such a large number of citizens' associations;

(b) would rather encourage and support citizens' association initiatives and colony-level projects;

(c) citizens are not now disparate and unorganized—they are organized and structured as registered societies (under the Societies Registration Act, 1860), and have regular elections, office-bearers, activities, and membership of 250–500 families each. In a democracy, they cannot be taken lightly either by the political or bureaucratic establishment. Citizens' associations have also evolved and formed federations, that is, federations of RWAs, MTAs, SCAs, NGOs, industrial associations, Vyapar Mandals, and so on. It will be difficult for the departments/civic agencies to turn the clock back, especially if future political leadership also feels the need to gain and keep the support of citizens to whom they have to go back at election time. On this count also, the sustainability of citizens' partnership in governance looks fairly stable and sustainable. This covers both the administrative and the political leadership—hence, point (v) below is also covered as sustainable, at least in the near to medium term.

5. When the Bhagidari project was initiated in the year 2000 with only 20 RWAs in addition to the general doubt which naturally prevailed, the elected representatives also were very doubtful and skeptical. However, after seeing the projects actually implemented in colonies, markets, and housing complexes over the past eight to nine years, the elected representatives have seen a soft democratic evolution take place, and they now help RWAs convince departments of the usefulness of their projects.

6. The effective role of the Bhagidari Cell: During the entire period (2000–2008) and during this specific sixth phase also, the small but effective Bhagidari Cell (which reports to the special secretary to CM and works under the overall guidance of the principal secretary to CM) has played a major role in functioning as a critical resource, communicator, planner, problem-solver, and builder of collaboration in doing whatever is necessary to translate the CM's vision of a new democratic evolution into implementable programs and projects on the ground. As far as the RWAs and MTAs are concerned, this Bhagidari Cell created trust and credibility in the process by being their ambassador with departments, civic agencies, and revenue districts, smoothening the path of change.

In summary, on the issue of sustainability, it would be fair to say that through the Bhagidari process, of involving and empowering citizens through different citizens' associations to be partners in governance, urban democracy in Delhi has evolved to the next level of development as a "working democracy" and not just a "voting democracy." By aggregating the "sustainability quotient" on all the above five factors, it would be fair to say that it is definitely better than a 50–50 probability of sustaining, and near a 70–75 percent probability of sustainability in normal democratic circumstances.

14

Scope for Replication of Building Citizens' Partnership in Urban Democratic Governance through Multistakeholder Large-group Dynamics

In terms of the scope for replication, the basic context of the Bhagidari project is the city of Delhi as the site of the processes utilized for building and sustaining citizens' partnership in governance. Hence, this falls under the rubric of improving the quality of urban democracy and urban governance. Therefore, based on this 10-year experience in Delhi, there appears to be good scope for replication in the metro cities, state capitals, and A-class cities of India (which are also major urban settings), provided the conditions provided below are largely met or can be developed. Other large and medium cities in the world (where there is at least a regular voting democracy) can also utilize multistakeholder large-group dynamics principles and processes to discover common ground and build a working democracy based on citizens' partnership in governance.

However, at the practical level of the issue of the scope for replication, the main necessary conditions required are the following.

1. The political leadership needs to have (i) a strong, genuine commitment to empower citizens and citizens' associations; (ii) a strong will to communicate directly with citizens; and (iii) a motivation to build a citizens' partnership in governance. The political leadership also needs to exhibit a consistent desire to upgrade the level of democracy, seek direct feedback and suggestions from citizens' associations, and even seek citizens' views on proposed policy changes (as the Delhi CM has sought feedback at more than 100 Bhagidari workshops, and also on policy matters like introduction of CNG, CAS, VAT, and so on).

   In case any other city in India meets this first requirement, it would fulfill the first necessary condition which augurs well for a good scope of replication.

2. Any other city that is interested in improving urban democratic governance will also need to encourage and nurture the formation of citizens' associations representing residential areas, market areas, senior citizens, trade associations, eco-clubs, and so on. These need to be given legitimacy by forming them as legally registered societies (under the Societies Act, 1860) and getting them to hold fair elections every two years, so that they can participate in the partnership-building for good governance.

3. Officials of all Civic Service Agencies and relevant departments, at all levels (including the field or cutting-edge level), need to be brought into the partnership-building process workshops with citizens' associations, along with a shift to citizen-centric administration and service delivery as the prime parameter of civic administration.

4. Merely holding conceptual training programs or seminars/conferences or grievance-meetings will not work for any successful replication. The reason is that with multiple stakeholders (with differing interests or opposing interests) and a past history of citizen frustration or aggression, most attempts at better communication (without the appropriate and proven processes) soon breakdown. Conceptual training programs on good governance also do not bring about any change. For change to take place, the processes have to be experiential, addressing both feelings/emotions as well as rational/cognitive aspects.

5. In the pilot phase and the Phase I stage of such a project, there will exist a wide range of attitudes and mind-sets in several stakeholders, including feelings of doubt, skepticism, opposition, pessimism, and so on. The political leadership needs to be able to

steer deftly by communicating a simple but clear mission that (i) in a democracy, citizens need to be genuine partners, on a daily basis, in a quest for good governance; (ii) in a democracy, in between elections also, citizens have a vital, central role as partners in good governance. The leadership needs to be genuine and sincere and should come across as credible in this joint effort to raise the level of democratic working on a day-to-day level. Even with this clarity and dedication, it will take two to three years for the doubts and skepticism to change and turn around to hope and confidence, as it did in Delhi. If a participatory change model is used, by involving all stakeholders in the large-group dynamics workshops and processes, there is a good scope for replication in other cities also.

Since the only globally proven processes consist of large-group dynamics (in which is embedded small-group dynamics) with multiple stakeholders, any city which wants to replicate any effective form of the Bhagidari project would need to utilize specialists who have experience and expertise in the two proven forms of large-group dynamics, that is, (i) Future Search; (ii) Large-group Interactive Workshops—experience in other cognitive processes of training or consulting cannot substitute for these requirements.

If these processes are applied and used with fidelity to the basic principles, then other cities can have a good scope of replicating the Delhi Bhagidari experience.

In fact other metros, state capitals, and A-class cities may have a better opportunity of building citizens' partnership in governance than Delhi because the Delhi government and CM do not even have land, police/law and order, the Municipal Corporation, NDMC, and so on directly under the state government—these report to the Central government (either to the Union Home Ministry in some cases or to the Union Urban Development Ministry in others). In other metro cities and state-capitals there is a unity of command (which does not exist in Delhi and which posed additional challenges in Delhi).

Hence, if the appropriate principles and processes of multistakeholder large-group dynamics are applied without dilution, other cities should have a good scope of replication of this model of urban governance.

In conclusion, the most vital factor in relation to scope for replication is the genuine and long-term commitment of the political leadership to a clear vision and mission of raising the level and quality of urban democracy by building citizens' empowerment and citizens' partnership in good governance. This also involves the willingness of the leadership to accept and consider and act on citizens' feedback and recommendations, which can be strong quite often. Given this kind of genuinely democratic leadership, which wants to empower citizens, with a strong role even in-between elections, there is good scope of replication of a citizens' partnership model of urban democratic governance—this represents an evolution from a "voting democracy" to a day-to-day "working democracy."

Appendix 1

Better Management— Better Public Service Award (2005): United Nations Public Service Award (2005)

Source: Please see the mention of the above award at http://unpan1.un.org/intra-doc/groups/public/documents/un/unpan020145.pdf

The copy of the certificate was provided by the Government of National Capital Territory of Delhi.

Appendix 2

Commonwealth
Association for Public
Administration and
Management (CAPAM),
UK: International
Innovations Awards
Programme: Certificate
of Achievement (2002)

Source: Please see the mention of the above award at http://delhigovt.nic.in/
newdelhi/bhagi.asp

The copy of the certificate was provided by the Government of
National Capital Territory of Delhi.

Appendix 3
List of Bhagidari Workshops

Workshop Number	Number of Days	Dates	Title
		2000	
1.	Three	March 1 to 3, 2000	Bhagidari Workshop on Civic Issues in Delhi
2.	Three	June 14 to 16, 2000	Bhagidari Workshop on Civic Issues in Delhi
3.	Three	September 28 to 30, 2000	Bhagidari Workshop on Civic Issues in Delhi
		2001	
1.	Three	February 1 to 3, 2001	Bhagidari Workshop on Civic Issues in Delhi
2.	Three	July 19 to 21, 2001	1st District Level—Delhi Large Group Workshop
3.	Three	July 26 to 28, 2001	2nd District Level—Delhi Large Group Workshop
4.	Three	August 23 to 25, 2001	3rd District Level—Delhi Large Group Workshop
5.	Three	August 30 to September 1, 2001	4th District Level—Delhi Large Group Workshop
6.	Three	November 27 to 29, 2001	5th District Level—Delhi Large Group Workshop

Workshop Number	Number of Days	Dates	Title
		2002	
1.	Three	May 2 to 4, 2002	6th District Level—Delhi Large Group Workshop
2.	Three	May 16 to 18, 2002	7th District Level—Delhi Large Group Workshop
3.	Three	September 12 to 14, 2002	Bhagidari Workshop on Industrial Associations
4.	Three	October 24 to 26, 2002	8th District Level—Delhi Large Group Workshop
5.	Three	December 19 to 21, 2002	Preparatory Bhagidari Workshop for Rural Areas
		2003	
1.	Three	January 16 to 18, 2003	Rural Bhagidari Workshop—I
2.	Three	January 30 to 1 February 2003	9th District Level—Delhi Large Group Workshop
3.	Three	March 27 to 29, 2003	Rural Bhagidari Workshop—II
4.	Three	June 19 to 21, 2003	Rural Bhagidari Workshop—III
5.	Three	June 23 to 25, 2003	Preparatory Bhagidari Workshop for Solid Waste Management
6.	Three	July 15 to 19, 2003	Preparatory Bhagidari Workshop for Solid Waste Management
7.	Three	August 19 to 21, 2003	Bhagidari Workshop on Civic Issues in Delhi
8.	Three	August 28 to 30, 2003	1st MCD Bhagidari Workshop on Segregation of Domestic Waste: Rohini, Najafgarh & Shahdara South
9.	Three	September 11 to 13, 2003	2nd MCD Bhagidari Workshop on Segregation of Domestic Waste: South, Central & West
10.	Three	December 18 to 20, 2003	3rd MCD Bhagidari Workshop on Segregation of Domestic Waste: Civil Lines, City & Sadar-Paharganj

Appendix 3 continued

Appendix 3 continued

Workshop Number	Number of Days	Dates	Title
		2004	
1.	Three	January 8 to 10, 2004	4th MCD Bhagidari Workshop on Segregation of Domestic Waste: Karol Bagh, Shahdara North & Narela
2.	Three	January 29 to 31, 2004	Delhi Jal Board Internal Bhagidari for Change Management
3.	One	June 19, 2004	MCD Pilot Ward Bhagidari Workshop
4.	One	July 9, 2004	MCD Pilot Ward Bhagidari Workshop
5.	One	July 17, 2004	MCD Pilot Ward Bhagidari Workshop
6.	One	July 24, 2004	MCD Pilot Ward Bhagidari Workshop
7.	One	July 31, 2004	MCD Pilot Ward Bhagidari Workshop
8.	One	August 7, 2004	MCD Pilot Ward Bhagidari Workshop
9.	One	August 21, 2004	MCD Pilot Ward Bhagidari Workshop
10.	One	August 28, 2004	MCD Pilot Ward Bhagidari Workshop
11.	One	September 4, 2004	MCD Pilot Ward Bhagidari Workshop
12.	One	September 11, 2004	MCD Pilot Ward Bhagidari Workshop
13.	One	September 18, 2004	MCD Pilot Ward Bhagidari Workshop
14.	One	September 25, 2004	MCD Pilot Ward Bhagidari Workshop
15.	Three	November 4 to 6, 2004	1st District Level Bhagidari Workshop Phase IV (RWAs & officers), South and South-West
16.	Three	December 2 to 4, 2004	2nd District Level Bhagidari Workshop Phase IV (RWAs & officers), North, North-West & Central
		2005	
1.	Three	January 6 to 8, 2005	3rd District Level Bhagidari Workshop Phase IV (RWAs & officers), East and North-East
2.	Three	February 17 to 19, 2005	4th District Level Bhagidari Workshop Phase IV (MTAs & officers), East, North, North-West & Central

Workshop Number	Number of Days	Dates	Title
3.	Three	March 10 to 12, 2005	5th District Level Bhagidari Workshop Phase IV (RWAs & officers), West & South
4.	Half	February 4, 2005	Domestic Solid Waste Segregation under YAP II
5.	Half	February 4, 2005	Domestic Solid Waste Segregation under YAP II
6.	Half	February 5, 2005	Domestic Solid Waste Segregation under YAP II
7.	Half	February 5, 2005	Domestic Solid Waste Segregation under YAP II
8.	Half	February 11, 2005	Domestic Solid Waste Segregation under YAP II
9.	Half	February 11, 2005	Domestic Solid Waste Segregation under YAP II
10.	Half	February 12, 2005	Domestic Solid Waste Segregation under YAP II
11.	Half	February 12, 2005	Domestic Solid Waste Segregation under YAP II
12.	Half	February 25, 2005	Domestic Solid Waste Segregation under YAP II
13.	Half	February 25, 2005	Domestic Solid Waste Segregation under YAP II
14.	Half	February 26, 2005	Domestic Solid Waste Segregation under YAP II
15.	Half	February 26, 2005	Domestic Solid Waste Segregation under YAP II
16.	Half	March 4, 2005	Domestic Solid Waste Segregation under YAP II
17.	Half	March 4, 2005	Domestic Solid Waste Segregation under YAP II
18.	Half	March 5, 2005	Domestic Solid Waste Segregation under YAP II
19.	Half	March 5, 2005	Domestic Solid Waste Segregation under YAP II

Appendix 3 continued

Appendix 3 continued

Workshop Number	Number of Days	Dates	Title
20.	Half	April 8, 2005	Domestic Solid Waste Segregation under YAP II
21.	Half	April 8, 2005	Domestic Solid Waste Segregation under YAP II
22.	Half	April 9, 2005	Domestic Solid Waste Segregation under YAP II
23.	Half	April 9, 2005	Domestic Solid Waste Segregation under YAP II
24.	Half	April 28, 2005	Domestic Solid Waste Segregation under YAP II
25.	Half	April 28, 2005	Domestic Solid Waste Segregation under YAP II
26.	Half	April 29, 2005	Domestic Solid Waste Segregation under YAP II
27.	Half	April 29, 2005	Domestic Solid Waste Segregation under YAP II
28.	Half	April 30, 2005	Domestic Solid Waste Segregation under YAP II
29.	Half	April 30, 2005	Domestic Solid Waste Segregation under YAP II
30.	Three	May 5–7, 2005	6th District Level Bhagidari Workshop Phase—IV, New Series
31.	Three	July 21–23, 2005	7th District Level Bhagidari Workshop Phase—IV, New Series
32.	One	August 3, 2005	Draft National Curriculum Framework
33.	Three	October 6–8, 2005	Large Group Workshop on Stree Shakti (Women's Empowerment)
2006			
1.	Three	January 12–14, 2006	Future Search Workshop: On Delhi 2010
2.	Three	May 25 to 27, 2006	Bhagidari Large Group workshop phase VI for RWAs & Officials of East, North-East & West Districts of New Delhi
3.	One	August 3, 2006	Bhagidari 'RTI' Workshop for RWAs & Officials of North-West, South-West, South & West Districts of New Delhi

Workshop Number	Number of Days	Dates	Title
4.	One	August 4, 2006	Bhagidari RTI Workshop for RWAs & Officials of East, North East, Central, North and New Delhi
5.	Three	October 12 to 14, 2006	Large Group Workshop on Improving Public Service Delivery
6.	Three	October 26 to 28, 2006	Multistakeholder Workshop on Vidya-laya Kalyan Samitis
2007			
1.	Half	February 2, 2007	Experience Sharing Workshop for RWAs/MTAs
2.	Half	February 3, 2007	Experience Sharing Workshop for Eco-clubs
3.	Half	February 3, 2007	Experience Sharing Workshop for Stree Shakti
4.	Half	February 3, 2007	Experience Sharing Workshop for Vidyalaya Kalyan Samiti's
5.	Three	February 13 to 15, 2007	Citizen's Partnership in Governance on Civic Issues
6.	Three	August 30, 31 & Sep. 1, 2007	Citizen's Partnership in Governance on Civic Issues
7.	Three	September 19 to 21, 2007	Citizen's Partnership in Governance on Civic Issues
8.	Three	November 1 to 3, 2007	Citizen's Partnership in Governance on Civic Issues
9.	Three	November 5 to 7, 2007	Citizen's Partnership in Governance on Civic Issues
10.	One	December 12, 2007	Bhagidari Review : Large Group Workshop
11.	One	December 13, 2007	Bhagidari Review : Large Group Workshop
12.	One	December 14, 2007	Bhagidari Review : Large Group Workshop
13.	One	December 15, 2007	Bhagidari Review : Large Group Workshop
14.	One	December 16, 2007	Bhagidari Review : Large Group Workshop

Appendix 3 continued

Appendix 3 continued

Workshop Number	Number of Days	Dates	Title
15.	One	December 17, 2007	Bhagidari Review : Large Group Workshop

2008

1.	Three	May 15 to 17, 2008	Citizens' Partnership in Governance on Civic Issues
2.	Three	July 29 to 31, 2008	Citizens' Partnership in Governance on Civic Issues
3.	One	April 7, 2008	Multistakeholder Workshop on Regularization of Unauthorized Colonies
4.	One	April 8, 2008	Multistakeholder Workshop on Regularization of Unauthorized Colonies
5.	One	April 9, 2008	Multistakeholder Workshop on Regularization of Unauthorized Colonies
6.	One	April 10, 2008	Multistakeholder Workshop on Regularization of Unauthorized Colonies

2009

1.	Three	September 17 to 19, 2009	Citizen Partnership in Governance on Civic Issues
2.	Three	October 22 to 24, 2009	Multistakeholder Workshop on Mission Convergence: Making Social Welfare Citizens Friendly
3.	Three	October 29 to 31, 2009	Citizen Partnership in Governance on Civic Issues
4.	Three	November 25 to 27, 2009	Citizen partnership in Governance on Civic Issue
5.	Three	December 17 to 19, 2009	Citizen partnership in Governance on Civic Issue

2010

1.	Two	March 18–19, 2010	Creating Success Stories : Large Group Workshop on projects Implementation through Partnership
2.	One	August 30, 2010	Large Group Workshop on Cleanliness Drive
3.	One	August 31, 2010	Large Group Workshop on Cleanliness Drive

Workshop Number	Number of Days	Dates	Title
		2011	
1.	One	January 6, 2011	Rogi Kalyan Samiti : Large Group Workshop on Public Hospitals
2.	One	January 7, 2011	Rogi Kalyan Samiti : Large Group Workshop on Public Hospitals
3.	One	June 28, 2011	Bhagidari Workshop on Civic Issues in Delhi
4.	One	June 29, 2011	Bhagidari Workshop on Civic Issues in Delhi
5.	One	June 30, 2011	Bhagidari Workshop on Civic Issues in Delhi
6.	One	July 1, 2011	Bhagidari Workshop on Civic Issues in Delhi
7.	Half	July 20, 2011	10 Lakh Trees : Large Group Workshop on Improving Delhi's Green Cover
8.	Half	July 20, 2011	10 Lakh Trees : Large Group Workshop on Improving Delhi's Green Cover
9.	Half	July 21, 2011	10 Lakh Trees : Large Group Workshop on Improving Delhi's Green Cover
10.	Half	July 21, 2011	10 Lakh Trees : Large Group Workshop on Improving Delhi's Green Cover
11.	Two	September 23–24, 2011	Jal Bhagidari : Large Group Workshop on Improving Water Supply
		2012	
1.	Two	February 24–25, 2012	Streetscape Plantations : Large Group Workshop on Improving Greenery
2.	Two	March 29–30, 2012	Streetscape Plantations : Large Group Workshop on Improving Greenery
3.	Two	May 22–23, 2012	Jal Bhagidari : Large Group Workshop on Improving Water Supply
4.	One	June 26, 2012	District Consultation Meet : Review & Suggestions for Improving Bhagidari
5.	One	June 27, 2012	District Consultation Meet : Review & Suggestions for Improving Bhagidari
6.	One	June 28, 2012	District Consultation Meet : Review & Suggestions for Improving Bhagidari

Appendix 3 continued

Appendix 3 continued

Workshop Number	Number of Days	Dates	Title
7.	One	June 29, 2012	District Consultation Meet : Review & Suggestions for Improving Bhagidari
8.	One	July 3, 2012	District Consultation Meet : Review & Suggestions for Improving Bhagidari
9.	One	July 4, 2012	District Consultation Meet : Review & Suggestions for Improving Bhagidari
10.	One	July 5, 2012	District Consultation Meet : Review & Suggestions for Improving Bhagidari
11.	One	July 6, 2012	District Consultation Meet : Review & Suggestions for Improving Bhagidari

Source: ACORD.

Note: The one and half day workshops were either for (i) review or (ii) for IEC (information/education/communication) purposes. Only five workshops were designed and conducted on the principles and processes of large-group dynamics with multistakeholders in 2009.

Appendix 4

List of Award Winning RWAs and MTAs for Their Successful Implementation of Projects on the Ground, in Partnership with Relevant Departments

List of Award Winning RWAs and MTAs for the Year 2003

S. No.	Prize	Name and Address of the RWA
1	First Prize	Federation of LP, Ext-II, H.B.71, Kiran Vihar, Delhi
2	First Prize	R-Block, Welfare Association, R-599, New Rajinder Nagar, Delhi
3	Second Prize	Panchsheel Co-operative, Group Housing Society, Panchsheel Club, New Delhi
4	Second Prize	Kallol Co-operative, G. H. S. Ltd, 35, LP Extension, Delhi
5	Second Prize	C-758, LIG DDA Flats, East of Loni Road, Delhi

Appendix 4 continued

Appendix 4 continued

S. No.	Prize	Name and Address of the RWA
6	Second Prize	Federation of RWAs of Vasant Kunj, New Delhi
7	Third Prize	C-Block, Dilshad Garden, Delhi
8	Third Prize	New Jagrook RWA, C-739, Delhi Admn. Flats, Timarpur, Delhi
9	Third Prize	B-9, RWA, Vasant Kunj, New Delhi
10	Third Prize	Mohalla Sudhar Samiti, C-5, Yamuna Vihar, Delhi

Special Commendations

S. No.	Name and Address of the RWA/MTA
1	Vishal Enclave Welfare Association, A-89, Vishal Enclave, Rajouri Garden, New Delhi
2	Hari Nagar Ashram RWA, 209, Hari Nagar Ashram, N/Delhi
3	Sadar Bazar RWA, 832/7, Sahid Mahal, Azad Market, Delhi
4	Jt. Forum Vasundhara CGHS and Institutions community Hall Vasundhara Enclave, Delhi
5	Pocket-A, Sarita Vihar RWA, A-266, Sarita Vihar, Pocket-1, New Delhi
6	Khan Market and Traders Association, 10B Khan Market, New Delhi 110003

List of Award Winning RWAs and MTAs for the Year 2004

S. No.	Prize	Name and Address of the RWA
1	First Prize	Dilshad Colony Residents Welfare Association, F-172, Dilshad Colony, Delhi-110005
2	First Prize	Federation of Group Housing Societies (LP Extension), 58, Delhi-110092
3	Second Prize	Defence Colony Welfare Association, The Gumbad, Defence Colony, New Delhi-110024
4	Second Prize	Joint Forum, Vasundhara Enclave, CGHS and Institutions, Vasundhara Enclave, Co-operative GHS, 14-A, Overseas Apartment, Vasundhara Enclave, Delhi-110096

S. No.	Prize	Name and Address of the RWA
5	Second Prize	Resident Welfare Association D-l, Vasant Kunj, Delhi
6	Second Prize	Kalkaji "Bhagidari" Coordination Committee, 9/7 Nehru Enclave, East Kalkaji Extension, New Delhi-110019
7	Third Prize	Khan Market Traders Association, 10-B, Khan Market, New Delhi-110003
8	Third Prize	Mayur Vihar Phase-I, Pocket-3, Apartment Owners Association, 73-D, Pocket-III, Mayur Vihar Phase-I, Delhi-110091
9	Third Prize	Sadar Zila Welfare Association, 1-223, Karampura, New Delhi-110015
10	Third Prize	Residents Welfare Association (Regd) Kamala Nagar, F-Block, 54 F, Kamla Nagar, Delhi

Special Commendations

S. No.	Name and Address of RWA
1	Rural Group of Singhu Village
2	Dilshad Garden, Pocket E, RWA
3	Gole Market Traders Association Phase-III

List of Award Winning RWAs and MTAs for the Year 2006

S. No.	Prize	Name and Address of the RWA
1	First Prize	Munirka Vihar Welfare Association, Munirka Vihar, New Delhi-110067
2	First Prize	Federation of Naraina Vihar, RWA Naraina Vihar, New Delhi-110028
3	Second Prize	North Delhi Residents Welfare Federation, Chandrawal Road, Delhi-110007
4	Second Prize	Federation of Triveni-II, Residents, Sheikh Sarai-II, New Delhi
5	Second Prize	Central Government Employee Resident's Welfare Association (Regd), Sector II (Blocks 18–42), DIZ Area, New Delhi

Appendix 4 continued

Appendix 4 continued

S. No.	Prize	Name and Address of the RWA
6	Second Prize	RWA, WP block Maurya Enclave, Pitampura, Delhi-110088
7	Third Prize	Maitri Edn. and Welfare Society, Sri Nagar, Shakurbasti, Delhi-110034
8	Third Prize	Bengali Market Traders Association (Regd) 2-3, Bengali Market, New Delhi-110001
9	Third Prize	New Krishna Nagar RWA, 25 New Krishna Nagar, Delhi-110051
10	Third Prize	Gram Vikas Mandal (Regd), Vill-Barwala, Delhi-10039

Special Commendations

S. No.	Name and Address of the RWA/MTA
1	Dilshad Colony Residents Welfare Association, Dilshad Colony, Delhi-110095
2	Mohalla Sudhar Samiti, C-5/51, Yamuna Vihar, Delhi-110053
3	G-Block RWA, G8, Naraina Vihar, New Delhi-110028
4	Riviera Apartment Owners Cooperative Housing Limited, North Riviera Apartment, 45 Mall Road, Delhi-110007
5	FIST RWA, Kasturba Niketan, Lajpat Nagar-II, New Delhi Sadar Bazar Traders Welfare Association, Sadar Bazar, Delhi

List of Award Winning RWAs and MTAs for the Year 2007

S. No.	Prize	Name and Address of the RWA
1	First Prize	The Delhi Sainik Co-op Housing Building Societies Limited, Sainik Vihar, Near Rani Bagh, Delhi-110034
2	First Prize	Green View Apartments Resident Welfare Association, 80-SFS Flats, Hari Nagar, New Delhi
3	Second Prize	Welfare Society (Regd), D-29, Marg 13, Saket, New Delhi
4	Second Prize	Dilshad Colony Association, F-172, Dilshad Colony, Delhi-110095
5	Second Prize	Residents Welfare Association (Regd), Sector C, Pocket 9, Vasant Kunj, New Delhi-110070

S. No.	Prize	Name and Address of the RWA
6	Second Prize	Jangpura Extn. Residents Welfare Association (Regd) 1 (LGF) Comercial Complex, K-Block, Near Post Office, Jangpura Extn., New Delhi
7	Third Prize	P&T Residents Welfare Association and Recreation Club, Atul Grove Road, T-18-C, Atul Grove Road, New Delhi-110001
8	Third Prize	Lawerence Road Resident's Welfare Association, Rani Jhansi Kunj, C-2 Pocket (MIG) DDA Flats C-2/65 A, Keshavpuram, Delhi-110035
9	Third Prize	(HIG, MIG, and LIG) DDA Flats Owners Association (Regd) Rani Jhansi Complex, 20 A, SFS, DDA Flats, Motia Khan, Pharganj, New Delhi-110055
10	Third Prize	Janpath Bhawan Market Association (Regd) Janpath Bhawan, New Delhi Janpath Market, New Delhi-110001

Special Commendations

S. No.	Name and Address of the RWA
1	Federation of Indraprastha Extn-II Housing Societies,71, Kiran Vihar, Delhi-110092
2	Resident Welfare Association (Regd) Mir Dard Lane, 362/96 or 195/4, Type-II, Mir Dard Lane, New Delhi-110002
3	Resident Welfare Association, D-l Vasant Kunj, D-l, Vasant Kunj, New Delhi
4	Raja Park Vikas Samiti, WZ-2187 Raja Park, Shakur Basti Delhi-1100034
5	Mohalla Sudhar Samiti, C-5 block C-5/51 Yamuna Vihar
6	Federation of Naraina Vihar RWA B-77 Naraina Vihar, New Delhi-110028
7	North Delhi Residents Welfare Federation 1618, Chandrawal Road, Delhi-110007
8	Central Govt. Employees RWA, Sector-11, (Block 18-42), Sector-II, Gole Market, DIZ Area, New Delhi
9	Rajinder Nagar Welfare Association (Regd) 28/7, Old Rajinder Nagar, New Delhi-110060
10	RWA, Double Storey, New Rajinder Nagar, 542, Double Storey, New Rajinder Nagar, New Delhi-110060

Appendix 4 continued

Appendix 4 continued

S. No.	Name and Address of the RWA
11	Munirka Vihar Welfare Association, Association Office Building, Main Parking Lot, Munirka Vihar, New Delhi-110067
12	Bengali Market Trader Association, 2-3, Bengali Market, New Delhi-110001
13	Basant Lok Community Centre Welfare Association (Regd) Vasant Lok, Vasant Vihar, New Delhi-110057
14	Gram Vikas Mandal, VIII, Barwala, Delhi-110039

List of Award Winning RWAs and MTAs for the Year 2011

S .No.	Prize	Name and Address of the RWA
1	First Prize	Narmada Apartments RWA (Regd), D-399, Narmada Apartments Alaknanda, New Delhi-110019
2	First Prize	Resident Welfare Association (Regd) B-5/26 Block, Paschim Vihar, Delhi
3	Second Prize	CA Block, RWA Shalimar Bagh, CA-70/D, Shalimar Bagh, Delhi-110088
4	Second Prize	Kendriya Sarkari Karamchari Awas Kalyan Sansthan, Block No. 101–108, Sector-IV, DIZ Area, Baba Kharak Singh Marg, New Delhi-110001
5	Second Prize	RWA, Double Storey, New Rajinder Nagar, 542, Double Storey, New Rajinder Nagar, New Delhi-110060
6	Second Prize	Okhla Industrial Estate Association (Regd), Exhibition Complex, Okhla Industrial Estate, Phase-III, New Delhi 110020
7	Third Prize	Residents Welfare Association (Regd) LIG DDA Flats, C-182, "Chitrakoot" East of Loni Road, Delhi-110093
8	Third Prize	Pandav Nagar Complex—Ganesh Nagar Welfare Samiti, B-Block, Gali No. 6, House No.39/A, Pandav Nagar Complex, Ganesh Nagar, Delhi
9	Third Prize	Dilshad Colony RWA (Regd), F-172, Dilshad Colony, Delhi-110095
10	Third Prize	Prithviraj Market Trader Association, 6 Prithviraj Market, New Delhi

Special Commendations

S. No.	Name and Address of the RWA
1	Resident Welfare Association A-I Block, Janakpuri, A-1/294, Janak Puri, New Delhi
2	Pragati Apartment Resident Welfare Association, Paschim Vihar, New Delhi-110063
3	Defence Colony Welfare Association, The Gumbad, Defence Colony, New Delhi-110024
4	Welfare Society, D-29, Marg 13, Saket, New Delhi-110017
5	Shastri Nagar Dev & Welfare Association, 85-86, Shree Geeta Bhawan, Mandir, Marg, Sarojini Park, Shastri Nagar, Delhi-110031
6	Federation of RWA, Mayur Vihar Phase-I, 49-B, Pkt-1, Mayur Vihar-I, Delhi-110091

Source: Bhagidari Cell, Government of NCT of Delhi.

Note: As per our information no awards were given in years 2008, 2009, and 2010.

Appendix 5

List of Projects by RWAs and NGOs Supported by the "Delhi Parks & Gardens Society"

S. No.	Name of RWA/NGO	Number of Parks	Area in Acres	Total GIA Amount in Rupees	District Zone
1	Netaji Nagar Vikas Samiti	3	1.017	49,250	South
2	Jor Bagh Association	20	6.252	323,655	South
3	Golf Link Association	23	9.078	475,470	South
4	Central Government Employees, FGH Block, Sarojini Nagar	23	2.017	166,499	South
5	Shalimar Bagh RWA, Pockets U and V,B-Block	14	2.84	251,820	North-West
6	Central Government Employee North-West, Moti Bagh	2	0.94	67,000	South-West

7	South Ganesh Nagar	4	0.55	89,000	East
8	A-Block, Preet Vihar	3	0.52	75,900	East
9	B1, Vasant Kunj	25	3.808	294,470	South-West
10	Sarojini Park Shastri Nagar	1	0.33	88,300	North
11	Kasturba Nagar RWA	3	0.84	127,600	East
12	Mayur Vihar, Pocket- B4, Phase-III	1	6.05	738,000	East
13	Rose Society of India	1	5.88	1054,000	South
16	Pocket-A1, Sector-17, Rohini	6	2.212	284,644	North-West
17	Defence Colony Welfare Association	7	2.212	559,550	South
19	Vasant Kunj, Sector-D, Pockets-7 and 8	12	2.67	271,398	South-West
20	Shastri Nagar Dev., Welfare Association, Sarojini Park	1	0.17	51,636	North
21	E-Block RBWA Naraina Vihar	1	0.6	34,260	South-West
22	F-Block RWA Naraina Vihar, Delhi	4	0.491	30,464	South-West
23	Federation of Naraina Vihar, RVA, B-Block	1	0.5	29,150	South-West
24	Apna Park Naraina Vihar, F1 Block	2	1.15	78,265	South-West
25	C-Block, Resident WA, Naraina Vihar	1	1.5	85,650	South-West
26	Manavsthali CGHS Ltd	1	0.16	25,576	East
27	RWA Block-E4, Sector-7, Rohini	4	2.08	218,600	North-West

Appendix 5 continued

S. No.	Name of RWA/NGO	Number of Parks	Area in Acres	Total GIA Amount in Rupees	District Zone
28	B-Block, C. R. Park RWA	1	0.7	55,000	South
31	Defence Colony Welfare Association	1	1.1188	84,462	South
32	Hauz Khas Apartment SFS Owners Welfare Association	14	3.834	168,268	South
33	Pocket K-1, C. R. Park	3	0.104	21,272	South
34	C-Block RWA Naraina Vihar	5	1.75	105,000	South-West
35	E-Block RWA Naraina Vihar	7	1.566	93,440	South-West
36	Surbhi Education and Welfare Society, Mayur Vihar, Phase-1 Extension	2	0.272	46,304	East
37	B-Block SMKPS Welfare Society, A-86, Gopal Vihar, Rohini	7	4.3	451,295	North-West
SUB TOTAL		**196**	**63.2118**	**6,043,903**	
	Financial Year 2010–2011				
38	Sarthak Shiksha Samiti, Geeta Colony	2	0.63	71,595	East
39	New Shine RWA, Geeta Colony	1	0.32	35,656	East
40	RW Avem Cultural Association Blocks C-1 and C-2, Sector-16, Rohini	11	1.63	220,594	North-West
41	Kanungo Co-op., Gr. Housing Society Ltd., 71, IP Extension, Patparganj	2	1.35	119,750	East
42	RWA Geeta Colony, 14/93 Geeta Colony	1	0.52	59,816	East

43	Janhit Awasiya Kalyan Samiti, New Seema Puri	1	0.7	73,500	North-East
45	RWA Varun Enclave Kondli	4	8.702	881,690	East
46	J-Block, RWA, C.R. Park	4	4.8	426,500	South
47	Pocket-40,C.R. Park RWA	1	1.976	166,200	South
48	H-Block, RWA, C. R. Park	2	1	98,000	South
49	RWA, Nehru Enclave East, Kalkaji Extension	3	0.98	96,100	South
50	Awas Welfare Association, Jal Vihar	10	9.75	791,250	South
51	Vishwakarma Co-operative Group Housing Society Ltd., B-17,Vasundhara Enclave	5	0.202	24,120	East
52	Parvatiya Vikas Co-operative Group Housing Society Ltd., B-16, Vasundhara Enclave	1	0.372	42,620	East
53	Mangal Co-operative Group Housing Society Ltd, 16 Vasundhara Enclave	4	0.619	64,615	East
54	ILA Co-operative Group Housing Society Ltd, B-7, Vasundhara Enclave	2	0.455	41,300	East
55	Dainik Janjug Naaph Co-operative Group Housing Society Ltd, C-01, Vasundhara Enclave	1	0.272	20,820	East
56	Puneet Co-operative Group Housing Society Ltd, B-10,Vasundhara Enclave	1	0.35	25,500	East

Appendix 5 continued

S. No.	Name of RWA/NGO	Number of Parks	Area in Acres	Total GIA Amount in Rupees	District Zone
57	Paryatan Co-operative Group Housing Society Ltd, B-4 Vasundhara Enclave	1	3	203,000	East
58	Vishal Co-operative Group Housing Society Ltd, 5, Vasundhara Enclave	2	0.097	14,820	East
59	Samrat Co-operative Group Housing Society Ltd, B-11,Vasundhara Enclave	3	0.376	31,560	East
60	Anekant Co-operative Group Housing Society Ltd, 23, Vasundhara Enclave	3	0.38	41,300	East
61	Pawittra Co-operative Group Housing Society Ltd,12,Vasundhara Enclave	1	0.62	48,200	East
62	Soochana Co-operative Group Housing Society Ltd,15,Vasundhara Enclave, Dollupura	1	0.088	14,980	East
63	KIRTI Co-operative Group Housing Society Ltd, Mayur Vihar-1 Extension, Vasundhara Enclave	2	0.42	69,900	East
64	West Kidwai Nagar, D-11/165 RWA	8	1.82	89,600	South
65	Hanuman Road Colony 38, RWA	1	1.25	73,750	New Delhi
66	Sarita Vihar, Pocket C, RWA	5	2.2	204,000	South
67	RWA Block-B1, Sector-17, Rohini	5	0.364	30,940	North-West

68	Social Development Welfare Society, Palam Extension	1	0.63	86,450	South-West
69	RWA Preet Vihar, B-Block	3	0.885	53,100	East
70	Pocket-A 3, Apartment Owners Association, Mayur Vihar, Ph-3	1	4.41	462,900	East
71	Manav Adhikar Sangharsh Committee, Aram Park, Shastri Nagar	1	0.16	19,600	East
72	Saraswati Kunj CGHS Ltd, 25 IP Extension, Patparganj	4	0.662	161,960	East
73	Kesheer Sagar CGHS Ltd, 45 IP Extension, Patparganj	2	0.207	20,595	East
74	Defence Colony Welfare Association, A-Block	1	1	79,000	South
75	Rohini MIG RWA, Sector-16, Block-1, Pocket-5, 7, and 8, Rohini	7	3.781	369,195	North-West
76	Shree Adarsh Sewa Samiti, Sector-11, Rohini	3	0.676	73,220	North-West
77	Defence Colony Welfare Association	1	0.9	36,000	South
78	RWA, Hemkunt Colony, GK, Part-1	2	1.53	118,450	South
79	Diplomatic Enclave Owners and Resident Association, 3, Malchha Marg, Diplomatic Enclave	14	7.665	234,950	New Delhi
80	RWA, Preet Vihar, G-Block	8	1.357	88,920	East
81	Sahyog Care for You, Paschim Vihar	3	1.11	80,600	North-West
82	Janak Puri, A-3 Block, Welfare Association	6	6.635	497,100	West
83	Akash Bharti CGHS Ltd, 24 IP Extension, Delhi	3	0.15	35,000	West
84	RWA, Pocket-A5, Sector-16, Rohini	1	0.321	30,470	North-West
85	RWA, Blocks-12 and 12A, Trilokpuri	4	0.43	84,450	East

Appendix 5 continued

S. No.	Name of RWA/NGO	Number of Parks	Area in Acres	Total GIA Amount in Rupees	District Zone
86	RWA, Block 18 , Trilokpuri	4	0.411	67,265	East
87	B-XI RWA, Vasant Kunj	4	2.587	225,350	South
88	RWA, D-Block, Sector-11, Rohini	11	0.646	74,370	North-West
89	Shastri Nagar D. and W. A. Geeta Bhawan Mandir Marg, Sarojini Park	1	0.175	38,000	East
90	Dayanand Co-operative House Building Society, Dayanand Vihar	5	1.666	121,460	East
91	Border Roads CGHS Ltd, IP Extension	3	0.255	39,175	East
92	Arjun Nagar House Owners Welfare Association	4	0.21	20,936	South
93	Yufsuf RWA	2	0.6	38,160	South
94	Block-4, Safdarjung Enclave Resident's Association	1	0.41	32,576	South
95	RWA Safdarjung Enclave, B-6 Block	1	0.31	21,216	South
96	RWA Block-A, Pocket-3, Sector-16, Rohini	5	0.259	17,495	North-West
97	Kallol CGHS Ltd, 35 IP Extension	4	0.316	44,296	East
98	Krishana Nagar RWA, Safdarjung Enclave	1	1.25	120,688	South
99	Jan Kalyan Vikas Samiti, Sarojini Park, Shastri Nagar	1	0.45	50,490	East
100	B-4 Block, South Zone, Safdarjung Enclave RWA	1	0.68	49,748	South
101	Safdarjung Enclave RWA A-2 Block	2	1.22	78,819	South

102	RWA, A-1 Block, Sector-16, Rohini	8	0.545	36,814	North-West
103	K-Block, C. R. Park, RWA	5	2.521	121,638	South
104	RWA, B-Block, Yojana Vihar	2	1.004	58,132	East
105	B-9, Rock View Apartments RWA, Vasant Kunj	6	1.386	66,880	South
106	Bougainvilla Apartments RWA, B-4, Vasant Kunj	3	0.748	73,728	South
107	Senior Citizen Forum, East Patel Nagar	1	2.5	133,125	West
108	Dilshad Colony RWA, Blocks-A, B, D, and E	1	1.15	133,780	North-East
109	Ashok Niktan RWA, I-Block, Naraina Vihar	4	0.6	55,740	South-West
110	G-Block RWA, Naraina Vihar	5	1.785	109,351	South-West
111	Preet Vihar, D-Block Garden Samiti	6	1.388	80,365	East
112	Golden CGHS Ltd, IP Extension	5	0.4	30,660	East
113	Highland Co-operative Housing Society Plot No. 8, Vasundhra Enclave	6	0.471	50,691	East
114	Abhyant Co-operative Plot No. 2, Vasundhra Enclave	1	0.237	18,222	East
115	Police Computer Co-operative B-16, Vasundhra	1	0.112	11,484	East
116	New Pragatisheel, Plot No. 81, Vasundhra Enclave	1	1.292	111,806	East
117	Habitat Co-operative B-19, Vasundhra Enclave	5	0.435	37,686	East
118	SD RWA D-2, Bhim Nagar, Safdarjung	1	3.39	141,854	South
119	Gramin Jeevan Vikas Society, 34/1, Yusuf Sarai	1	0.83	59,067	South

Appendix 5 continued

S. No.	Name of RWA/NGO	Number of Parks	Area in Acres	Total GIA Amount in Rupees	District Zone
120	ISI CGHS Ltd, Manak Sadan, Manak Vihar	2	0.657	51,040	East
121	RWA Savita Vihar	2	1.73	127,167	East
122	RWA Sec-C, Pocket-3, Vasant Kunj	6	1.27	100,278	South
123	Hargobind CGHS Ltd, Vasundhara	3	1.5	119,350	East
124	Retited Government Servants RWA, Pocket D-15, Sector-7, Rohini	2	0.142	12,592	North-West
125	Panchsheel Enclave RWA, Blocks-B, C, and D	4	2.492	127,191	South
126	Vasant Kunj, Sector-D, Pockets 3 and 4, RWA	33	7.477	376,350	South
127	Deepali RWA, Deepali Pitampura	5	3.44	199,176	North-West
128	New Delhi Apartments Co-operative HR society, 7, Vasundhra Enclave	1	0.284	24,446	East
129	Panchsheel Enclave RWA, Blocks-A and A-1	1	1.67	88,952	South
130	RWA, Block-D, Pocket-3, Sector-16, Rohini	2	0.635	42,894	North-West
131	West Enclave (NW) Pitampura, Dev. Association A-41, Parijat Apartments West Enclave	3	4.17	441,684	North-West
132	Abul Fazal Co-operative Gr. Hr. Society Ltd 22, Vasundhra Enclave	2	0.407	34,565	East
133	Indian Naval Employees CGHS P. No. 14, Vasundhra Enclave	1	0.112	9,985	East
134	Anupam CGHS Ltd, B-13, Vasundhra Enclave	1	0.5	49,950	East

No.	Description				Region
135	Overseas CGHS P. No. B-18, Vasundhra Enclave	1	0.118	8,332	East
136	Deluxe CGHS Ltd, B-5, Vasundhra Enclave	3	0.261	24,612	East
	TOTAL	**344**	**141.156**	**1,1274,562**	
137	General CGHS, 37, IP Extersion, Patpar Ganj	5	0.367	30,749	East
138	RWA, Pocket B-5, Sector-7, Rohini	1	1.143	113,210	North-West
	Financial Year 2011–2012				
139	Parivar CGHS, 30, IP Extension, Patpar Ganj	4	0.271	21,690	East
140	Neel Kanth CGHS, 46, IP Extension, Patpar Ganj	3	0.617	60,224	East
141	Masjid Moth, RWA, DDA Flats, Masjid Moth, Phase-I	11	0.909	35,088	South
142	RWA, B-8, Vasant Kunj	6	1.006	98,106	South
143	Green Glade Apartments, RWA, B-2, Vasant Kunj	8	1.089	108,287	South
144	B-3&4, Vasant Kunj, RWA	7	2.877	160,815	South
145	RWA, B-Block, East of Kailash	5	1.18	64,435	South
146	RWA, C-1, Vasant Kunj	24	4.602	260,548	South
147	RWA, C-4, Vasant Kunj	4	0.587	39,323	South
148	CSP Flats, 54 East of Kailash, RWA	4	0.464	37,344	South
149	Mandakini Enclave, RWA, Alaknanda	2	1.9	210,775	South
150	Avasiya Kalyan Evam Vikas Samiti, B-Block, Saraswati Vihar	1	2.94	214,226	North-West

Appendix 5 continued

S. No.	Name of RWA/NGO	Number of Parks	Area in Acres	Total GIA Amount in Rupees	District Zone
151	Agrasen CGHS, 66, IP Extension, Patpar Ganj	4	1.182	82,440	East
152	ABHYAAS, 60-D, Pocket-A, Mayur Vihar, Phase-II	23	7.358	446,028	East
153	RWA, B-5 Block, Paschim Vihar	3	1.7	140,930	West
154	RWA, Sector-D, Pocket-8, Vasant Kunj	8	0.434	33,441	South
155	Samachar CGHS Ltd, Mayur Vihar, Ph-I Extension	3	1.21	89,059	East
156	RWA, Sector-16, Rohini	2	1.649	123,890	North-West
157	Niligiri Apartments Welfare Association, Alaknanda	9	3.325	160,431	South
158	Vardhaman CGHS Ltd, Vardhaman Apartments, Plot no. 3, Mayur Vihar, Ph-I Extension	3	0.245	28,686	East
159	Rosewood Apartments CGHS Ltd, Plot no. 4, Mayur Vihar, Ph-I Extension	3	0.249	26,917	East
160	AD-Block, Shalimar Bagh, RWA, AD/91A, DDA Flats, Shalimar Bagh	23	2.849	204,456	North-West
161	Janhit RWA, E-193, New Seemapuri	2	1.5	144,800	North-East
162	Achiever Social Association, Block-4, Khichripur Colony	11	2.162	216,910	East
163	A-Block, RWA, Sector-11, Rohini	4	0.784	63,960	North-West
164	RWA, Block-C-5D, Janak Puri	7	1.477	116,018	West
165	C-3 Block (Private Construction) Janak Puri, RWA	4	6.42	406,218	West

166	Saraswati Vihar, E-Block, RWA	4	4.36	271,444	North-West
167	RWA, DDA Flats Double Storey Garhi, East of Kailash	5	0.532	46,204	South
168	RWA, Mangal Apartment, G-Block, Kalkaji	8	0.335	24,164	South
169	CA-Block, Shalimar Bagh, RWA, CA-70-D	8	2	140,800	North-West
170	RWA, D-1, Vasant Kunj	24	6.196	341,457	South
171	Nirman Co-operative Gr. Housing Society Ltd, Mayur Vihar, Ph-I Extension	3	1.04	90,216	East
172	Vasant Co-operative Gr. Housing Society Ltd, Mayur Vihar, Ph-I Extension	1	0.41	28,739	East
173	RWA, B-7, Vasant Kunj	9	1.347	95,992	South
174	Himmat Puri RWA, 33/259, Himmat Puri	10	0.947	82,246	East
175	Arur Co-operative Gr. Housing Society Ltd, Mayur Vihar, Ph-I Ext.	3	0.28	20,712	East
176	Glaxo Co-operative Gr. Housing Society Ltd, Plot no. 14, Mayur Vihar, Ph-I Extension	3	1.089	89,052	East
177	Leiah Co-operative Gr. Housing Society Ltd, B-15, Vasundhara Enclave	3	0.123	11,622	East
178	Ratnakar CGHS Ltd, Plot ncs 4–21, Dwarka	1	0.78	58,162	South-West
179	LIG Government Servants Co-operative House Building Society Ltd, Sunder Vihar	6	5.108	338,454	West
180	RWA, G-20, Sector-7, Rohini	1	1.16	78,358	North-West

Appendix 5 continued

Appendix 5 continued

S. No.	Name of RWA/NGO	Number of Parks	Area in Acres	Total GIA Amount in Rupees	District Zone
181	Sardar Patel Enclave, RWA, 20 Points Program Colony, Pooth Kalan Extension, Sector-23, Rohini	4	4.35	425,298	North-West
182	Varishth Nagrik Sanskritik Sangthan, 32/14-II, East Patel Nagar	1	0.232	36,291	North-West
183	RWA, Pocket-B, Dilshad Garden	2	1.02	78,744	North-East
184	RWA, DDA Flats Pocket-1,Sec-23, Dwarka	1	2	151,800	South-West
185	Sanmati CGHS, Plot no. 19A, Sector-6, Dwarka	1	0.35	34,765	South-West
186	Parwana CHGS Ltd, Parwana Apartments, Mayur Vihar, Ph-I	1	2	115,800	East
187	Dronacharya CGHS Ltd, Drona Apartments, Mayur Vihar, Ph-I Extension	1	0.14	14,106	East
188	Sushant Vihar Sudhar Samiti, Sushant Vihar, Ibrahimpur Extension Uttarakhand Chowk Road	1	0.12	14,922	North-West
189	Udaan Awareness and Education Society, 36–182, Trilok Puri	5	0.472	31,884	East
190	C. R. Park(M, N, and P Blocks), RWA, M-37, LGF, C. R. Park	1	0.22	18,615	South
191	RWA,Vasant Kunj, Sector-D, Pocket-2	14	3.135	167,264	South
192	Senior Citizen Welfare and Uplift Association, Giri Nagar, Kalkaji	6	1.12	75,656	South
193	Jagdish Prasad Saxena Memorial Society, E-65, South Extension, Part-1	2	0.642	114,100	New Delhi
194	Manav Adhikar Sangharsh Committee, 96-A, Aram Park, Shastri Nagar	1	1.884	127,264	East

195	RWA, Block-17, Trilok Puri	4	0.435	37,780	East
196	Janata CGHS, Meera Bagh	5	3.395	217,070	West
197	Mangol Puri Development Welfare Society, G-332, Mangol Puri	6	1.859	161,454	North-West
198	Manavsthali CGHS Ltd, 6,Vasundhara Enclave	1	0.84	74,636	East
199	CD-Block, LIG Flats, RWA, Hari Nagar	1	2.15	178,980	West
200	Dharmik Samaroh Evem Mandir Nirman Samiti, A-360, Bunkar Colony, Ashok Vihar, Ph-IV	25	5.939	411,179	North-West
201	Vasant Vihar Welfare Association, Pocket-D/7	3	2.75	94,112	South
202	Vishrantika CGHS Ltd, Plot no. 5A, Sector-3, Dwarka	3	0.432	25,012	South-West
203	Tihar Employees Welfare Association, Kiran Suvidhaghar, Old Residential Complex, Tihar Jail	16	3.89	352,846	West
204	Puja CGHS Ltd,77, IP Extension, Patpar Ganj	3	0.323	29,810	East
205	Rehayasi Jan Kalyan Samiti, Kailash Apartments, Plot no. 2, Sector-4, Dwarka	4	0.564	35,656	South-West
206	Anand Vihar Welfare Association, BL-119, L-Block, Hari Nagar	2	1.78	129,062	West
207	Sunder Apartments RWA	7	2.909	188,930	North-West
208	Gazipur Vikas Samiti, 72-A, DDA Flats, Gazipur	15	4.213	386,398	East
209	Shree New Anamika CGHS Ltd, Plot no. 25B, Sector-4, Dwarka, Phase-1	1	0.939	67,368	South-West

Appendix 5 continued

S. No.	Name of RWA/NGO	Number of Parks	Area in Acres	Total GIA Amount in Rupees	District Zone
210	RWA, 19-Block, Kalyan Puri	5	0.986	92,134	East
211	Lahore Colony, Shastri Nagar Janhit Samiti, 147, New Lahore Gali no. 5, Shastri Nagar	1	0.1	14,220	East
213	CEL CGHS Ltd, B-14, CEL Apartments, Vasundhara Enclave	4	0.461	33,660	East
214	Akhil Bhartiya Samaj Kalyan Sangh, 5/128, Khichri Pur	8	0.889	88,510	East
215	RWA, Block-9, Khichri pur	9	1.378	134,020	East
216	Bhirochi, CGHS, Bhera Enclave	1	1.3.2	83,200	North-West
217	JP-Block, RWA, Maurya Enclave, Pitampura	1	2.438	150,280	North-West
218	Aashirwad CGHS Ltd, Plot no. 114, IP Extension	1	0.216	16,460	East
219	OCS Friends CGHS Ltd, OCS Apartments, Mayur Vihar, Ph-I	2	0.447	30,881	East
220	Green Park Association, G-6, Green Park Extension	1	0.89	39,730	South
221	LD-Tower Apartments, RWA, LD-Block, Pitampura	3	0.62	44,200	North-West
222	RWA,DDA Flats, East of Kailash	7	1.13	79,100	South
223	CC-Block, RWA, Hari Nagar	8	3.93	286,100	West
224	Delhi Janta Sewi Sangathan, B-6, Ashok Market, Hastal Colony, Uttam Nagar	12	2.15	195,500	South-West
225	BW Shalimar Apartments, RWA, BW-3B, Shalimar Bagh	11	3.97	250,700	North

226	RWA, A1-Block, Janakpuri	1	1.36	86,600	West
227	Desh Prem Society, 12/190, Shop no. 5, Geeta Colony	1	0.229	18,320	East
228	Mayur Vihar, Pocket-A, Ph-II, RWA	8	5.363	334,780	East
229	Pharma, RWA, 88, IP Extension	3	0.195	11,700	East
230	RWA, New Seelampur	3	1.294	112,637	North-East
231	GTB Enclave, LIG, RWA, Pocket-E	8	4.383	350,640	North-East
232	Taj Sartaj CGHS Ltd, Taj Enclave, Link Road, Geeta Colony	11	0.779	86,820	East
233	Lakshy Development Society, 6/363, Khichripur	4	0.45	42,500	East
234	Varishth Nagrik Sanskritik Sangthan, East Patel Nagar	1	0.787	44,350	West
235	Avasiya Welfare Asociation, C-3 Block, Ashok Vihar-II	2	1.498	94,880	North-West
236	RWA, Block-no.18, Trilok puri	7	0.553	53,270	East
237	RWA, Pocket-A, DDA Flats, Hari Nagar	3	0.555	46,400	West
238	Dharmik Sewa Samiti, B-1/74, New Kondli	10	1.072	98,480	East
239	RWA, Group-7, DDA Flats, A1/77-116, Mayur Vihar, Ph-III	7	4.829	291,740	East
240	Sandesh Vihar, RWA, 106, Pitampura	2	1.664	106,840	North-West
241	Maurya CGHS Ltd, 95, IP Extension	3	0.28	20,300	East
242	S-Block Welfare Association, 5-473, Greater Kailash-I	1	2.7	113,000	South
243	B-Block Welfare Association, Kalkaji	6	0.759	39,950	South

Appendix 5 continued

S. No.	Name of RWA/NGO	Number of Parks	Area in Acres	Total GIA Amount in Rupees	District Zone
244	Sagar CGHS Ltd, 113, IP Extension, Patparganj	9	0.304	18,240	East
245	RWA, Rishi Nagar, Shakur Basti, WZ-362/B-6, Gali no. 8, Rani Bagh	2	2.729	199,530	North-West
246	Nav Sanjivan CGHS Ltd, Plot no. 1, Sector-12, Dwarka	1	0.792	51,020	South-West
247	Gram Vikas Samiti Alipur, 34, Alipur	1	4.4	404,000	North-West
248	Jhilmil DDA Flats, RWA, 24B, Satyam Enclave, Jhilmil	6	1.63	146,700	East
249	RWA, B-10, Vasant Kunj	11	1.447	76,350	South
250	Gram Vikas Samiti, 69, Village Madan Pur, Dabas	1	1.23	110,700	West
251	Wazirpur III SFS Flats, RWA, Shakti Apartments, Ashok Vihar, Ph-III	7	1.432	92,420	North-West
252	Mayur Vihar, Pocket-III, Apartments Owner Association, 16A, Pocket-III	11	2.533	151,980	East
253	Citizen Forum, RWA, GD Colony, A-664, Mayur Vihar, Ph-III	1	1.67	100,200	East
254	RWA, A-2 Block, A-2/54, Paschim Vihar	2	1.414	84,840	West
255	Azad Yuva Ekta Club, Basti Vikas Kendra, Peera Garhi Road	1	3.53	319,700	West
256	Suryodaya Apartments, RWA, Pocket-8, DDA MIG Flats, Sector-12, Ph-I, Dwarka	4	2.029	123,740	South-West
257	Matri Mandir Samity, Safdarjung Enclave, B-2 Block	1	0.91	38,400	South
258	Bharat Nagar Social Welfare Association, 27	2	0.57	39,900	North-West

259	Dewdrop Welfare Society, House no. 65, Ground floor Pocket-10, Sector-20, Rohini	1	0.342	23,940	North-West
260	RWA, Mayfair Garden, Hauz Khas	6	1.57	49,100	South
261	Shakti Co-operative House Building Society, Blocks-B and C, Shubham Enclave, Paschim Vihar	1	1.352	73,791	West
262	Ashalat Pur Janakpuri	5	1.68	134,400	West
263	Lok Kalyan Vikas Samiti, Sawan Park Extension, Ashok Vihar-III	3	1.288	79,280	North-West
264	Resident Security and Development Society, C-53, Shakti Nagar Extension	4	1.674	102,440	North-West
265	Ishwar CGHS Ltd, Plot no. 4, Sector-12, Dwarka	3	0.535	34,100	South-West
266	Sunny Valley CGHS Ltd, Plot no. 27, Sector-12, Dwarka	3	0.917	55,020	South-West
267	RWA, Pocket-B, Sarita Vihar, B-498	3	1.68	100,800	South
268	All India Panchayat Parishad, 368, Balwant Rai Mehta Panchayat Bhawan, Panchayat Dham, Mayur Vihar, Ph-I	1	4	324,000	East
269	RWA, Sector-16, Rohini	2	1.649	123,890	North-West
270	A-Block, RWA, Sector-11, Rohini	4	0.784	63,960	North-West
271	Great Capital CGHS Ltd, Plct-15, Sector-6, Dwarka	1	0.518	33,080	South-West
272	East End Enclave, RWA, 9, Laxmi Nagar	2	1.38	98,600	East
273	A, B, C, D-Blocks, RWA, B-66, New Rajinder Nagar	2	0.95	59,000	Central

Appendix 5 continued

S. No.	Name of RWA/NGO	Number of Parks	Area in Acres	Total GIA Amount in Rupees	District Zone
274	Green Valley CGHS Ltd, Plot no. 18, Sector-22, Dwarka	1	1.95	119,000	South-West
275	Azad Gramin Vikas Samiti, 47 Salahpur Majra Dabas	4	4.28	344,902	North-West
276	Janki Devi Foundation and Industrial Development	3	1.35	83,000	East
277	Universal Brother Hood CGHS Ltd, Sector-12, Dwarka	5	1.136	70,160	South-West
278	RWA AP Block Maurya Enclave, Pitampura	13	5.984	365,040	North-West
279	RWA Tower Apartment Pocket SD, Pitampura	13	3	184,000	North-West
280	RWA DU Block, Pitampura	1	0.399	23,940	North-West
281	Ispat CGHS Ltd, Sector-4, Dwarka	3	1.105	66,300	South-West
282	Kala Vihar CGHS Ltd, Mayur Vihar Ph-1, Extension-II	7	0.553	33,180	East
283	C. R. Park, C-Block, RWA	1	0.91	45,500	South
284	Shahdara CGHS Ltd, Sector-5, Dwarka	5	0.381	22,860	South-West
285	Nava Kairali CGHS Ltd, Sector-3, Dwarka	3	0.922	55,320	South-West
286	New Jyoti CGHS Ltd, Sector-4, Dwarka	2	0.923	55,380	South-West
287	Sanchar Vihar CGHS Ltd, Sector-4, Dwarka	3	0.496	29,760	South-West
288	Gold Croft CGHS Ltd, Sector-11, Dwarka	2	0.968	58,080	South-West

289	Farm View Apartments RWA	3	0.862	68,960	South
290	Shree Balaji, CGHS Ltd, Sector-6 Dwarka	2	0.9	54,000	South-West
	SUB TOTAL	**747**	**249.719**	**17,737,833**	
	GRAND TOTAL	**1,287**	**454.0868**	**35,056,298**	

Source: Data provided by Delhi Parks & Gardens Society, New Delhi.
Notes: Payments were made by check or through RTGS.

*GIA = Grant-in-aid

Appendix 6
Some Examples of Projects Implemented through RWAs/MTAs Initiative

S. No.	Names of RWAs/ MTAs	Projects Implemented through RWAs/MTAs Initiative
1	Residents Welfare Association, Dilshad Colony	• Collection of ₹1.84 crore* and working with DJB for water and sewer system installation • Construction of roads and drains in colony in collaboration with MCD • Opening a branch of Kendriya Bhandar under the Bhagidari program • Installation of piped natural gas • Setting-up a Senior Citizen Center
2	New Krishna Nagar Residents Welfare Association, New Krishna Nagar	• Distribution of about 500 medicinal saplings in Bhagidari meeting of East District • Supply of 60 green plants to SBI, Krishna Nagar Branch, and for its customers as well
3	DDA Flats Owner Welfare Association Rani Jhansi Complex, Paharganj	• Removal of encroachment in the surrounding area of DDA complex Motia Khan by big cluster of *jhuggies* • Revival of the parks

*₹1.84 crore = ₹1,84,00,000

S. No.	Names of RWAs/ MTAs	Projects Implemented through RWAs/MTAs Initiative
4	Residents Welfare Association, Pocket-D, Dilshad Garden	• Raising the height of boundary wall and its grit plastering through the Councillor Fund in association with MCD • Construction of foot path • Installation of 15 sodium lights from MLA Fund and two others from Councillor Fund. Another 15 lights were purchased through contribution made by members of the RWA itself • Two watchman cabins installed at entry gates of colony for ₹ 28,000 from members contributory fund • Helping people in getting their ration card/voter ID cards, and so on from government offices • Plantation undertaken around the boundary wall of the pocket
5	Joint Forum of Vasundhara Enclave Co-operative Group Housing Society, Vasundhara Enclave	• Worked with DJB for covering of the open drain adjacent to Hindon, Soochna, Leiah, Anupam Apartments, and so on • Supply of gas through pipelines • New Pragatisheel Apartment, Vasundhara Enclave distributed more than 1,500 saplings for planting in parks • Constructing a community hall on a piece of land allotted in August 2005 • BSES street lights of Vasundara Enclave made fully operational
6	Krishan Ganj Sheesh Mahal Rihaishi Kalyan Samiti, Shivaji Azad Market, Teliwara	• Laying of sewer line, water pipeline near Masjid Sheikh Gamo and in Shyam Gali, Teliwara • Repair and replacement of street lights in Tokri Walan, Teliwara, Kishan Ganj, Shish Mahal, Azad Market • Removal of garbage and malba from public places • Setting up of check collection center of BSES • Removal of illegal encroachment on government land at Pul Mithai Azad Market and converted into park by horticulture department
7	Haveli Hisamuddin Haider Welfare Society, Ballimaran	• 200 ration cards were distributed to senior citizens and sick persons • Shortage of teaching staff matter taken up with deputy director of education (central); finally five teachers were posted in school

Appendix 6 continued

Appendix 6 continued

S. No.	Names of RWAs/ MTAs	Projects Implemented through RWAs/MTAs Initiative
8	Vasant Vihar Welfare Association, Vasant Vihar	• Completion of "Sewerage Water Recycling Project" • Conversion of a dumping ground (for malba) into beautiful parks
9	Residents Welfare Association, Surajmal Vihar	• Charitable dispensary "Madhru Jyoti" for providing medical facilities at nominal cost • Construction of four-storeyed community hall • Development of parks and plantation activity in parks • For safety, boundary walls constructed, security guards posted at gates and servants and tenants verification done
10	Residents Welfare Association, Mansarover Garden	• Health awareness camp for detection and prevention of blood sugar, blood pressure was organized in association with Sandoz Pvt Ltd, Mumbai and Krishna Polyclinic Camp
11	Sehyog Residents Welfare Association, Sector 6, Rohini	• Maintenance of street lights and drainage • Plantation in Bhagwan Parshuram Park
12	Tri Nagar Residents Welfare Association, Shanti Nagar	• Iron gates fixed at entry points
13	Central Market, Welfare Association, Surajmal Vihar	• Development of four parking places around market • Development of parks, plantation in these parks and around pathways of market • Halogen lights installed by BSES, damaged wires, bulbs replaced, sub-station of market locked to avoid pilferage of electricity
14	Navyuvak Gaon Mukandpur Gram Vikas Samiti, Mukandpur, Badli	• Got water pipe laid down by DJB for water supply
15	Residents Welfare Association, D Block Ashok Nagar	• BSES Camp organized and 1,288 new power connections provided to avoid pilferage in power consumption

S. No.	Names of RWAs/ MTAs	Projects Implemented through RWAs/MTAs Initiative
16	Residents Welfare Association, C-5 Block, Yamuna Vihar	• Three high mast poles installed in parks • Iron gates erected on Wazirabad side of colony • Segregation and management of wastes is taking great stride and moving towards green future • DJB changed water pipelines and sewer lines of two back lanes have also been replaced • Verification of tenants done with help of Police • Controlled the menace of stray dogs, monkeys, and cattle with assistance of MCD • Helping senior citizens and widows in getting financial help of ₹20,000. Also old age pension by Delhi government
17	Kingsway Camp Welfare Association, 45 Mall Road	• Saplings planted around the boundary wall of complex for greenery and to control pollution • Waste segregation method is adopted very effectively • Rain water harvesting and water conservation plan also in process of implementation • Campaign like "Say No to Plastic Bags," "Say No to Fire Crackers," and so on • Parking place facility arranged for each individual • Water and electricity bills payment at a single point
18	Central Employees Residents Welfare Association, Gole Market	• Development of a "Model Park" • Active in water conservation. Rain water harvesting location identified with CPWD officials
19	Janhit Residents Welfare Association, Pocket –I, Dilshad Garden	• Boundary wall with barbed fences constructed all around pocket and Iron gate installed at entry points • BSES ensured fixing of high mast light at nodal points • 500 saplings of flower and medicinal plants have been planted • Two tube wells provided for watering parks • 60 benches fixed for senior citizens in parks • Dustbins placed at several points • Parking places fixed for residents

Appendix 6 continued

Appendix 6 continued

S. No.	Names of RWAs/ MTAs	Projects Implemented through RWAs/MTAs Initiative
20	C-Block (1–50) Dilshad Garden Residents Welfare Association, Dilshad Garden	• Bhagidari Platform used to accomplish the long pending works • Replacement of old damaged pipelines for getting sufficient water supply in association with DJB • New Sewer lines laid down • Well maintained parks, playgrounds • Medical check up for residents through Escorts Heart Research Institute • Converting school of C-Block, through VKS, into an ideal learning place and cleaning of Dhalao
21	Residents Welfare Association, Subzi Mandi	• Repair and maintenance of streetlights and sewer lines • Laying of new water pipelines
22	Dalit Welfare Association, Joharipur Extension	• Construction of Pucca Nallah by funds of residents • Main road of the colony was also repaired to keep green and clean area
23	Residents Welfare Association, Pocket-E, Dilshad Garden	• Installation of iron gates at entry points, expenses incurred by residents, security guards also deputed • Encourage removal of encroachment • Parks well maintained • Plantation drive undertaken to improve ecology; separate dustbins placed for biodegradable and non-biodegradable wastes • Street lights repaired
24	DAV Education Welfare Society, Pocket-12, Sector-21, Rohini	• Maintenance of street lights and sewer lines • With the cooperation of DDA and Horticulture Department more than 150 saplings planted and 500 plants distributed among students of local schools
25	Federation of RWA, Saket	• Replacement of sewer lines, widening of roads, maintenance and beautification of local parks. • Ensuring uninterrupted power supply in locality, additional electric poles, and sodium lights have been installed • Decongestion of traffic by introducing one-way traffic inside Saket • Maintenance of local parks

S. No.	Names of RWAs/ MTAs	Projects Implemented through RWAs/MTAs Initiative
26	Rani Jhansi Complex, Motia Khan, Paharganj	• Improved condition of government school of area through Vidyalaya Kalyan Samiti • Nearly ₹140,000 spent on upgradation of infrastructure and greening and beautification of school; a water filter with cooling system installed for the students and staff
27	Residents Welfare Association, Greater Kailash-II	• Roads were re-carpeted and pavements repaired with association of area MLA • Own tennis court, a skating track constructed through MP Fund • Through Central Groundwater Board, rain-water harvesting at four sites in the colony has been approved out of which projects at two sites already completed by RWA
28	Residents Welfare Association, DB-Block DDA Flats, Hari Nagar	• RWA worked with Horticulture Department to turn barren parks of the area into well-maintained parks • Through Bhagidari, improved water for area with laying of additional four water pipelines • Replacement of old transformers with high capacity transformer • Laying of underground cables • Iron gates installed on all entry points
29	Federation of Naraina Vihar Residents Welfare Association, Naraina Vihar	• Achieved success in developing some of the well maintained parks • In association with PWD, MCD, traffic police, and CM office has resulted into widening of Ring Road at Naraina Sector where bottleneck of the road was causing serious traffic jam • Sewer line has been laid down for benefit of some part of Naraina village in association with DJB • Opening of water bills collection and correction center in C-Block • In association with Federation, the Central Ground Water Board has identified locations for water harvesting. Estimates for the project have been finalized and sent to DJB for further action

Appendix 6 continued

Appendix 6 continued

S. No.	Names of RWAs/ MTAs	Projects Implemented through RWAs/MTAs Initiative
		• In a management and civil defense program residents were taught about protective measures in case of natural calamities like earthquake and fire
30	Gram Sudhar Sainik Samiti, Village & PO Issapur	• In association with DC (revenue) District South-West and MCD completed the unfinished Dhalao • With Irrigation and Flood Control Department carrying out development works in local ponds • Construction of 2 km long nallah to remove dirty water of drains of the village
31	Federal Welfare Association, Sadh Nagar, Palam Colony	• Awareness campaigns to check spread of dengue and malaria mosquitoes • Workshops organized on waste management under Bhagidari initiative and demonstration were made regarding method of solid waste segregation and conversion of household waste into manure
32	Bijwasan Gram Vikas Samiti, Bijwasan	• A new Barat Ghar and renovation of the *chaupal*
33	Residents Welfare Association, WP Block, Pitampura	• Installed iron gates on all the entry points • Boundary wall of district park raised • Boundary wall of colony fenced with barbed wire • A tube well installed in pump house to get adequate water supply; work of laying CI Pipes in progress to solve problem of contaminated water • During cleanliness campaign three parks were planted with new grass, seasonal flowers, and various kinds of trees. Handmade nests were also placed in parks for attracting various kinds of birds • All tube lights replaced with halogen lights in streets. High-mast lights were installed in two of the parks • All drains were covered with concrete slab to prevent stagnant water from spreading all over the colony

S. No.	Names of RWAs/ MTAs	Projects Implemented through RWAs/MTAs Initiative
34	North Delhi Residents Welfare Federation, Chandrawal Road	• Removal of garbage in the ridge, and leveling of land • Construction of boundary wall and gates • Completion of rain water harvesting unit having a capacity of 5,000 liter at Malkaganj under My Delhi I Care Fund
35	Neghban Residents Welfare Association, Azad Market	• Installation of 10 electric poles at Main Road, Azad Market
36	Residents Welfare Association, Karampura	• Conversion of an unattended park into a beautiful park for women • Shifting of urinal from Karampura Commercial Complex to another place with proper construction • Removal of construction waste from opposite MCD office • Construction of a wall by the side of nallah by E-Block, Karampura • Setting-up of a machine for payment of water bills to DJB at E-Block, Karampura • Setting-up of electronic LCD machine in B-Block, Karampura for payment of power bills to BSES
37	Jan Kalyan Samiti, C-3, C-4, Yamuna Vihar	• Provision of drop box to pay IGL bills • Arrangements for car parking
38	Residents Welfare Association, Zafrabad	• Tree plantation in the area under Green Delhi Project • Verification of tenants in collaboration with Delhi Police
39	Residents Welfare Association, Singhu Village	• Construction of Road • Development of Park
40	Vasant Kunj B-9 Residents Association, Vasant Kunj	• Implementation of Solid Waste Management Project • Garbage collection from each flat • Implementation of Vermi-culture Composting Project

Appendix 6 continued

Appendix 6 continued

S. No.	Names of RWAs/ MTAs	Projects Implemented through RWAs/MTAs Initiative
41	Munirka Vihar Association, Munirka Vihar	• Replacement of old PVC water supply pipe with normal metal pipe • Boring of the tube well • Installation of a high-capacity motor in the pump house
42	Federation of RWA, Mayur Vihar, Phase-I	• Installation of street lights on Khudi Ram Bose Marg
43	Rihayasi Welfare Samudayik Samiti, Harsh Vihar	• Construction of drains • Electrification of the area
44	Krishna Market Paharganj Residents and Shopkeepers Welfare Society, Paharganj	• Installation of street lights under My Delhi I Care Fund
45	Youth Welfare Association, Vijay Park, Maujpur	• Laying down sewers in the left out streets of Vijay Park • Construction/improvement of almost all streets of Vijay Park • Covering of drains on the main road of Vijay Park
46	Residents Welfare Association, South Ganesh Nagar	• Development and maintenance of park • Signage boards in every road and alley in the colony • Arrangement of two Samarsebal
47	Golf Link Association, Golf Links	• Procurement of fitness equipments under My Delhi I Care Fund for establishment of gymnasium at Community Centre, Golf Link
48	Kendriya Sarkari Karamchari Awas Kalyan Sanstha, Baba Kharak Singh Marg	• Procurement of fitness equipments for establishment of gymnasium at Sector-IV, Baba Kharak Singh Marg under My Delhi I Care Fund
49	Shahdara Residents Welfare Association, Farsh Bazar, Shahdara	• Starting of Senior Citizen Manoranjan Kendra at Anaaj Mandi, Shahdara, under My Delhi I Care Fund

S. No.	Names of RWAs/ MTAs	Projects Implemented through RWAs/MTAs Initiative
50	Narmada Apartments Residents Welfare Association, Alaknanda	• Installation of two iron gates under My Delhi I Care Fund
51	Ghee Mandi Gali Halwai Traders Welfare Association, Ghee Mandi, Paharganj	• Distribution of 50 dustbins amongst the shopkeepers

Source: Bhagidari Report: *Eight Years of Success—Glimpses of Partnerships Progress; and Monthly Newsletters* both by Bhagidari Cell and Government of NCT of Delhi.

In addition, several RWAs/MTAs have carried out the following regular activities:

- Organizing health melas (fairs/exhibitions)
- Organizing free medical check-up camps
- Distribution of woolen clothes to the poor in winter
- Organizing dengue-malaria awareness camps
- Organizing disaster management workshops
- Organizing plantation drive for green environment
- Collection of property tax to facilitate easy payment by citizens
- Provision of drop boxes for collection of water and electricity bills
- Nukkad natak on the issues of "Clean Yamuna" (street plays for IEC)
- Organizing city cleanliness drives
- Organizing blood donation camps
- Celebration of national days
- Cultural and sports activities in the area
- Collection and distribution of ration cards
- Drive for verification of domestic servants, salesmen, and security guards by local police

Appendix 7

Examples of the "Difficulties" and "Agreed Solutions" Shared by the Participating Citizens' Associations in Bhagidari Workshops during 2000–2002 on Power Issues with DVB (Electricity Board of Delhi)

Difficulties

- No responsible official is available at the time of breakdown
- Difficult residents are beyond the control of RWAs
- Absence of meeting between DVB and RWAs; lack of communication

- Complaints not attended to by duty in-charge
- Errors/wrong operation by DVB staff
- Lack of coordination between working timetable of different grids
- Indifference of the lower staff of DVB
- Members of RWAs are not available in their area around the clock
- RWAs representative may not be given sufficient time to note the timings of breakdown, as this is a never-ending process
- No office or paid staff to record breakdowns, loads shedding, and its restoration round the clock and preparing weekly and fortnightly statements to send the same to DVB
- Dispute between RWAs and DVB regarding duration of breakdown time
- Financial assistance to RWAs
- DVB makes technical distinctions between breakdown, load-shedding, transformer-failure, grid-failure, and so on—whatever be the cause, the supply has been broken to the citizens
- Authenticity and accuracy of meter reading is not reliable
- No proper meter reading by DVB
- RWAs do not have the expertise and resources to monitor misuse and cannot take up the responsibility
- RWAs may give undue favor to any influential residents
- Financial implication in installing extra transmission lines, power houses, and transformers
- Proper/complete procedures are not known to bonafide/domestic users and RWAs
- RWAs do not always have the knowledge of each occupant and also not their load requirement
- Process of meter name change and load enhancement is very lengthy
- Who will be held responsible for wrong reading and billing; one JE is handling a number of RWAs
- DVB staff not regular in their duties and blames their seniors on non-availability of necessary stores and materials
- How can RWAs manage the work of DVB staff; at most they can supervise and report back
- In colonies where there are more than one resident's association, problem of identification of RWAs may come
- Harassment by local areas' staff of DVB of those who report violations
- Noncooperation of DVB staff with RWAs

Agreed Solutions

- To remove unauthorized connections frequent raids should be made with the help of police; MTA surprise inspection should also be made by DVB officials and office-bearer of MTA. In case of default, once in a month, heavy penalty should be imposed.
- Single-point system to be introduced by DVB and further distribution to the individuals to be done by MTA.
- The procedure for getting new electric connection could be simplified and limited to one-window approach.
- Formation of joint working group of DVB and MTA for checking of excess load and unauthorized tapping and on the spot sanctioning of load addition and new connections.
- Popularizing the use of unconventional methods, that is, use of solar energy for generating electricity for common use in markets by MTA.
- The shopkeepers should use the electricity to minimum extent—high-voltage bulbs and halogen lights should be discouraged, and energy saving devices should be encouraged. Use of AC and neon signs during peak hours should be strictly banned.
- MTA should ensure closure of all shops at the scheduled time.
- A Joint Committee of MTA and DVB to educate shopkeepers on curbing consumption.
- Trained/responsible official must be posted at complaint corners.
- Prior intimation for scheduled power cut should be given to RWAs.
- Frequent meetings should take place between DVB and RWAs
- Telephone numbers (residential and official) of the officials should be provided.
- Provide streetlights at crucial points to be working on standby generators.
- Coordination between working timetable of different grids is a must.
- A breakdown team should be ready each time.
- DVB complaint center should honestly display the problem on the notice board.
- There shall be a policy circulated by DVB whereby the demand can be compared with the sanctioned load of the area, which will facilitate in working out the duration of the load shedding in a particular area.

- There should be local camps to sort out the problems of the residents in coordination with RWAs.
- DVB to reduce the gap between demand and supply (augment power from other surplus states).
- DVB should train the field staff to be responsive, well behaved, well versed, and polite.
- Proper distribution of load should be sanctioned in consultation with the RWAs.
- Prompt action shall be taken to intimate RWAs of power failure/breakdown.
- Nodal officers from DVB shall inform RWAs on telephone well in advance, if load shedding is for more than 30 minutes.
- DVB should check theft of electricity. Theft prone areas to the identified and maximum load shedding enforced there. As far as possible, no load shedding should happen at residential areas.
- All telephones provided at complaint centers should be always kept in working order by DVB to ensure proper response to general consumer's problem.
- High rise flood lights should be installed at vulnerable points to ensure safety of shopkeepers and visitors.
- Provision for alternate arrangement during breakdown must be ensured for safety of market areas.
- Initially improved type streetlight should be done by DVB and after that streetlight to be maintained, and switching on/off to be done by MTAs.
- Glow signs should be provided in and around market areas.
- Standard pattern of poles and light equipment for beautiful and uniform look.
- Proper regulation for on/off system and regular maintenance to save energy.
- Check on theft of street/road light in association with market associations.
- If Market Traders Associations want more lighting for beautification, it can be provided on "pay and use basis".
- DVB should be ready to install new and more beautiful designs of poles and lights, ducting for cables and other services.
- Guidelines should be issued by the DVB to RWAs for enhancement of load, and meter-name change.
- The documentation of change of meter name and enhancement of load should be verified and authenticated by RWAs.
- Periodical review of pending cases by RWAs with DVB officials.

- Individual applications to be routed through RWAs to save time and avoid unnecessary harassment.
- RWAs can assist the consumer with proper guidance and correct procedure supplied by DVB.
- RWAs can help DVB for smooth functioning within a time frame and also can create awareness regarding merit and demerits of meter name-change and load enhancement.
- DVB should organize local colony/area camps in coordination with RWAs. RWAs should identify such premises where name change of meters and load enhancement is required.
- Load verification should be carried out by DVB along with the representative from RWAs.
- Misuse of electricity should be reported by DVB to RWAs for its remedial measures and to facilitate load enhancement.
- Name-change form/load enhancement form to be made available in the office of RWAs. Complete application form will be submitted by RWA in the office of DVB twice a month.
- Commercial formalities for name change/load enhancement should be displayed in the office of RWA.
- RWA should be empowered to recommend the name change as well as for load enhancement.
- There should be regular interaction between RWAs and DVB officials to solve day-to-day problems.
- Complaint center of the DVB to be made functional in all the areas. These complaint centers should maintain the complaint register properly, area wise, and time wise. Complaint centers should be computerized and made automatic like airlines and railways.
- A meeting should be held by RWAs and officers of the DVB periodically.
- DVB shall engage full-time workers for the RWAs or give financial assistance to the RWAs for the same.
- DVB should install some automatic devices to record the exact timings of failure and restoration.
- RWA representative will note the time and duration of power failure/breakdown in supply and enter it in the power register next day.
- Electric complaint office should be computerized so that the exact time of failure of supply is noted.
- RWA should be allowed to construct an office in one of the parks or permitted to use a room in the community hall for coordinating with all civic agencies and utilities.

- Block-wise feeding to be done by DVB and information to be given to RWAs whenever feeding is altered.
- Reporting of power failure time/restoration time be intimated immediately to complaint center of DVB—name of officers to whom the information have been given should also be entered in the power diary.
- There must be an executive engineer in regional complaint center who knows the information regarding supply of electricity/disturbance and he can inform the same to RWA office.
- Weekly pre-titled register of breakdown/shut down and restoration charts to be supplied by DVB and also to be collected by DVB after the weekend for follow-up action.
- DVB should give advance information/intimation about date and time of shut down.
- DVB should provide to RWAs a list of names of staff deployed for maintenance and attending to complaints by name, designation, phone number, and address.
- DVB should also provide residence and office telephone numbers of the concerned officers.
- Standard format of power diary to be evolved mutually by RWAs and DVB.
- Public announcement by DVB of the load shedding with date and time of a particular area.
- Feeder-wise distribution chart showing the houses or group of houses being serviced by individual feeders be given by DVB to the RWAs.
- Only maintaining record through the RWAs is not sufficient, reported actions should be pursued vigorously till the implementation is ensured, since DVB has its own limitations.
- An official of DVB should visit the office of RWA once in a fortnight to handle problems and signature should be kept in power diary.
- Self-reading of meter by owner/residents; this should be tabulated/compiled by RWAs and sent to DVB.
- DVB should appoint a private agency for meter reading.
- Person deputed for meter reading should be authorized by RWAs and DVB.
- Cases of faulty meters should be brought to the notice of DVB immediately.
- Meter reading to be done by RWAs through a person trained by DVB.

- Advance technology to improve reliability of reading and billing should be adopted by DVB, like MTNL.
- Meter reading should be done on a percentage basis of the revenue collected.
- DVB should have a mobile van with computer and printer for reading, so that the billing and collection can be done simultaneously.
- RAs shall ensure periodical meter readings on meter cards maintained at individuals residence.
- DVB shall ensure at least half yearly actual meter reading in coordination with RAs staff.
- RWAs should be ready to pay enhanced charges.
- There should be a check on corruption by DVB officials.
- Procedures may be simplified and settled timely as recommended by RA.
- In case of tenant, RWA should come forward for justification for name change and additional load.
- DVB should issue an acknowledgement for submission of application, and time should be fixed for sanction of requirement.
- All the required document of application should be checked at the time of receipt of application and any discrepancy should be pointed out on the spot.
- Transparency with proper guidelines.
- Meter reading should be displayed on notice board of RWA.
- Incentive should be increased for meter reading.
- Meter sheets with the particulars of the connection with opening meter reading, and so on should be supplied by DVB.
- Meter reading cards in duplicate should be made for each consumer and be given to RWAs; one card should remain with the consumer and the other with the DVB; duplicate cards having reading will be regularly collected from RWAs and returned after updating the record of DVB.
- Periodic checking by DVB officials, who will have to sign meter reading cards in token of working of meter, and confirming the intactness of the seals and glass of the meter.
- Consumer should be authorized to get his defective meter replaced with a new private meter duly tested by DVB through a private authorized technician with the concurrence of RWA.
- Meter reading should be collected by DVB staff on a particular day as decided between RWA and DVB.
- Regular/periodical meetings should be held between DVB staff and RWAs to sort out most repetitive grievances.

- Camps or *adalats* should be held at regular intervals to clear backlog of problems.
- The DVB local staff should also mark their attendance with RWAs.
- RWAs should maintain diaries of complaints and actions taken/not taken which DVB should monitor.
- Duty register of staff, with the name of standby staff, should be provided by DVB to RWAs.
- RWAs should train their volunteers to have a check on the DVB staff randomly and give remarks on complaint register.
- Feedback should be kept confidential but RWAs must appreciate the good work done by DVB officials.
- RWAs should not be given such powers so that they take undue advantage.
- DVB should provide update list of all area staff to avoid entry of unauthorized person.

Phase II

- Delivery of bills should be made through courier services.
- Collection centers should be increased near every market/localities to facilitate the collection.
- Check collection boxes should be placed at collection center/market.
- Self-billing and depositing in authorized banks.
- Bills should be supplied one week before the payment.
- Bills should be supplied after correction.
- Association to give the list of their members with their members' address and connection numbers to DVB.
- Mobile van should be provided in market on a fixed date/time to collect the bills.
- Number of bill collection centers should be increased.
- MTA should collect check and drafts from markets and submit to DVB at exclusive counters.
- Bills to be handed over to MTA office well in time.
- Sufficient time should be given for collection of the bills by MTAs and payment of the same to DVB.
- DVB staff should collect the payment from associations' office on a fixed date and should furnish the individual receipts in MTAs offices.

- Residents should be educated that load enhancement will certainly improve the supply position.
- Meter-name change will be fruitful in other legal implication.
- Area-wise camps should be arranged.
- Minimum guarantee charges should be reduced to encourage load enhancement.
- NOC from DVB regarding "no-dues certificate" should be issued prior to sale of property; registrar should ask for these no dues certificate at the time of sell/transfer of property.
- Instruction should be issued to DVB to set up "single-window" as a system is computerized.
- DVB should organize SEHYOG program along with RWAs in the colony along with departments of DVB like finance, technical, and accounts, and so on (under one roof).
- Residents should be educated through meetings for regularizing their connected load by depositing necessary charges to DVB.
- Minimum formalities/paper work should be required by DVB and necessary charges should be recovered in installments through their bills.
- DVB should provide RWAs with all the proper guidelines for meter-name change and load enhancement.
- DVB may organize camps for meter-name change and load enhancement in association with the RWAs.
- A checklist should be provided to RWAs for ensuring completion of applications.
- Load enhancement charges should be allowed to be paid in minimum 10 installments with routine bills.
- RWAs should arrange consumer guides in bulk and distribute among residents and motivate them to get the name change/load enhancement done.
- At time of increasing the load actual consumption of the consumer should be taken into account, total points should not be considered.
- Meter-name changing and enhancement of load form, along with load receiver, should be available at RWAs office (recognized association).
- Text report filled by consumer must be verified by RWAs authorized person in place of licensed contractor of Delhi Administration.
- All these processes must be finalized at zonal office in place of district office.

- In case of litigation the decision taken by RWAs should be recognized by the court.
- RWAs can only assist in meter-name change and cannot help/assist DVB in load enhancement, this being an individual perspective.
- All prescribed forms should be available with RWAs.
- As far as load enhancements are concerned, no user will come forward through RWAs; the process for load enhancements is to be reexamined and it should be assessed on the basis of actual average consumption of electricity and connected load.
- The load enhancement may be allowed without name change in the interest of tenant/occupant.
- DVB staff and RWA should jointly inspect the premises to check the irregularities regularly.
- Application form and procedure be simplified by DVB to avoid lengthy cumbersome procedure and request should be directly entertained by DVB on merits.
- Bonafide requests for load enhancement may be entertained by DVB on first-come-first-served basis, duly endorsed by RWA and should be sanctioned by DVB subject to total sanctioned load for the colony.
- While RWA welcomes the concept of coordination, it may not be made compulsory for such occupants/owners who do not want RWAs' assistance or intervention as legal and personal aspects will also be involved.
- RWA can do door-to-door survey for load enhancement.
- RWAs should insist for sanction of enhancement of load as per minimum requirement.
- Power companies should deploy their staff once in a month at RWA office to interact with the residents.
- Application for load enhancement and meter-name change should be sent directly to DVB by the consumer with a copy to RWAs.
- Consumer should reach RWAs first to know how to fill up the forms with relevant documents.
- RWAs should persuade the landlords to issue the NOC to the tenants.
- Powers should be given to RWAs for better performance.
- Moral education to DVB staff.
- Additional funds for small jobs to be undertaken by RWAs.
- Views/complaints given by RWAs should be kept confidential.
- A register be maintained for monitoring complaints in the monthly meeting with senior officials.
- Competent officers should have regular coordination with RWAs.

- Regular meeting of all DVB local staff with RWAs.
- Time and date for periodical meeting with RWAs may be fixed.
- Residential and office telephone numbers may be provided.
- Company staff should be cordial and should not react negatively.
- Staff should be punctual.
- Repair and maintenance staff should have proper knowledge of local cable network.
- RWAs must know the functioning of the department.
- The company to provide feedback to RWAs on action taken.
- Organizing monthly meetings to have proper coordination between staff and RWAs.
- The RWAs should issue the compliance certificate and compliance should be time-bound.
- DVB officers should have full control and watch over working of their field staff.
- Accountability should be fixed.
- RWAs should convey the performance to nodal officer.
- RWAs to suggest ways for improving efficiency.
- Strict action is required to be taken in case of unsatisfactory performance.
- Government should provide more line staff for quick rectification of faults.
- Staff should wear uniform with identity card/name plate at the time of duty hours.
- Availability of required material like cables, jumper and conductor, and so on must be ensured in complaint center.
- The intimation regarding transfer of staff should be sent to the concerned RWAs.
- Copy of rotation chart of the staff should be provided to RWAs..
- Appreciation/complaint about the field staff should be asked from the RWAs.
- Fortnightly visits by the senior officers of the DVB to the RWA office and locality.
- Provision of extra line staff at local complaint center in evening/ late hours.
- Replacement of old underground cables and overhead conductors.
- Sufficient T&P with material should be made available along with vehicle to rectify the complaints and problems on priority basis.
- Compulsory redressal of the problem within a specified timeline should be ensured by a competent official.
- In cases of delayed action responsibility should be fixed.

- RWA should report to DVB in case of suspicion of fraudulent abstraction of energy; reading should be taken by meter reader or individual should give their own meter reading.
- Random checking by DVB to encourage support to RWA.
- There should be periodical review of the rate of remuneration.
- RWAs will take responsibility of correct reading from their own paid official; amount received from DVB shall go to RWA.
- Self-assessment of reading by residents can be implemented and proper verification can be done by DVB officials periodically.
- Increase in remuneration to get efficient and reliable meter reader.
- Proper training by DVB and sample check of the meters by DVB to reduce malpractice.
- Remuneration to be increased to minimum of ₹4 per meter reading.
- Insurance cover to be provided to the meter reader.
- Meter reader should be engaged by DVB only; they should however work in close coordination with RWAs.
- Meter reading should be taken in the presence of consumer and should be supported by signature of both.
- RWA should select such persons who are honest and have good behavior as meter reader.
- Power Distribution Company and RWAs should keep constant watch on the private meter reader and undertake surprise checking of certain percentage of readings.
- Coordination committee should be formed and meeting should be held periodically/monthly/bimonthly.
- This task should be given to private sector along with distribution of electricity.
- Private sector may take help of RWAs in recording meter reading and the same should be counter-signed by the RWAs.
- New electronic meter should be installed by DVB.
- MTA to evolve its own internal introspection and cleansing mechanism.
- Nexus pointed out by the MTA between illegal users and concerned government officers should be dealt seriously.
- In case MTA does not participate actively, then it should be made accountable in case even if one illegal user is detected by the system.
- Political vote bank culture is the main reason for unauthorized electric connection and privatization is the only solution.

- Awareness should be created among the citizens that unauthorized connection and over drawing of electricity is illegal and direct loss to the national progress/exchequer.
- Procedure for sanctioning of connection and additional load process should be simplified at one window service and deterrent laws should be enacted to deal with defaulters.
- Underground cabling system may be adopted where possible.
- Heavy penalty should be imposed on all unauthorized consumers; no political interference should be allowed.
- One window service for sanction of load/connection and simplifying the procedures for grant of additional load.
- Local camps should be organized in coordination with the MTAs for enhancement/regularization of additional load.
- Regular raids should be conducted to detect theft of electricity in coordination with MTAs.
- Procedures should be simplified for execution of enhancement of load and system should be augmented on top priority.
- DVB should arrange to hold camps at market areas for regularizing unauthorized load at the site on one window service basis.
- MTAs need to be made aware and educated by DVB about the benefits of availing correct enhanced load that load directly link with the system improvement.
- Representatives of MTAs should accompany or be a member of Theft Raid Teams to bring transparency in the system.
- Camp should be organized by DVB with the help of association to enhance the load in approved areas on the pattern of unauthorized colonies.
- Load welfare association should intimate DVB about unauthorized connection and help them to get regularized; if not, he should be heavily penalized.
- The procedure for getting regularization of electricity meter/enhancement of power should be simplified and done in stipulated timeframe.
- MTAs should adhere to the time schedule of opening and closing of shops, factories, and so on.
- For improvising the power factor, the shunt capacitors should be installed and the part of the premises where light is not required, the fans, and so on should be switched off.
- Use of ACs for long hours should be discouraged; neon light and use of power for advertising purposes should be banned.
- All shops and commercial establishments must close by 7:00 p.m. positively; heavy fine and deterrent action on defaulter.

- Use of electric bulbs consuming more power to be discouraged/banned in all places of use—homes, offices, markets, marriage parties; instead use tube-lights and CFL lamps; street lights to be switched on and off timely use automatic switches.
- Less use of high-power lighting for advertising display and no-use-after-closure-of-shops' research should be regularly carried out for development; low-consumption appliances with efficient results.
- Show windows should be lighted but minimum at the demand of consumer; CFL should be used in place of tube/bulbs.
- MTAs should watch and inform the local authorities if rules are found violated.
- Special encouragement should be given to the traders/MTAs who abide by the rules.

Source: *Report on "Bhagidari"—the Citizen–government Partnership*, Phase I: January 2000 to June 2001 and Phase II: July 2001 to October 2002 (documentation reports sponsored by the Administrative Reforms Department, Ministry of Personnel, Pension & Public Grievances, Government of India).

Note: Since different table groups were working on the same issue, many points are common, thus, indicating the common ground that emerges during the Bhagidari workshops. They have been shared in its original form to give the flavor of democracy at work through this process.

Appendix 8

Examples of Feedback Given by the Participating Citizens in Bhagidari Workshops in 2007 and 2010 on Power Issues (Post-power Reforms) (for Discoms)

Positive Points Given by Stakeholders in the Bijli Bhagidari Workshop of BRPL

- Availability of power supply is good
- Very prompt urgent attention regarding any type of electricity fault
- Satisfied with the customer services and commercial department for taking prompt actions
- Commercial/businesses are up to the mark
- There has been distinct improvement in power supply and load shedding/outages have been considerably reduced
- Process of payment of bills has improved much and simplified

- New connections procedure has been simplified
- Load shedding is less as compared to earlier
- Complaint centers (customer-care stations) have been provided across the city
- BSES staff has started speaking soft language
- Quick response
- Easy bill payment
- Supply of electricity has improved
- Consumer's complaints attended in reasonable time
- Payment collection system made very easy
- Improvement in fault rectification time and supply restoration
- Improvement in customer-care service/response
- Initiation of door-step services
- Better maintenance of equipments
- Better consumer services in giving new connections
- More consumer-friendly and better coordination between staff and public
- Customer-care services are improved and good
- Easy to take new connection and bill deposition by improved services
- Voltage or quality of supply improved
- Availability of power supply is by and large satisfactory
- Customer-care services have partly improved
- In spite of the increase in input rates, tariff rates are still reasonable and stable
- Response of managers when meeting personally or telephonically is quite positive
- Bills are received in time
- Various payment options introduced by BRPL are consumer-friendly and convenient
- Customer care is far better now
- It is a good service provided as it provided all kinds of information related to BRPL
- They attend to customers very quickly
- Officers are mostly cooperative
- Door-step services by BRPL are very customer-friendly
- Senior BRPL officers are very positive and helpful and attentive to consumer's suggestion and grievances
- Bill distribution system and cash collection counters/centers are very excellent in working
- Response time to complaints lodged personally at BRPL complaint centers is excellent and within time

- There is improvement in customer-care relations
- Common helpline number
- Improvement in power distribution after privatization
- Officers are responsive
- Better electricity distribution
- Satisfactory complaints recording at the complaint centers
- Improved and constant electric supply voltage
- Customer-care service has been improved
- Uninterrupted power supply
- Releasing of new connections and so on has become easy
- Improvement in customer care
- Payment of bill made easy
- Calculation of bills made transparent
- Supply improved
- Bills payment is easy
- There is some improvement in attending to the faults

Note: Since different table groups were working on the same issue, many points are common, thus indicating the common ground that emerges during the Bhagidari workshops. They have been shared in its original form to give the flavor of democracy at work through this process.

Positive Points Given by Stakeholders in the Bijli Bhagidari Workshop of BYPL

- Quick redressal of problems
- Door-step service provided
- Supply of electricity improved
- SMS facility for different nature of complaints
- Replacement of oil type filled transformers by dry type transformers
- Personalized and timely solution to customer's needs
- The position of supply is satisfactory and complaints redressal by the BYPL staff is very good
- Very caring attitude towards consumers/RWA in all respects
- Demand and supply is better than before
- Customer satisfaction
- Quick response to consumer complaints
- Better power supply
- Better electric supply
- Bill payment options are easy

- Simplified procedure of new connections
- Uninterrupted power supply
- Better online services and quick disposal of problem
- Better management services of streetlight
- Bill payment is hassle-free now queues are short
- Breakdowns have drastically reduced
- Voltage stability is much better
- Electricity is available round the clock
- Easier and faster new connection installation through DSS where in consumer can get connection on one phone call
- Payment of bills are faster and easier due to multiple payment options
- Service has certainly improved to a great extent
- Distribution of electricity has improved
- Insulated overhead conductors in the distribution system are a good move both to check theft and safety
- Good payment facility
- Supply reliability is excellent
- Interaction between officials and consumers is good
- Reliability of supply is good
- Involvement of RWAs as Bhagidars in the process
- Almost uninterrupted power supply
- Quick removal of faults
- There is indeed improvement in the working of BYPL in providing continuous supply of electricity
- The customer services provided by BYPL are very good
- The setting up of customer-care centers is a good initiative
- The starting of door-step services is appreciable
- Uninterrupted power supply and treatment of public-care units is worth praising
- Quick response
- Timely resolution of complaints
- We can easily approach the authorities
- Customer can get easy and fast information
- Improvement in rectification of breakdown
- Services have substantially improved vis-à-vis pre-bases era
- Customer-care services are good
- Better billing and payment collection system
- DSS—a good improved initiative
- Role of PROs are commendable as they are constantly updating information with RWAs

- The higher staffs of O&M and business are very cooperative and their performance is commendable
- Supply position particularly on street light has improved tremendously
- Upgrading of payment facilities from time to time
- Excellent neat and clean building, customer-care centers, and so on for visiting consumers
- Most cooperative officers—always prepared to extent cooperation
- Reliable power supply
- Billing system improved
- Proper maintenance
- Announcement before shutdown
- Customer-care systems improve with the help of IT system
- Customer-care services have improved considerably
- Good relation between consumers and the staff
- Complaint sections inform actual status of the outages duration

Note: Since different table groups were working on the same issue, many points are common, thus indicating the common ground that emerges during the Bhagidari workshops. They have been shared in its original form to give the flavor of democracy at work through this process.

Positive Points Given by Stakeholders in the "Srijan" Workshop of NDPL (Now Tata Power Delhi Distribution Limited)

- Streamlined work culture of NDPL
- Easy bill payments
- Better work ambience
- Uninterrupted power supply
- Prompt service of any complaint and staff is very cooperative
- Better facilities for consumer at consumer care center, particularly for senior citizens
- Fast redressal of consumer complaints
- Good behavior of staff towards consumers
- Improvement in supply conditions in terms of breakdowns
- Dedicated consumer care and cash collection center
- Improvement in work environment and behavior change of staff
- Power supply has improved
- Procedures are simplified

- Better response to consumer complaints
- Paying bills is easier
- Regular supply
- Much better service
- Quick in action
- Appreciated in cash collection centers
- New HT connections are easily available
- Reduction in corruption, post privatization
- Improved consumer services (especially, cash counter and consumer-care center, CRO cooperative attitude, and so on)
- Improvement in quality of services and power supply
- Consumer-oriented approach, better consumer complaint redressal mechanism
- Better payment facilities
- Services towards consumers have improved ethically; uninterrupted power supply and customer relationship has improved
- Timely attending to the general complaints
- Bills depositing has become an easy job; more consumer-friendly atmosphere in offices
- Theft controlled to some extent
- Better services in providing new connections, easy payment of bills, timely redressal of complaints, and senior citizens are properly cared for
- Excellent power distribution management system resulting in less power cuts
- NDPL has very cordial relations with consumers
- Prompt rectification of complaints
- Well-maintained consumer-care center
- Efficient bill payment facilities
- Improved power supply (low power cut and no voltage fluctuation)
- Reliable power supply
- Improvement in resolution of no current complaints and correction of bills, as well as increase in payment collection avenues
- Employees are very cooperative and friendly and reduction of corruption
- Quality of electricity has improved
- Number of complaints have reduced and are attended on priority
- Behavior of officials is very courteous
- Payment avenues
  - Easy bill
  - Drop box

- ◆ Cash collection centers
- ◆ ATPM
- Reduction in load shedding
- Transport and consumer-friendly organization
  - ◆ Bhagidari meeting
  - ◆ Timely disposal of consumer complaints
  - ◆ 100 percent consumer information on Web site
- Reliable power supply
- Good arrangements for collection of bills
- Quick redressal of power supply complaints
- More consumer-friendly and socially conscious attitude to community needs
- Positive attitude of staff and management towards best continuity of supply, less breakdowns, and so on
- Excellent billing system and positive attitude of staff towards complaint redressal
- Quality and quantity of electricity improved substantially
- Innovative technology adopted by NDPL, that is, unmanned grid, AMR, breakdown facility
- Easy bill payment system, drop box, easy bill counters, check payment, and e-payment

Source: Report on NDPL Srijan Workshop, 2007 and Bijli Bhagidari Workshops, 2010.

Note: Since different table groups were working on the same issue, many points are common, thus indicating the common ground that emerges during the Bhagidari workshops. They have been shared in its original form to give the flavor of democracy at work through this process.

Appendix 9

Listing by Citizens' Associations and Officials of Transformational Citywide Developments in Delhi over the Period from 2000 to 2012

West District (June 26, 2012)

- Flyovers
- Bhagidari
- Time-bound civic services
- Various pension schemes
- Chacha Nehru Sehat Yojana (Children's Health Scheme)
- Laadli Scheme (Girls Education and Welfare Scheme)
- My Delhi I Care Fund
- Plantation—Green Delhi
- Sports and stadiums
- Regularization of unauthorized colonies
- Kerosene-free Delhi
- Anna Shri Yojana (food subsidy for the poor)

- Educational/technical institutions
- E-governance/computerization of various departments
- Improvement of infrastructure
- City beautification
- Low-cost housing schemes
- Outstanding leadership
- Introduction of CNG for pollution reduction
- Low frequency of power cuts
- Low-floor buses with AC
- Improvement of roads/highways
- New Airport Terminal T-3 which is world class
- New sports complexes
- Introduction of consumer courts
- Building of new malls/shopping complexes
- Better environment/reduced pollution
- Improved traffic conditions
- Better education facilities for all
- Manifold increase in green cover of city
- Better road network with number of new flyovers
- E-governance
- Awareness about disaster management
- Delhi RTI Act
- Introduction of Bhagidari
- Improvement in social service sector by introducing various schemes
- Improved standard of life
- Shopping malls
- Improved sanitation, door to door garbage collection
- Successful organizing of Common Wealth Games 2010
- Improved water distribution network
- Better health services
- Successfully completion of Commonwealth Games
- Phasing out of diesel buses and introduction of CNG green buses
- Construction of tallest building in Delhi (MCD)
- Introduction of e-PDS system in Food and Supply Department
- Computerization/online services in different departments
- Implementation of Janahar Yojana for urban poor
- Regularization of unauthorized colonies
- Establishment of super-speciality hospitals
- Establishment of Delhi Technological University
- CNG transportation
- Laadli Yojana (Girls Education and Welfare Scheme)
- SLA of various certificates in Delhi government

- Online MCD taxation and self-assesment
- Electricity supply in Delhi by privatization in distribution
- Midday Meal
- Jan Aahar Yojana
- BRT Corridor
- Commonwealth Games
- Rainwater harvesting
- SC/ST training programs
- Airport metro
- No signal on Ring Road
- Less power cuts
- Water supply increased
- Education standard improved
- Better roads
- Stadiums
- Information technology
- Kerosene-free state
- Per capita income increased
- More residential accommodation
- Transport system improved
- Bhagidari Yojana
- Chacha Nehru Sehat Yojana (Children's Health Scheme)
- Amdani Yojana
- Pollution-free Delhi
- Plantation
- Sanitation
- Disaster management
- Laadli Scheme (Girls Education and Welfare Scheme)
- Rainwater harvesting
- Kerosene free Delhi
- Anna Shri Yojana (Food subsidy for the poor)
- Bread and Break Fast Scheme
- Midday Meal
- RTI
- Academic improvement
- CNG autos and taxis
- Radio taxis
- Flyovers and underpasses
- Widening of roads
- Improvement in power supply
- Increased forestation
- Improvement of traffic management

- Participation of citizen in government
- Implementation of RTI Act
- Implementation of Citizen Charters
- Commonwealth Games
- Starting of Sarvodaya School Pratibha Vidyalaya—education field
- Pension for senior citizens, widows, and handicapped
- Financial help for marriage of daughter of widow
- My Delhi I Care Fund has been increased from ₹5 lakh to ₹5 crore—a great thing provided for development works to be taken up by RWAs
- Regular/monthly meeting of RWAs with area MLA
- Chacha Nehru Sehat Yojana (Children's Health Scheme)
- Flyovers
- Footover bridges
- Underpasses/subways
- Beautification of Delhi/Parks developed in Delhi
- Parking facilities provided in Delhi
- CNG stations
- Introduction of RTI Act 2005
- Trifurcation of MCD
- BRT Corridor
- Division of MCD
- Improvement in education
- Increase of electricity supply
- Laadli Yojana (Girls Welfare Scheme)
- Renovation of Bus stops
- Old-age homes
- Increase of old-age pension
- RTI Act
- Development of ponds
- Direct contact with the government in the form of Bhagidari
- Environment improvement (more greenery)
- Broad and clean roads
- Sufficient streetlights
- Improvement in public transport (metro/DTC)
- Improvement in education
- More flyovers to decongest the traffic problem
- Chacha Nehru Sehat Yojana (Children's Health Scheme)
- Improvement in stadiums
- Clean fuel
- PNG in Delhi

- Appointment of consultant for sewage system
- Improvements of roads
- Pollution control
- Introduction of PNG
- Maintenance of parks and gardens
- Improvement of drainage system/rainwater
- Improvement in medical facilities
- Renovation/new school buildings
- Education facilities to weaker sections of society
- Laadli Scheme for girls (Girls Education and Welfare Scheme)
- Availability of indoor/outdoor games facility
- Pension for widows and senior citizens/weaker sections of society
- Multilevel parking
- Improvement in supply of electricity supply
- Improvement of sewerage systems
- Number of hospital increased
- Citizen charter introduced
- Kerosene-free Delhi
- Chacha Nehru Sehat Yojana (Children's Health Scheme)
- Bhagidari funds increased from 50 lakh to 5 crore, in each district
- Plantation of trees
- Entertainment homes for senior citizens
- Introduction of online complaints/other services
- Lowfloor AC buses introduced
- CNG
- IGL supply provided in most locations of Delhi
- Lumpsum amount for marriage of widow's daughter
- Commonwealth Games held in Delhi because of which development of Delhi has improved to a large extent
- Replacement of blue line buses with LPG-AC and low-floor buses
- Construction of BRT corridor from Moolchand to MB Road
- Construction of subways and subways, underpasses, and flyovers
- Increase of greenery from 5 percent to 27 percent in Delhi
- Improvement of electricity supply system
- Renovation of several stadiums during Commonwealth Games 2010
- Participation of RWA/Bhagidari for various works
- Renovation of IGI Airport of international standard
- Distribution food in schools at primary education level
- Better medical services
- Development of national highways

- Increase in water reservoirs, water bodies, and rainwater harvesting
- Better management of solid waste
- Ban on plastic bags
- Improvement in public transport system
- Improvement in infrastructure
- Transparency in the system
- Reliable power supply
- Improved transportation system
- Reduction in pollution by introduction of CNG
- Introduction of PNG (Piped Natural Gas)
- Development growth increased
- Per capita income grew three times
- Green Delhi Campaign
- Facility Centers 40 to 124
- Online driving licence facility
- Introduction of NPR
- Increased tap water 645 to 850 MGD
- Admission of EWS children in public schools
- Mapping of utility/services under the geo-spatial mapping department
- Bed and breakfast services
- Ho-Ho Bus Service (Hop on Hop off)
- Chacha Nehru Sehat Yojana (Children's Health Scheme)
- Improvement in health care services
- Door-to-door collection of domestic waste
- My Delhi I care Fund amount increased 10 times
- Generation of power from waste
- Iconic signature bridge under construction
- Successful CWG Games
- Another Dilli Haat
- Ornamental streetlights
- Anna Shri Yojana introduced (food subsidy for the poor)
- Strengthening of Bhagidari
- Completion of 5,000+ RWA Projects
- Social Service Sector Allocation
- Laadli Yojana (Girls Education and Welfare Scheme)
- Old/Widow pension
- Improvement in horticulture
- Improvement of ISBT
- Decentralization of MCD
- Disaster management plan
- Metro rail (Phase I–II)

- Barapula Flyover
- DTC CNG buses (air conditioned)
- Laadli Yojana (Girls Education and Welfare Scheme)
- RTI Act 2005
- Recycling plant for water
- Bhagidari participation
- Electricity supply improvement
- Multilevel parking
- Old-age homes
- Midday Meal Scheme
- New court buildings
- Self-assessment of property tax
- Rogi Kalyan Samiti
- Chacha Nehru Sehat Yojana (Children's Health Scheme)
- Upgradation of Road
- World's largest millennium bus depot in Delhi
- Introduction and increase in metro network
- Construction of flyover for easing traffic
- Improvement in power sector supply
- Introduction of CNG in Delhi—DTC become world biggest CNG fleet
- PNG supply in houses
- Establishment of technology and management institution
- Good sports stadium developed in Delhi
- Forest cover area developed/increased in Delhi
- Improvement in health sector
- Development of new industrial blocks
- Better electricity
- Better education
- Introduction of CNG
- Ban on use of polythene/plastic bags
- Enactment of Delhi Excise Act, ban on Tobacco Act, and Delhi Prevention of Defacement of Public Property Act
- Various welfare schemes like Laadli, Chacha Nehru Sehat Yojana Midday Meal, increase in old age pension, and so on
- Houses for weaker sections
- Issuance of provisional certificates to unauthorized colonies
- Hosting of successful Commonwealth Games
- More tree plantation
- Privatization of Electricity Board
- Trifurcation of MCD
- Bhagidari Scheme

- Enhancement in level of education
- Successful implementation of Jan-Aahar Project
- Improvement in public transportation system
- Disaster management awareness increased
- Improvement in parking facility
- Condition of basic infrastructure has been improved
- Successful implementation of Laadli Yojana Project (Girls Education and Welfare Scheme)
- Time-bound services in Delhi Government offices
- Citizens Charter
- Increase in greenery in entire Delhi
- Implementation of EWS Scheme in Schools
- Reduction of pollution level
- Sports facility development
- Improvement in medical facility especially for BPL families
- Improvement in electricity and water supply
- Underpasses
- Signal-free roads
- Electronic signal with digital time indication
- Increase in greenery/parks
- Reduction in air pollution
- Increase in amount of pension for senior citizens
- Chacha Nehru Sehat Yojana (Children's Health Scheme)
- Collection of garbage by mobile vans
- Ornamental lights
- High mask lights
- Better education facility in schools
- Free treatments in hospitals for BPL families
- Trifurcation of MCD for good governance
- Development of infrastructure
- Shifting of industries from residential area
- Increase in number of dispensaries/hospitals
- Super specialties hospitals
- Covering of open drains
- Introduction of RTI Act
- Introduction of Bhagidari Scheme
- CNG and AC buses
- More flyovers
- More parks
- Better roads
- Shopping malls
- Increase in green-cover area

- Increase in DTC buses
- Removal of blue line buses (killer buses)
- Feeder bus services for metro
- Commenwealth Games
- More community centers
- Increase in the number of hospitals
- Increase in number of schools
- Improvement in the result of CBSE Xth Board Exams
- Improvement in the result of CBSE XIIth Board Exams
- Upgrading of schools from secondary to senior secondary
- Increase in the number of engineering/medical colleges
- Converting shed to proper schools buildings
- Right to Information Act
- Old-age pension
- Midday Meal Scheme
- More engineering colleges
- Introduction of CNG
- Gas pipeline
- Improvement in power supply
- Mobile health service
- South Delhi Ring Road made signal free
- More community centers
- Improvement in education
- Time-bound civic services
- Online driving Licence
- Online property tax
- Online electricity and water bill
- More stadiums
- Commonwealth Games
- Bus terminals
- ITI schools
- Regularization of unauthorized colonies
- Electricity to unauthorized colonies
- Reduction of pollution level
- Green Delhi
- Cleanliness of Yamuna
- Privatization of DESU
- Farmers' compensation increased
- Alternative plots to farmers
- More sports colleges
- Rail
- Electricity

- Improvement in earnings
- Flyovers
- Traveling time reduced
- Water improvement and water saving
- Colleges
- Improvement in hospital facilities
- Improvement in school studies
- CBSE X Class—result improvement
- Scholarships schemes for minority classes
- Unauthorized colonies passed—regularized
- Improvement in facilities to girls in education
- Improvement in poor women's health—financial assistance during pregnancies and deliveries and good diet
- Bhagidari improvement
- School gyms
- Park gyms
- Sports facilities
- Covering of garden nallahs
- Improvement in roads
- Delhiites privileged with Commonwealth Games
- Super-speciality hospitals
- Dilli Haat in Janakpuri
- Guru Tegh Bahadur structure near Sindhu Border
- Improvement in Subzi Mandi
- Provision of vegetables/fruits in Mother Diary at much lower rates
- Improvement in licencing facilities
- Provision of Jeevan Centers
- Increase in pension for senior citizens, and so on
- AC buses
- PNG gas
- Night shelters
- Chacha Nehru Sehat Yojana (Children's Health Scheme)
- Midday Meals
- Various festivals/melas
- Public transport
- Power supply
- Streetlight
- Subway and overhead bridges
- Primary education
- Rehabilitation of JJ clusters
- Green environment
- E-governance

- Citizen Charter
- Stadia.
- Rainwater harvesting
- T-3 Terminal—airport metro
- Laadli Yojana (Girls Education and Welfare Scheme)
- Chacha Nehru Sehat Yojana (Children's Health Scheme)
- Property tax by self-assessment
- Introduction of RTI Act
- BRT
- Right to time-bound services by the government
- Increase in forest cover area
- Introduction of AC buses
- Chacha Nehru Sehat Yojana (Children's Health Scheme)
- Kerosene-free Delhi
- Improvement in the students life in general
- Regularization of unauthorized colonies and provisional certificate
- Distinct improvement in supply of electricity
- Improvement in DTC buses by introducing buses of better quality
- Use of CNG in transport system has reduced pollution
- Ring Road has been made signal free to a large extent
- Improvement in education in government schools
- Bypass roads for vehicles Haryana to Delhi to UP in order to reduce pollution in Delhi
- Construction of footover bridges/overhead bridges and underpasses
- Improvement in water supply
- New initiative to develop old city (Shahjahanabad)
- Plantation of trees
- Adhaar Card
- Standard of education in government schools improved
- Rajiv Ratan Awas Yojana
- Improvement of electricity supply
- Munak Nahar for water supply
- Improvement of roads
- Number of underground water reserviors increased
- Metro rail expansion
- Flyovers and underpasses
- Bawana Power House (GAS)
- Air pollution control
- Old-age Pension Scheme
- Laadli Yojana (Girls Education and Welfare Scheme)
- Increase in per capita income

- Increase in beds in hospitals
- Chacha Nehru Sehat Yojana (Children's Health Scheme)
- Unit area system in house tax
- Improvement in infrastructure
- Midday Meal
- Bhagidari Andolan
- Kerosene-free Delhi
- Discoms
- Disaster Management
- Solar Energy
- Signal-free Ring Road
- Issuance of Citizen Charter
- Ecosystems in Delhi Schools
- Low-floor AC buses
- Improvement in Green Belt
- Improvement in health services
- Education for all
- Construction of flyovers
- Rainwater harvesting
- Control on unauthorized construction
- Relocation of polluting Industries
- World-class airport
- New sports stadiums
- Midday Meal Scheme
- Reduction in air pollution
- Better law and order
- Implementation of EWS Scheme
- Better waste management
- Yamuna Action Plan
- Disaster Management Scheme
- Better Infrastructure
- E-governance
- Multilevel parking
- Road transportation
- Replaced Kerosene oil with LPG
- Trifurcation of MCD
- CNG-based public transport system has reduced pollution
- Metro rail introduced to ease traffic congestion
- PNG for kitchens as replacement of LPG
- Education for all children
- Development of new railway stations
- Sodium and mercury lamps for streetlights

- Metallic bus quene shelters
- New hospitals opened
- Additional Delhi government dispensaries
- Laadli Yojana for girls
- Additional night shelters for needy persons
- Additional power supply for residents and shops
- Pension for senior citizens, widows, and handicapped
- Concessional bus passes for senior citizens
- Ban on use of plastic bags
- Assistance for marriage of widow's daughter
- Introduction of Delhi RTI Act
- Bhagidari Scheme introduced
- Kerosene-free Delhi
- Chacha Nehru Sehat Yojana (Children's Health Scheme)
- My Delhi I Care Fund raised to 5 crores
- Citizens Charter and time-bound service level agreements
- Deelopment of new roads, bus lanes
- Anganwari centers
- Free lunch and uniform in schools
- Samajik Suvidha Sangam
- Trifurcation of MCD
- Aawaz Uthao initiative to stop violence against women
- Old Parents Care by Children Act
- Rashtriya Swasthya Beema Yojana
- Participation of senior citizens in government schemes
- Promotion of ISM system
- Eradication of Polio
- New master plan for Delhi
- Yamuna Cleanliness Program
- Unauthorized colonies legalized
- Water conservation at homes
- Rainwater harvesting
- Subsidy on solar/cell-based gadgets
- Administrative reforms department in Delhi government
- Concrete roads
- Covering of drains
- Buses for rural areas and NCR
- Environment cleanliness with free plantation
- Computerized DTC bus passes
- Uninterrupted power supply
- Low-floor bus fleet
- Delhi Government Employees Health Scheme

- Concession to women in various schemes
- Overhead bridges/underpasses
- Low-floor non-AC/AC buses
- CNG/PNG provision
- Improvement in electricity supply
- Laadli Yojana (Girls Education and Welfare Scheme)
- Kerosene-free Delhi
- Chacha Nehru Sehat Yojana (Children's Health Scheme)
- Citizen Charter
- Financial help to senior citizens/widows and economically weaker sections
- Green Delhi and Clean Delhi
- Women empowerment
- RTI Act
- Solid-waste management
- PPP Scheme
- Commonwealth Games
- Better sanitation
- Improvement in medical facility
- Improvement in education system
- Rainwater harvesting
- Mushrooming of flyovers
- Right to Education
- Commonwealth Games
- Use of CNG in Vehicles
- Introduction of Bhagidari Scheme
- Right to Information
- Footover bridges and subways with escalators
- Increase in number of inter-state bus depots
- Relocation of industrial units from residential areas
- Waste collection vehicles
- Regularization of commercial shops in residential areas
- Introduction of road tax
- Modernization of bus shelters
- Opening of more institutions for higher education/professional degree colleges
- Successful completion of three terms of office by CM Ms Sheila Dikshit
- Improvement of banking infrastructure such as ATMs, and so on
- Mushrooming of shopping malls
- Disaster management
- Introduction of e-governance

- Electric crematoriums
- CNG buses/autorickshaws to reduce pollution
- Increase in CNG stations
- Privatization of electricity
- FOBs and underpasses and green paths
- Increase in water supply
- Modernization of bus shelters
- Widening of roads
- Improvment in pass percentage of government/MCD schools
- Introduction of RTI Act
- Introduction of Citizen Charter
- Increase in number of public toilets
- Improvement in streetlights
- Covering of nallahs (large drains)
- Lifting of garbage through private contractors
- Linked buses for metro
- Trifurcation of MCD
- Management of Common Wealth Games
- Introduction Bhagidari Scheme
- Introduction of PPP
- Introduction of Laadli Scheme (Girls Education and Welfare Scheme)
- Increase in pension for senior citizens
- Self-assessment of property tax
- Network of flyovers
- CNG/PNG service
- Better power supply
- Laadli Scheme (Girls Education and Welfare Scheme)
- Pension for widows
- Service-level agreements for various services
- Opening of Jeevan Centers
- Construction of old-age homes
- Construction of underpasses and footover bridges
- Right to Education Scheme
- Reservation of seats for EWS students for admission in private schools
- Free treatment for BPL cardholders in government and recognized private hospitals
- Revamping of roads taken from MCD, by the PWD
- Renovation of Connaught Place
- Bhagidari Scheme
- Subsidy in electricity for consumption upto 200 units

- Unit area method for calculation of house tax
- Free books for SC/ST children
- Polio-free Delhi
- Gift of metro rail
- Improvement in electricity supply
- Improved DTC buses/services
- Improved airport
- Improved education
- Clean city
- Improved Railway Station
- Decentralization of inter-state bus terminal
- E-governance
- Citizen Charters
- Implementation of Bhagidari Yojana
- Kerosene free
- Successful Commonwealth Games
- Good developments
- Less power cuts
- Better road and parks
- Less pollution
- Laadli Scheme to promote more education for girls
- Polio drops facility
- CNG for domestic use
- Signal-free ring road
- Dwarka to Noida Route red-light free
- BRT corridor
- Public transport fully converted to CNG
- Mordernized DTC low-floor buses of international standards
- Battery operated rikshaw/buses
- Metro feeder buses
- Pollution-free city
- Multilevel parkings
- IGI Airport
- Railway stations
- Underground reservoirs
- Beautification of city
- Laadli Yojana (Girls Education and Welfare Scheme)
- Senior citizen pension
- Commonwealth Games
- RTI for citizens
- Streetlights
- Property tax (self-assessment)

- Reduction of VAT on petrol
- New stadiums during CWG
- Delhi tourism
- Trauma centers
- Improved electricity/water supply
- Improved waste disposal
- Chacha Nehru Sehat Yojana (Children's Health Scheme)
- Recreational centers for senior citizen
- Regularization of unauthorized colonies
- Freehold rights for resettlement colonies
- Sewarage system improvements
- Bus service DTC (low-floor and AC)
- E-banking
- National highways development
- Kerosene-free Delhi
- Introduction of Jeevan Services
- Chacha Nehru Sehat Yojana (Children's Health Scheme)
- Streetlights
- Pension for senior citizen and widows
- PNG supply
- CNG implementation
- Social justice
- Anna Shri Yojana (food subsidy for the poor)
- Night shelters for homeless people
- Implementation of anti-domestic violence act for women security
- Pollution-free Delhi—use of CNG in buses, other vehicles
- Removal of old blue line buses
- Pension for handicapped
- Beautification of parks
- Improvement in education system
- Unit system in house tax introduced
- Introduction of Adhaar Cards
- Better power supply
- Parks and tree plantation
- CBSE results
- New railway terminals
- New ISBT (Inter-state bus terminals)
- Adhaar biometric cards
- Rainwater harvesting
- More cooking gas connections
- Time-bound Service Act
- Sports stadiums

- Flats for EWS people
- International standard Terminal 3 Airport
- Signal-free roads and Terminal Airport
- Solar energy
- CNG pumps
- Signal-free Ring Road
- Increased number of hospitals
- Night shelters for homeless
- Increase in number of UGRs
- Road signage boards
- Programs to prevent Yamuna pollution
- Education loan
- Short stay homes for destitutes
- Promoting cultural developments
- Separate ghat for last dip of dead bodies at River Yamuna
- Promoting regional languages
- Cancer Research Centers
- Orphanage homes
- Awareness about TB/AIDs
- Vocational/working women's colleges
- Eco-friendly rickshaws
- Online provision of SC, OBC, income certificate, and so on
- Online service for Voter ID Card (new)
- Electricity bill with full detail like, load, security deposit by consumer in English as well as in Hindi (BYPL)
- DJB supplying clean and pure water
- DTC issuing electronic computerized passes

North-West District (June 27, 2012)

- Pollution-free Delhi
- Introduction of metro rail
- Road over bridge
- Construction of BRT
- Ration Card—online
- Bhagidari
- Increase of old-age/widow pension
- Increase of number of schools
- Number of hospital increased
- Rationing of water
- Better supply of electricity

- Kerosene-free Delhi
- Polio free
- Chacha Nehru Sehat Yojana (Children's Health Scheme)
- Introduction of Adhaar Card
- All departments working online
- My Delhi I Care Fund
- Increase of percentage of police force
- Construction of new stadiums
- Hosting of Commonwealth Games
- Delhi—a model city
- RWA fund introduced
- Introduction of Anna Shri Yojana
- Living standard high
- Better transport services
- Per capita income increased
- Population increased
- Free signals due to flyovers
- Awareness in general public
- Voting system better
- Electronics system introduced for voting
- Awareness in women
- To help ladies—women helpline
- Awareness about AIDS
- Construction of new buildings
- Better functioning of RTI system
- Introduction of Citizen Charter
- Encouragement of games
- Green Delhi
- Metro network
- Successful completion of Commonwealth Games
- Increase in green cover
- Construction of new roads
- Reduction in pollution
- Reduction in power cuts
- Computerization of government records
- Kerosene-free Delhi
- Anna Shri Yojana (food subsidy for the poor)
- Pension to senior citizens
- RTI
- Smart Card
- Adhaar Card
- Citizens Charters

- Night shelters
- Dense carpeting of roads
- Cleanness of Yamuna river
- Health services improved
- High class buses
- Midday meals for children
- Chacha Nehru Sehat Yojana (Children's Health Scheme)
- Computerization of banking facilities
- Availability of mobiles to message
- Ration Card online
- Online reservation of rail tickets
- IGL gas
- PNG gas
- CNG autos
- Trifurcation of MCD
- Easy bills
- Construction of chopals
- Bhagidari
- Commonwealth Games
- Polio-free Delhi
- Kerosene-free Delhi
- Citizen Charter
- Trauma center
- Under bridges
- Underground parking
- Pollution-free Delhi
- Laadli Yojana for children (Girls Education and Welfare Scheme)
- Assistance for wedding of widow's daughters
- Booster pumps
- Tubewells
- Better electricity supply
- Malls
- High-mark lights
- Traffic signal timings
- Road dividers panels
- Satellite channels
- International Airport
- Highways
- Water supply
- Stadiums
- Lifestyle
- Subways

- Metallic road (foot path)
- Multi storey building
- Improvement in roads
- Signal-free roads
- Sodium lights on main roads
- Construction of barapula elevated road
- Construction of Geeta Colony Road (river bridge)
- Construction of stadiums (new)
- Construction of hostels for Commonwealth Games in East Delhi near Akshardham Temple
- Delhi University
- CNG AC buses
- Delhi Police line
- Privatization of electric supply
- Shopping malls
- Medical service improved
- Senior citizen recreation Centers
- Bhagidari introduced
- Introduction of RTI Scheme
- Trifurcation of MCD
- Construction of Nakul Highway
- Delhi has increased number of buses three times
- Delhi has metro network covering 180 km
- Electric supply is near normal 24 hours a day
- DTC has non-polluting buses now
- Delhi has become world-class city by way of flyovers and roads
- DJB has improved water supply
- Free education to girl child has improved literacy level
- Laadli Yojana has improved life of girl child
- Support to girls for marriage has given confidence
- Pension Scheme is very good for senior citizens/widows
- Special healthcare for senior citizens
- DTC support to senior citizens
- Green cover has increased is in spite of population growth
- Number of schools have increased
- Delhi University has increased admissions
- Disposal of waste is being organized
- Unauthorized colonies shall be given development fund now
- Bhagidari cell has done wonderful job in cooperations
- Pollution is under control now, despite more vehicles
- Per capita income has increased
- Pucca houses for *jhuggi* dwellers

- Rainwater harvesting
- Management of traffic
- Overall age of citizen has increased due to CNG buses
- Less power cuts
- Metro-feeder buses
- Better streetlights
- Better roads
- Better piped water
- Collection of bills (Jeevan)
- PNG cooking gas
- Pollution control
- Sewer lines improved
- Gramin seva
- Door-to-door collection of garbage
- Traffic management
- E-ticketing by DTC
- Ho-Ho bus for Delhi darshan
- MCD trifurcation
- Delhi development
- Online payment facility
- Sports achievement
- Regular electric supply
- Regular water supply
- Online complaint is registered
- Removal of old diesel polluting vehicles
- My Delhi Green Delhi
- Online driving licence, and so on
- Providing better electricity in partnership with NDPL and BSES
- DTC passes to senior citizens
- BPL Card for below poverty line people
- Introduction of discom system (power reform)
- Beautification of parks
- Organizing Commonwealth Games successfully
- Lighting streetlights
- Right for education
- Free meal in schools
- Bill collection center (Jeevan)
- Polio eradicated
- Introducing Bhagidari in every department
- Infrastructure development
- CNG buses good for environment
- Phasing out of diesel buses

- Online payment of House Tax
- Citizen Charter implementation
- Increase in per capita income
- Increase in number of collages/polyclinics
- DJB UGRs increased
- Flyovers and underpasses increased
- Increase in city forest area
- Roads better
- Education system inproved through new schools
- Better result in government schools
- Improvement in environment
- Development of parks
- Door to door collection of garbage
- Increase in number of hospitals
- Underpasses/overbridges
- Elevated roads
- Lighting of public roads
- Stadiums/swimming pools
- District parks
- Hospitals in each district
- Increase in forest area
- IGL services
- IGI airports
- Pension for senior citizens and widows (poor citizens)
- Engineering technology and medical colleges
- Education pass precentage increased
- More housing to EWS people
- Less power cuts
- Improvement in waterflow
- Good sanitation
- Education increased
- Streetlights improved
- Cleanliness in hospitals
- Pension for senior citizens/widows/handicapped
- BPL Scheme
- Admission of EWS children in public schools
- Herbal park
- Improvement in primary/secondary schools
- Multilevel parking
- Traffic improvement
- Right to Education Act implementation
- First tech university in Delhi

- Multilevel parking
- Street vender policy for clean Delhi
- Regularization of unauthorized colonies
- New power plant in Bawana
- Gramin sewa
- VAT online
- Education online
- BRT corridor
- Light better than before (streetlighting)
- More DTC, CNG/AC buses
- Transport—metro rail
- Transport—more flyovers/footover bridges/subways
- New stadiums
- Metro rail network 187 km
- AC buses—(5,775 buses with DTC)
- BRT (Bus Rapid Transit System)
- RTI information
- New international airport
- Development of NCR
- Social networking through Facebook
- Fast-track courts
- Provision of CNG/PNG
- Bhagidari
- Streetlight functionality
- Green Delhi
- Energy clubs
- New hospitality
- Recreation center
- Tourism
- Introduction of CNG stations for vehicles
- Privatization of electricity
- Improvement in infrastructure across Delhi
- Opening of new hospitals
- Reduction in pollution levels
- CNG auto-rickshaws
- Plantation of 1 million trees
- Success of Commonwealth Games
- Concept of mono rail
- Better employment
- Sports facilities improved
- Introduction of door-to-door garbage collection
-       r supply improved

- Signal-free roads
- Elevated roads
- Pollution level at its lowest level due to use of CNG
- Construction of more stadiums
- Introduction of new hospitals
- PNG supply system
- Introduction of Laadli Yojana (Girls Education and Welfare Scheme)
- Introduction of underpass roads
- Introduction of green revolution
- Introduction of Jeevan Centers
- Introduction of bus passes to senior citizens
- Introduction of education loan to ST/SC/OBC students
- Introduction of Jan Ahaar Yojana
- Introduction of NPR Cards
- Introduction of Mahila Samajik Suvidha Kendra
- Low power cut (electricity supply uptime is 98 percent across Delhi)
- Greenery and tree-cover much improved
- Wide roads
- Better water supply
- Better streetlighting
- PNG
- Sulabh Sauchalya
- Old-age homes
- Self-assessment property tax
- Mobile
- Better medical facilities
- Metro rail
- Lower power cuts
- CNG in three wheelers/taxis
- DTC CNG/AC buses
- Streetlights
- Good environment with reduced pollution
- More parks + greenery
- Jan Aahaar Yojana
- Old-age pension (for the poor)
- Rural Development Board
- Delhi Bed and Breakfast Scheme
- Laadli Yojana for girls education
- Bhagidari Yojana
- Water treatment plants (additional)

- Rainwater harvesting CWG
- DTC bus stands/shelters (new designs)
- Midday meals (for school children and the poor)
- VKS in Delhi government schools
- Pension for handicaps
- Mobile libraries
- Mobile dispensaries
- SC/OBC certificates
- Yamuna action plans
- Introduction of discom (power reforms)
- Under bridges
- Right to Education
- Right to Information Act
- CNG
- Quality roads
- Rainwater harvesting system
- Trifurcation of MCD
- Recycling of waste
- Metro rail in Delhi
- Eighty-four night shelters
- ESLA system
- PNG (Piped Natural Gas)
- New stadiums
- Rainwater harvesting in Delhi
- Pension to poor widows
- Midday meals (for school children)
- Mediation center
- Dispensaries increased
- New flyovers
- Municipal Corporations in Delhi
- Constitution of RWAs
- Right to Education
- RTI
- Kerosene-free Delhi
- PGC
- CIC
- LPG gas
- CNG–PNG facility
- Improved electricity service
- Digital television
- Police protection towards senior citizens, children, and women
- Training to women for self defense

- Free midday meals (for school children and the poor)
- Polio eradication
- Improvement in electricity supply
- Holding of lok adalat of different departments
- Opening of Jeevan service counter
- Education loan facility
- Opening of new colleges
- Opening of new hospitals
- Introduction of PNG
- Right to Information Act
- No power cut in the working hours
- Government schools increased
- Helpline for pensioners
- Better sewerage system
- Increase in hospitals
- Uninterrupted electricity supply
- Clean Delhi Metro Rail is pollution free
- Pollution-free Delhi
- Expansion of schools
- AC buses by DTC
- Pension of widows
- Signal-free roads
- Online service of house tax
- Plantation in Delhi
- Kerosene-free Delhi
- Elevated roads
- New ISBT
- PNG in residence
- Increase in numbers of government hospital
- PDS improved
- Improvement in health-care schemes, infrastructure, transportation, pollution control, education, per capita income, road condition, law and order, public distribution, electricity supply, water supply, and overhead bridges
- Metro network
- House tax online
- Development of parks
- Communication
- Computerization
- Women empowerment
- Reduction in crime rate
- Bhagidari strengthening

- Industrial development
- Malls and multicomplexes
- Garbage collection van and bioenergy plant
- Rainwater harvesting
- Underground water storage
- Child-care programs
- Free education to EWS
- GST introduction CNG supply
- Polio eradication
- Transport system improved
- Laadli Yojana started (Girls Welfare Scheme)
- Old-age pension (for the poor)
- Help for marriage of poor family girls
- So many road bridges constructed
- Underpasses provided
- Greenery increased by plantation upto 27 percent of city area
- Parking facilities increased
- Recreation centers provided for senior citizens
- Colony parks improved by providing flowers and shrubs
- Underground parking provided at so many places
- Condition of electric supply improved
- Funds provided to RWAs directly for various projects
- Dense carpet roads even in the small colonies
- Production is being given to water bodies of villages
- Internet provision given in all government offices
- Encouragement is given for games
- Free education for children upto 5th class
- Encouragement given to girls for joining school
- CNG
- Flyovers/underbridges
- Eco-clubs
- Water supply
- Roads widened
- My Delhi I Care Fund
- Metro rail/feeder buses
- More signal free drive
- Reduced pollution
- BRT corridor
- Less power cuts
- More greenery
- Easier driving licenses
- Increased schools and colleges

- More night shelters
- Laadli Yojana
- Pension for senior citizen
- Commonwealth Games
- Bhagidari
- Chacha Nehru Sehat Yojana (Children's Health Scheme)
- More medical colleges/hospitals
- Improved water supply
- More parks
- More schools/universities
- Increase of police stations
- Horticulture
- Water system
- Flyovers/underpasses
- Government hospitals
- Education free
- Free meals at school
- Division of MCD
- Multilevel parking
- Footover bridge
- Colleges increase
- Community centers increased
- Night shelters
- New hotels/guest houses
- Concession to senior citizens
- AC buses introduced
- Bus shelters
- Sign boards good
- Old-age pension
- Laadli Scheme (Girls Education and Welfare Scheme)
- Traffic vehicle number improved
- Police patrolling increased
- Development of IGI Airport of the level of international standard
- E-SLA
- RTI implementation
- Public Grievance Commission established
- Police complaint authority
- Enhancement of welfare schemes
- Improvement in sports facilities
- Improvement in distribution of power supply
- Mobile dispensary
- Number of dispensary increased

- Super-speciality hospitals
- Child labor district task force
- Shifting of polluting industries
- Introduction of SAFAL outlets (for lower cost vegetables and fruits)
- Improvement in education standard
- Regularization of unauthorized colony

North-East District (June 29, 2012)

- Pollution-free Delhi
- Introduction of metro rail
- AC buses
- Roads and overbridges
- Construction of BRT
- Ration Card—online
- Bhagidari
- Laadli Yojana (Girls Education and Welfare Scheme)
- Increase of old-age/widow pension
- Increase of number of schools
- CNG
- Number of hospital increased
- Rationing of water
- Better supply of electricity
- Kerosene-free Delhi
- Polio free
- Chacha Nehru Sehat Yojana (Children's Health Scheme)
- ₹25,000 for marriage of widow's daughter
- Free food to children
- Introduction of Adhaar Biometric Card
- Online all departments
- My Delhi I Care Fund
- Increase of percentage of police force
- Construction of new stadiums
- Hosting of Commonwealth Games
- Delhi became model city
- Introduction of Anna Shri Yojana (food subsidy for the poor)
- Living standard high
- Better transport services
- Per capita income increased

- Signal-free flyovers
- Awareness in general public
- Voting system better
- Electronics system introduced for voting
- MCD trifurcation
- Awareness in women
- Women helpline
- Awareness about AIDS
- Better functioning of RTI system
- Introduction of Citizen Charter
- Green Delhi
- Successful completion of Commonwealth Games
- Construction/widening of new roads
- Better mobility
- Reduction in power cuts
- Computerization of government records
- Kerosene-free Delhi
- Anna Shri Yojana (food subsidy for the poor)
- Pension to senior citizens
- RTI
- Smart/Adhaar Card
- Citizens Charters
- Night shelters
- Dense carpeting of roads
- Cleanness of Yamuna River
- Better transportation facilities
- Health services more provided
- High-class buses
- Midday meals for children
- Chacha Nehru Sehat Yojana (Children's Health Scheme)
- Computerization of banking facilities
- Availability of mobiles to message
- Ration Card online
- Online reservation of rail tickets
- IGL/PNG gas
- CNG auto-rickshaws
- Trifurcation of MCD
- Easy bills
- Commonwealth Games
- Polio-free Delhi
- Kerosene-free Delhi
- Citizen Charter

- Trauma Center
- Underbridges
- Underground parking
- Pollution-free Delhi
- Rainwater harvesting
- Financial help for wedding of widow's girls
- Booster pumps
- Tubewells
- Better electricity supply
- High-mask lights
- Traffic signal timings
- Road dividers panels
- Electronic bus stands
- Satellite channels
- International airport
- Metallic road (foot path)
- Multi-storey buildings
- Signal-free roads
- Sodium lights on main roads
- Improvement in greenery
- Construction of Barapula Elevated Road
- Construction of Geeta Colony Road (river bridge)
- Construction of stadiums (new)
- CNG, AC buses
- Delhi Police line
- DTC low-floor buses
- Privatization of electric supply
- Shopping malls
- Medical service improved
- Senior citizen recreation centers
- Laadli Yojana (Girls and Welfare Scheme)
- Introduction of RTI Scheme
- Trifurcation of MCD
- Construction Nakul Highway
- Delhi has increased number of buses three times
- Electric supply is near normal 24 hours a day
- DTC has non-polluting buses now
- Delhi has improved roads
- Delhi managed Commonwealth Games nicely
- DJB has improved water supply
- Free education to girl child has improved literacy level
- Laadli Yojana has improved life of girl child

- Support to widows for girl's marriage
- Pension Scheme is very good for senior citizens/widows
- Special healthcare for senior citizens
- DTC support to senior citizens of old-age group
- Green cover has increased despite population growth
- Delhi University has increased admissions
- Disposal of waste is being organized
- Unauthorized colonies shall be given development fund now
- Bhagidari Cell has extended good cooperation
- Pollution is under control now in spite of increased vehicles
- Per capita income has increased
- Pucca houses for *jhuggi* dwellers
- Rainwater harvesting
- Management of traffic
- Overall age of citizens increased with CNG introduction
- Less power cuts
- Metro feeder bus
- Better streetlights
- Better roads
- Garbage pick up vans
- Better piped water
- Collection of bills (Jeewan)
- PNG cooking gas
- Pollution control
- Introduction of low-floor buses
- Sewer lines improved
- Gramin seva introduced
- Door-to-door collection of garbage
- Pollution control
- Traffic management
- E-ticketing by DTC
- Ho-Ho bus for Delhi tour
- RTI
- MCD trifurcation
- Infrastructure development
- Online payment of bills
- CWG
- Sports achievement
- Regular electric supply
- Regular water supply
- Online complaint is attended
- Removal of old diesel polluting vehicles

- My Delhi is Green Delhi
- Introduced CNG
- Replacement of old DTC bus and low-floor buses
- Online driving licence, and so on
- Providing better electricity with partnership with NDPL and BSES
- Laadli Yojana (Girls Education and Welfare Scheme)
- Pension Scheme for senior citizen and widows
- Provided DTC pass to senior citizen BPL
- BPL Card for below poverty line people
- Introduction of discom system (power reform)
- Beautification of parks
- Successfully organizing Commonwealth Games
- Lighting (streetlights)
- Right to Education
- Free meal in schools
- Bill collection center Jeewan
- Introducing Bhagidari in every departments
- Infrastructure development
- CNG buses for good environment
- Phasing out of diesel buses
- Improvement of electricity
- Online payment of house tax
- Citizen Charter implementation
- RTI
- Increase in per capita income
- Increase in number of collages
- Polyclinics increased
- DJB UGRs increased
- Flyovers/footover bridges and underpasses increased
- Increase in city forest area
- Birth and death certificates provision improved
- Roads in better shape
- Education system improved—new schools, better results
- Improvement in environment
- Development of parks
- Increase in number of hospitals
- Elevated roads
- Lights improved in public roads
- Stadiums/swimming pools
- Jan Aahaar Yojana
- Free provision of school uniform
- School buildings

- DTC buses low-floor/AC buses
- District parks
- Hospitals in each district
- Increase in forests
- IGL services
- IGI airports
- Engineering technology and medical colleges
- Education pass percentage increased
- More housing schemes
- Increase greenery
- Improvement in water flow
- Good sanitation
- Education increased
- Streetlight improved
- Good electricity by BSES
- Good treatment in hospital
- Cleanliness in good hospitals
- Pension for senior citizens/widows/handicapped
- BPL Scheme
- EWS children's school admission
- Herbal park
- Good condition of roads
- Improvement in primary/secondary schools
- Multilevel parkings
- Traffic improvement
- Right to education implementation
- First tech university in Delhi
- Multilevel parking
- Mall culture
- Street vendor policy for clean Delhi
- Regularization of unauthorized colonies
- New power plant in Bawana
- Gramin sewa
- VAT online
- Education online
- BRT corridor
- Light—better than before
- Transport—more DTC CNG/AC buses, metro
- Transport—more flyovers, subways, and FOBs
- New stadiums
- Metro network increased to 187 km
- AC buses—DTC (5,775 buses with DTC)

- Bus Rapid Transit System
- Flyover and underpasses
- New international airports
- Creation of mall culture
- Development of NCR
- Social networking through Facebook
- Fast-track courts
- Pension for widows
- DTC facilities
- Provision of CNG/PNG
- Streetlight functionality
- Energy clubs
- New hospitals
- Recreation center
- Supply of power dependable
- Tourism
- Privatization of electricity
- Improvement in infrastructure across Delhi
- Opening of new hospitals
- New stadiums
- Reduction in pollution levels
- CNG autorickshaws
- Plantation of 1 million trees
- Success of Commonwealth Games
- Concept of mono rail
- Better employment
- Sports facilities improved
- Introduction of door-to-door garbage collection
- Water supply improved
- Pollution level at its lowest level due to use of CNG
- Construction of more stadiums
- Introduction of new hospitals
- PNG supply system
- Introduction of Laadli Yojana (Girls Education and Welfare Scheme)
- Underpasses/roads
- Introduction of green revolution
- Introduction of Jeewan centers
- Introduction of Bhagidari Yojana of Delhi Government
- Introduction of bus passes to senior citizens
- Introduction of education loan to ST/SC/OBC students
- Introduction of Jan Aahaar Yojana

- Introduction of PNR cards
- Introduction of Mahila Samajik Suvidha Kendra
- Less power cuts (electricity supply uptime is 98 percent across Delhi)
- CNG
- Greenery and tree cover much improved
- Better streetlighting
- PNG
- Sulabh Shauchalya (public conveniences)
- Better transport services
- Old-age homes
- RTI Act
- Self-assessment property tax
- Better medical facilities
- Old-age pension for the poor
- CNG three-wheeler/taxi
- DTC CNG/AC buses
- Better roads
- Streetlights improved
- Environment improved with reduced pollution
- Widows/old-age pension (for the poor)
- Rural development board
- Delhi Electricity Regulatory Commission
- Bhagidari Yojana
- Water treatment plants (increased capacity)
- Rainwater harvesting
- Commonwealth Games
- Midday meals (for school children and the poor)
- VKS in Delhi government schools
- Pension for handicaps
- Mobile libraries
- Mobile dispensaries
- SC/OBC certificates
- Yamuna action plans
- RTI Act
- Introduction of discom (power reforms)
- Low-floor buses
- Under bridges
- Right to Education
- Right to Information Act
- Quality roads
- MCD trifurcation

- Recycling of waste
- Metro rail in Delhi
- Eighty-four night shelters
- E-SLA system
- PNG (Piped Natural Gas)
- CNG vehicles
- New stadiums
- Rainwater harvesting in Delhi
- Laadli Yojana (Girls Education and Welfare Scheme)
- Midday meals (for school children)
- Mediation centers for poor families
- Dispensaries increased
- Three Municipal Corporations in Delhi
- Constitution of RWAs
- Bhagidari Scheme in Delhi
- Right to Education
- Kerosene-free Delhi
- LPG gas
- Metro rail introduced
- AC buses introduced by DTC
- Improved electricity service
- Digitalization of television
- Police protection towards senior citizens children and women
- Training to women for self defense
- Polio eradication
- Improvement in electricity supply
- Holding of lok adalat of different departments
- Opening of Jeewan service counter
- Education loan facilities
- Opening of new colleges
- Opening of new hospitals
- Introduction of PNG
- Right to Information Act
- No power cut in the working hours
- Government schools increased
- Helpline for pensioners
- Better sewerage system
- Increase in number of hospitals
- Uninterrupted electricity supply
- Clean Delhi—metro rail is pollution free
- RTI Act 2005
- Expansion of schools

- Pension for poor widows
- Signal-free roads
- Citizen Charter
- Online service of house tax
- Plantation in Delhi
- Kerosene-free Delhi
- Elevated roads
- New ISBT
- AC bus
- CNG vehicles
- PNG in residence
- PDS improved
- Improvement in health-care schemes, infrastructure, transportation, pollution control, education, per capita income, road condition, law and order, public distribution, electricity supply, water supply, and overhead bridges
- House tax online payment
- Development of parks
- Communication
- Computerization
- Women empowerment
- Reduction in crime rates
- Industrial development
- Malls and multicomplexes
- Garbage collection van—bioenergy plant
- Underground water storage
- Child-care programs
- Free education to EWS category
- Transport system improved
- Laadli Yojana started (Girls Education and Welfare Scheme)
- Help for marriage of poor family girls
- Underpasses/parking facilities increased
- Recreation centers provided for senior citizens
- Colony parks improved by providing flowers and shrubs
- Under ground parking provided at so many places
- Condition of electric supply improved
- Funds provided to RWAs directly for various development works
- Dense carpet road constructed even in the small colonies
- Internet provision given in all government offices
- Encouragement is given for games
- Free education for children up to 5th class
- Encouragement to girls to join schooling

- Rainwater harvesting
- Roads widened
- My Delhi I Care fund
- Metro rail
- More signal-free drive
- Reduced pollution
- Better bus service
- BRT corridor
- Less power cuts
- More greenery
- Increased schools and colleges
- More night shelters
- Pension for senior citizen
- Commonwealth Games
- Bhagidari
- Easy arrear to many offices
- Chacha Nehru Sehat Yojana (Children's Health Scheme)
- More medical colleges/hospitals
- More and better roads
- Improved water supply
- More universities
- Increase of police stations
- Horticulture
- Underpasses
- Government hospitals
- Bhagidari Scheme
- Division of MCD
- Multilevel parking
- Footover bridges
- Colleges on the increase
- Community centers increased
- Night shelters increased
- Concession to senior citizens
- Bus shelters improved
- BRT require improvement
- Good sign boards
- Better VIP security
- Low-floor buses
- Development of IGI Airport of the level of international standard
- E-SLA
- RTI implementation
- Public Grievance Commission established

- Enhancement of welfare schemes
- Improvement in sports facilities
- Improvement in power supply
- Mobile dispensary
- Number of dispensary increased
- Super-speciality hospitals
- Shifting of polluting industries
- Introduction of SAFAL outlet
- Improvement in education standard and school results
- Improvement in water supply
- Regularization of unauthorized colonies

South District (July 3, 2012)

- Improvements in DTC
- Old-age home
- Sulabh toilets
- Laadli Yojana (Girls Education and Welfare Scheme)
- E-governance
- Improvements in light and electricity
- Residential flats for weaker society
- Pensions for old age, widow, handicapped, poor person
- BPL Cards/financial assistance
- Stadium/sport facilities
- Greenery and parks
- Right to Education
- Medical facilities
- Introducing Bhagidari system
- Metro
- Transport improvement
- Metro feeder services
- Improvement in light
- Improvement in education
- Better facilities in hospitals
- Bus passes for senior citizens
- Education loans
- Single window system
- Commonwealth Games
- Revolution in shopping malls
- Development of parks
- Pollution free environment

- Adhaar Cards
- Better water supply
- Radio taxis
- Connectivity to airports by metro
- Better and new railway stations
- Contribution of citizens in government
- Underpasses and overbridges with elevators
- Barapula road from Nehru Stadium
- Drinking water quality improved
- Improvement in government schools results
- Introduction of new stadiums
- Improvements in light and electricity
- Residential flats for weaker sections of society
- Flyovers and underpasses
- Pensions for old age, widow, handicapped, and poor person
- BPL Cards/financial assistance
- Adhaar Cards
- Greenery and parks
- Right to Education
- Medical facilities
- Introducing Bhagidari system
- Transport improvement
- Metro feeder bus services
- Improvement in streetlighting
- Improvement in education
- Better facilities in hospitals
- Underground parking
- Stadium for Commonwealth Games
- Specialized hospitals, trauma centers
- CNG/AC low-floor buses
- Polluting trucks were sent outside Delhi
- CNG filling stations
- New schools, air conditioned schools
- Higher education and technical and management institutes
- Privatization of electricity and round the clock supply
- E-governance
- ATM services
- Laadli Yojana (Girls Education and Welfare Scheme)
- Automatic traffic signals
- BRT corridor
- Citizen Charters
- Lok Adalat

- Tourist Volvo buses
- Organizing Commonwealth Games
- Polio eradication from Delhi
- Mother and child welfare schemes
- Green Delhi
- RTI
- Service-level agreement (96 time-bound services by government)
- Jal Suvidha Kendra (Help Centers for water issues) by DJB
- Formal and non-formal education for children
- Widow pension scheme streamlined (for the poor)
- Grant of widows daughter's marriage (for the poor)
- Janahar scheme for low-cost food (for the poor)
- Angan Bari Scheme provided
- Provision for handicapped persons
- Metro services provision and improvement
- RTI Act
- Provision of LPG and CNG gas
- Improvement of senior citizen welfare
- Provision of two old-age homes
- Sunday clinic for senior citizens
- Senior citizen security cell by Delhi police
- Metro rail—world-class services
- Footover bridges with escalators
- Good quality of education
- New buses shelters
- World-class airport
- Renovated footpaths
- Uninterrupted electricity supply
- Increase in number of schools
- Introduction of rain-water harvesting
- Covering of open drains
- Increase in greenery and tree cover in Delhi
- Provisions for Laadli Plan (for girls education and welfare)
- RTI Act
- Opening of new power plants
- Development of NCR (National Capital Region)
- Introduction of Grameen Sewa (rural transport system)
- Introduction of E-governance
- BRT (Bus Rapid Transit system) on pilot test
- Introduction of CNG
- Reduction in pollution level
- Improvement of roads by using latest technology

- Increase in number of flyovers
- Improvement in power supply
- Installation of world-class infrastructure at metro stations
- Increase and modernization in DTC bus fleet
- Improvement in education facilities
- Introduction of E-SLA
- Introduction of online facilities in government departments
- Introduction of Citizen's Charter
- Improvement of sports facilities after CWG
- Pollution reduced by CNG use
- Chacha Nehru Sehat Yojana (Children's Health Scheme)
- Comfortable air conditioned buses
- Better housing facilities for JJ colonies
- Improvement of infrastructure in schools
- Kishori Yojana (Young Woman's Welfare Scheme)
- Deworming of school children
- Development of parks
- Improvement in streetlighting
- Increase in eco-clubs
- RWA development
- Senior citizen facilities
- Awareness regarding disaster management
- Computer education in schools
- City forest development
- Rainwater harvesting
- Ladies compartment in Delhi metro rail service
- Police helpline for ladies
- Power cuts reduced
- Metro rail introduced all over Delhi
- Good governance started through Bhagidari
- Roads improved as well as green/plantation developed
- BPL limit increased
- Education system improved
- Good steps for carrying out development work in authorized colonies
- Commonwealth Games organized well
- Public transport on CNG
- Excellent roads
- Less power cuts
- Improved water supply
- Rainwater harvesting
- Solar power plants

- Pension for senior citizen
- Public delivery system (for rations)
- Bhagidari Scheme
- Adhaar Cards
- Improvement in pollution level
- Excellent parks and forest cover
- Multistorage parking
- Midday meal and scholarship for students
- New universities set up
- Technical education for women
- Fifty percent reservation for women in MCD elections
- Loan facilities for weaker sections of society
- ESI and EPF implementation
- E-governance
- Eco-clubs
- Vidyalaya Kalyan Samiti (School Welfare Committee)
- Shopping malls
- Welfare for poor widow's daughter marriage
- Kerosene-free city
- Woman welfare and empowerment schemes
- Garden of five senses
- Yamuna river cleaning
- Sonia Vihar Plant for water treatment
- PNG
- Underpasses
- Water supply increased
- Electricity supply and distribution better
- CBSE results better
- Stadiums increased
- Forest cover increased
- Number of parks increased
- Metro network
- Community centers built
- Successful organization of Commonwealth Games in 2010
- Laadli Scheme (Girls Education and Welfare Scheme)
- Pension for senior citizens
- Security better
- Roads are better
- Ring road is red light free
- Number of flyovers built
- Regularization of unauthorized colonies
- Welfare schemes for women, children, and the poor

- Delhi is kerosene free
- Living standard is up
- Chacha Nehru Swasthya Yojana (Children's Health Scheme)
- Anna Shri Yojana (food subsidy for the poor)
- Introduction of CNG
- Domestic gas pipelines
- E-governance
- Old-age homes for the poor
- Control in electricity and water thefts
- Midday meals for children and the poor
- Footover bridges/subways
- Covering of drains
- Signal-free Ring Road
- Air conditioned buses
- Less electricity cut even in summer
- Pollution-free roads
- Improvement in parks greenery
- Construction of night shelters
- Improvement in bus shelters
- Concession to senior citizen and ladies
- Boring and tube well construction
- Streetlight system improved/better
- PNG introduction in Delhi
- Girls Education and Welfare Scheme
- Special benefit given to handicap persons
- Improved in parking system in main markets
- Special attention to RWA
- Sports grounds/clubs for children
- Water improvement by DJB
- Commonwealth Games successfully conducted
- RTI Scheme
- Trauma center set up
- Air conditioned buses
- Privatization of electricity distribution
- Improved power situation
- New airport of global standard
- Laadli Scheme (Girls Education and Welfare Scheme)
- Increase in pension of handicapped poor and senior citizens
- Sonia Vihar Water Treatment Plant
- New power grid
- BRT
- Improved road network

- More underpasses
- Commonwealth Games successfully managed
- More funds to RWAs
- Development of parks
- E-ticketing of railways
- Gas pipeline
- Twenty-five percent reservations for poor children
- Single admission for IITS
- Midday meals for school children
- Uniform to school children
- Indraprastha university set up
- Improved health services
- Technical education of women only
- Metro link to airport and station
- Adhaar Card Scheme
- Registry of property online
- Sarv Shiksha Abhiyaan (Education for All Scheme) for education improvement
- Segregation of waste
- Improvement of New Delhi railway station
- BRT corridor
- Bus shelters
- Bus services improved
- Water supply (Sonia Vihar Water Treatment Plant)
- Interstate bus terminals
- Tree cover increased
- Pollution control improved
- CNG for the entire public transport
- Commonwealth Games held to showcase Delhi
- Bore wells
- Solar traffic signals
- Railway station improvement
- Hospitals added
- Medical colleges added
- Midday meals in schools
- Trauma center set up
- Increase in number of recreation centers
- Telephone density 90 percent
- Gas pipeline
- LPG replaced kerosene
- E-governing
- Citizen Charter

- CNG use in vehicles
- International airport construction (upgradation)
- Laadli Yojana for the girl child
- Indraprastha university set up
- Opening of Technical University for Women
- Development of roads
- Jan Aahar Yojana
- Citizen Charters
- Free education for children upto 10th class in government schools
- Increase in sports facility
- Increase in green belt/forest area
- Anna Shri Yojana (food subsidy for the poor)
- Chacha Nehru Sehat Yojana (Children's Health Scheme)
- Increase in government hospitals
- Commonwealth Games organized successfully
- Decrease in pollution level
- Pension for handicapped
- Increase in housing by DDA/Delhi government
- Rehabilitation of slum clusters
- Implementations RTI Act
- Subways and footover bridges
- Development of parks
- Widening of roads
- Installation of new streetlights
- Elevated roads constructed
- Water reservoirs constructed
- Opening of new colleges/universities
- Tent schools converted into SPS schools
- Marriage grants to daughters of widows
- Midday meals for school children
- Jan Aahar (scheme for providing food for the poor)
- Laadli Yojana (Girls Welfare Scheme)
- Piped gas supply to houses
- Enhancement in old-age pensions
- Introduction of BRT corridor
- Women compartment in Delhi metro
- Vocational institutions increased
- New district courts set up
- All womens police stations set up
- New bus terminal at IP estate
- Anand Vihar Railway Station
- E-governance

- Underpasses constructed
- Overbridges constructed
- Commonwealth Games well organized
- Cluster buses introduced
- BRT corridors
- New police stations
- New educational institutions (university)
- DTC own shelters
- E-registry by revenue department
- New stadiums
- New city forests
- Distribution of power through PPP model
- Covering of drains
- PNG introduction
- Development of parks
- Clubs in school
- New community centers set up
- My Delhi I Care Fund
- Pulse Polio Yojana
- New hospitals
- Trifurcation of MCD
- Free education for girls
- Online passports
- Metro rail of world-class quality
- DTC transport quality and quantity
- Pollution control
- Flyovers smoothen traffic across Delhi
- Number of stadiums increased
- Underpass roads
- Green Delhi with 27 percent tree cover
- Number of engineering colleges increased
- Hospitals increased
- More universities set up
- Public conveniences increased and modernized
- Laadli Education Scheme (Girls Education and Welfare Scheme)
- Delhi Metro
- CNG buses
- Piped gas for households
- Lesser power cuts
- Increased water supply
- BRT corridors
- New police stations

- New educational institutions
- Distribution of power
- T-3 IGI Airport of global standard
- PNG introduction
- Introduction of CNG
- Cluster buses
- New police stations
- Metro service
- DTC buses renovation
- Improvement in electricity supply
- Flyovers (11 to 75 numbers)
- Quality drinking water
- Introduction of new stadiums
- BRT corridor
- Barapula road (from Nehru stadium to outer Ring Road) reduces travel time
- Improvement in government schools
- Gas pipelines
- Midday meals for school children
- Vocational education
- Old-age homes
- E-government
- Jan Aahar
- Plantations to reduce pollution
- Low-floor buses
- Green Delhi by plantations
- Less power cuts
- Pensions to old-age/disabled poor
- Improvement of streetlightning
- Awareness through Bhagidari
- Improvement of roads
- Creation of new forest areas
- Laadli Scheme (Girls Education and Welfare Scheme)
- Stadiums built
- BRT corridor
- Hospitals
- T3 Airport of world standard
- Trifurcation of MCD
- Shopping malls
- Green environments
- Discoms
- Better road lights

- Vast improvements in transport systems
- Vast improvements in electricity supply
- Number of hospitals increased
- Fall in the crimes
- Higher education institutions increased
- Progress in the rural developments
- Improvement in IT sector
- RTI Act applicable
- Less power cuts
- Water situation is better
- More schools in Delhi
- E-filling of electricity bills
- Pass percentage increased in schools
- Multilevel companies
- IT sectors increased
- Laadli Yojana (Girls Education and Welfare Scheme)
- More BPL schemes for the poor
- Midday meals for school children
- Per person income increased
- Plantation increased
- Right to education increased
- Flyovers built across Delhi
- AC buses
- Pulse polio drops
- Underpasses
- More traffic signals
- Specialty hospitals set up
- World-class airport
- Broadening of roads
- Better patrolling by police
- Pension to poor/old people
- RTE (Right to Education)
- Computerization in public administration
- Old-age homes increased
- New Delhi Station has been modernized
- Metro rail service
- Sports stadiums
- CNG stations
- PNG supply
- Covering of nallahs
- Bus stands (Sarai Kale Khan)
- Expansion of water supply (Ganga Jal Supply)

- Power plant in Bawana
- New hospitals
- Multilevel parking introduced
- Footover bridges built
- Trifurcation of MCD
- Eco-friendly car parking
- BRT corridors
- Low-floor AC buses
- BRT corridors
- Electricity reform successful
- New stadiums set up
- Development of roads
- Midday meals
- New railway station
- Trauma centers set up
- Navodya schools set up
- Community centers set up
- Footover bridges built for pedestrian convenience
- Commonwealth Games successful
- Connectivity of NCR much better
- District courts set up
- RTI
- Laadli Scheme (Girls Education and Welfare Scheme)
- Adhaar Card
- Good education in Delhi
- Elevated road built
- Footover bridges built
- CNG
- Twenty-four hour electricity after power reforms
- Rainwater harvesting structures set up
- Signature bridge being built
- E-registration of property
- E-SLA
- Footover bridges
- Increase of flyovers
- Development of water bodies
- New hospitals set up
- New education institutes set up
- Introduction of Micro Irrigation System
- Old-age pensions for the poor, widows, and handicapped
- Adhaar
- Introduction of online bill payment

- E-ticketing
- Beautification of Delhi
- Metro rail service
- Wide roads with proper traffic signals and crossing
- Footover bridges and subways
- Increase in greenery
- CNG buses and autorickshaws for reducing pollution
- Pension increased
- Covering of open drains
- Multilevel car parking
- IGL gas pipeline
- Improvement in electricity
- Better education in government schools
- Eco-clubs in schools
- Improvement in Delhi Police services
- More sewage treatment plants
- Sonia Vihar Water Treatment Plant has increased water availability
- Broadening roads
- Old-age homes
- Parks and gardens—improved and increased
- Barapula Nalla elevated road—first of its kind
- PNG
- Delhi Technology University set up
- Introduction of PPP for electricity reform
- BRT
- Ring Road without traffic lights
- Improvement in power supply
- Improvement of roads
- Free education up to class 10
- Bhagidari/district-level meetings
- Frequent meeting with CM
- Better roads
- More power grids
- Improved power supplies
- Greener Delhi
- Asola Wild Life Sanctuary
- Night shelters for EWS
- Children homes
- Trauma centers
- Midday meal
- CWG village
- Elevated roads

- New railway stations
- Old-age homes
- RTI
- Public convenience increased
- New stadiums built
- Reduction of pollution
- Improvement of traffic
- Parking facilities improved
- Trauma centers set up
- Child and women development schemes doing well
- Laadli Scheme (Girls Education and Welfare Scheme)
- Fast-track family courts for women
- Formal/non-formal schools for children
- Newly constructed home at Narela
- Coaches reserved for women in metro
- Good implementation of RTI/ACT

South-west District (July 4, 2012)

- Improvement in greenery
- Reduced air pollution
- Increase in number of flyovers to improve traffic congestion
- Increase in number of over/under pass for pedestrians
- Covering of big storm water drains
- PPP Scheme for power reform successful
- Introduction of PNG
- Increase in number of colleges in Delhi
- Increase in number of hospitals in Delhi
- Improvement in government school education system
- Holding of successful Commonwealth Games
- Beautification of Delhi
- Introduction of Pension Scheme for widows and senior citizens
- Increase in per capita income of Delhi
- Metro rail
- Road construction, bus service improved
- Electricity improved
- Old-age homes
- Pension for widow and handicapped
- Construction of hospitals
- CNG-use reduced pollution
- Tree plantation

- Education result excellent
- Park development
- Lighting especially streetlight
- Roads development
- Hospitals
- Reliability of power supply—99 percent
- Successfully meeting of peak demand from 3,000 megawatt (MW) in 2002 to 5,500 MW in 2012
- Installation and operation of Pragati Power Project
- Installation of Bawana Power Project
- Drastic energy loss reduction from 55 percent to 18 percent
- Introduction of metro rail
- Introduction of low-floor buses
- Introduction of AC buses for public
- Introduction of Chacha Nehru Sehat Yojana (Children's Health Scheme)
- Introduction of Kishori Yojana
- Introduction of My Delhi I Care Fund
- Old-age homes
- RTI introduction
- Air pollution reduced with CNG use
- Improvement in road construction
- Widening of roads
- Increase in primary health centers in rural areas of south-west district, Delhi
- Construction of overhead bridges for crossing roads
- Construction of stadium
- Parks and garden society
- Increase in plantation in Delhi
- Increase in efficiency of electricity supply
- Increase in minimum wages for skilled and unskilled workers
- Metro
- School and colleges construction
- Bridges construction
- DTC diesel buses converted to CNG
- Subway construction
- New medical colleges
- Education level improved in government schools
- Low-floor buses
- AC bus service
- Privatization of DVB resulting in improvement in power situation
- Pension of senior citizen and the needy

- Passing an act in 2007 for maintenance and protection of parents and senior citizens
- Free meals in schools for poor children
- Good maintenance of schools and colleges
- Improved infrastructure
- Radio taxis
- Delhi greenery improved
- Security walls and gates developed in residential areas
- Cemented roads within blocks
- Pollution-free Delhi city
- Schools infrastructure improved
- AC buses and shelters
- Upgradation of transport system
- Upgradation of electric/power system
- Installation of CNG gas system
- Increased number of educational systems
- Constructions of flyovers
- Ring Road has been made red-light free
- Super metro service
- Pollution-free environment
- More trees planted
- Public infrastructures have been excellently developed like FOBs, flyovers, and so on
- Hospital facilities improved
- Development of industries
- E-governance system
- Introduction of AC DTC buses
- Plantation of more trees made Delhi pollution free
- Introduction to Laadli Scheme
- Introduction to Pension Schemes
- Improvement in electricity supply
- Improvement in primary education
- Commonwealth Games
- Elevated roads
- Subways
- Polio eradication achieved
- Improvement in BRT corridor
- Jan Ahaar
- E-governance
- Senior citizen's pension
- Trifurcation of MCD
- Laadli Yojana (for girls welfare)

- Kishori Scheme (for girls health)
- World largest millennium bus depot
- Construction of new parks
- Plantation and greenery
- Sulabh facility (public convenience)
- Airport new terminal (T3) has started
- BPL facility
- Metro rail
- Old-age homes
- Improvement of education up secondary level
- Environment (through plantation)
- Rehabilitation of sewer (deep sewer of main roads)
- AC buses (low floor)
- Commonwealth Games successfully held
- Self-assessment of property tax
- Easy bill facility
- Improvement communication
- Non polluting DTC/CNG
- Construction of flyovers and subways
- BRT corridors
- Upgradation of stadium
- Provision of footover bridge/escalators
- Civic amenities such as toilets improved
- Midday meals
- Facilities in government schools
- Upgradation of streetlighting
- Pension scheme for weaker sections of society
- Upgradation of water supply system
- Upgradation of sewerage disposal system
- Introduction of Jan Ahaar
- Implementation of strict pollution norms
- CNG—the world's largest public transport system without diesel
- Suvidha centers (Citizens Help Centers)
- Implementation of Maintenance and Welfare of Parents Act 2007
- E-registration of properties of Mehrauli sub-registrar office
- Plying of AC and cluster buses
- BRT corridor, as a pilot project to reduce bus travel time
- Information technology improvement in quality of education
- Barapula road—elevated road to reduce travel time
- Excellent performance of DTC buses and travel facilities
- Increase in electricity performance through power reform
- Increase of water supply

- Ban of diesel-run commercial vehicles in Delhi
- Widow/handicapped person's pension
- Commonwealth Games
- Reservation in public/private schools for EWS (Economically Weaker Sections)
- Implementation of RTE
- Implementation RTI 2005
- Bhagidari workshop organization
- Free treatment in government hospitals for BPL (below poverty line)
- Lakhs of trees plantation
- Privatization of electricity distribution
- Issue of provisional certificate to unauthorized colonies
- E-governance system
- Numerous unauthorized colonies have come up and government has been trying its best to provide better civic facilities
- Plantation has added beauty in green Delhi
- Commonwealth Games have boosted the morale in Delhi, capital of India
- Beautiful subcity like Dwarka planned by Government of Delhi
- Decentralization of labor and consumer courts
- Computerization of driving license in Delhi
- Bifurcation of district courts in Delhi
- Improvement in government school and colleges
- IGI Airport provided with T3 terminal of world class

North District (July 5, 2012)

- Delhi Metro
- Reliable power supply
- PNG supply
- Kerosene-free Delhi
- BRT
- Flyovers across Delhi
- CWG Games
- State-of-the-art bus shelters
- Radio Taxi
- T-3 Airport (world class)
- Citizen Charter
- Multilevel car parking

- Upgraded streetlighting
- CCTVs in public places for safety
- Eco-clubs in schools
- Separate bin for biodegradable waste
- Cleaner Yamuna
- Signature bridge
- Expansion of ISBT
- Bed and breakfast private guest houses
- E-SLA
- New stadiums
- Low-cost housing
- Revamping of railway station
- New plant in Bawana for power generation
- Laadli Yojana (for girls welfare)
- Pension for poor citizens
- My Delhi I Care Fund
- Relocation of slums JJ Clusters
- Old-age homes set up
- Electronic meters for power
- Connectivity in NCR
- Pulse Polio Scheme—eradicated polio
- Adhaar Card
- Motor license facility
- E-registration of property
- RTI
- Chacha Nehru Sehat Yojana (Children's Health Scheme)
- Midday Meal
- Footover bridges
- New look to Connaught Place
- DDA sports complexes
- Upgradation of IP and Rajghat power stations
- E-stamping
- Metro rail
- Improved roads
- Increase in green cover/tree cover
- Improvement in education
- Improvement in electricity
- Improvement in Connaught Place
- Metro rail system
- Enhancement of DTC

- Public distribution system enhancement (EPDS for rations to below the poverty line)
- Greenery enhancement
- Improved result of government schools
- Increased hospital facilities
- Convenience in depositing bills, and so on (Jeevan Centers)
- New district courts
- Increase in amusement parks
- Laadli Scheme
- Increase in old-age pension
- Cash subsidy on LPG for BPL families
- Capacity of DJB improved for water supply
- Expansion of power supply system
- RTI Act 2005 implementation
- E-SLA (96 time-bound services by government departments)
- Expansion of electoral registration office
- Midday meal in government schools
- Free distribution of books and study materials in government schools
- Free education for upto 14 years in government schools
- New universities set up
- Commonwealth Games managed well
- Better roads/parks
- Increase in green cover
- Birth and death registration online
- E-SLA started
- Better transport facilities
- Polio free Delhi
- Immunization coverage increased
- Door-to-door garbage collection
- Kerosene-free Delhi
- Financial assistance for widows
- Bhagidari
- Better hospitals including super-speciality hospitals
- Trifurcation of MCD
- Fifty percent seats reserved for women councillors
- Successful conducting of CWG-2010
- Ambedkar Awas Yojana for Safai Karamchari (welfare scheme for sanitation workers)
- Rajiv Ratan Niwas Yojana (for labor welfare)
- Better consumer care service
- Free books and uniform for MCD students

- My Delhi I Care Fund increase
- Chacha Nehru Sehat Yojana (Children's Health Scheme)
- Biometric attendance for employees in MCD
- Mechanical sweeping of roads
- Solar light/energy increases
- Twenty-five percent reservation for EWS
- Regularization of unauthorized colonies
- DOTS treatment for TB
- Education level
- Number of colleges and schools increased
- Health service better
- Laadli
- Jan Aahar
- Signal-free Ring Road
- Sports complex
- Old-age homes
- Park development
- Community center
- Per capita income growth
- Bhagidari Yojana
- Citizen Charter
- Commonwealth Games held
- Tree plantation
- Environmental awareness
- Footover bridges constructed
- No power cuts
- Good air conditioned buses
- Good roads built
- Development in education systems at all levels
- Implementation of RWA projects
- Pollution-free city
- Improvement in traffic control
- RTI Act
- CNG-based total public transport system
- Unani hospital set up
- Commonwealth Game
- Battery operated rickshaws
- Senior citizen transport subsidy
- Senior citizen pension
- Metro rail facility very good
- Regularization of unauthorized colonies in Delhi
- District courts set up

- Rashtra Mandal Commonwealth Games
- Adhaar Card
- Biometric Card
- Delhi Government Health Scheme
- Free uniform/books for students in government schools
- Road construction better
- Paper recycled in 200 schools
- Iconic Signature Bridge in Delhi when complete
- Cleanliness of Yamuna Project started
- Online e-governance
- Reduction in air pollution through use of CNG in all public transport
- Decongestion of traffic through road widening
- Construction of underpasses/overbridges
- Increase in greenery through massive plantation
- Improvement in sewage mechanism of city
- Laadli a pioneer step in education of the girl child
- Health-care facilities, a complete positive turn around
- Privatization of electricity, a boon for Delhi
- CWG, enhancement of our reputation internationally
- Social welfare pensions (for weaker sections of society)
- Polio eradication
- Dengue/malaria control
- Construction of flyovers and subways
- Development of roads
- Improvement of streetlights
- Induction of low-floor AC and non-AC buses
- Introduction of Laadli Scheme (Girls Education and Welfare Scheme)
- Improvement in drainage system
- Increase in green area
- Midday Meal in government schools
- Increase in electricity production and supply
- Increase in per capita income
- Improvement in standard of living
- Introduction of mobile libraries
- Night shelters for poor people
- Beautification of parks
- Construction of rainwater harvesting system
- Better parking facilities
- Improvement in medical facilities
- Increase in drinking water processing capacity

- CNG—public transport system
- Footover bridges/escalators constructed
- Commissioning of 140 MGD Sonia Vihar Water Treatment Plant
- Huge increase in water supply networks and rehabilitation of sewer lines
- Commonwealth Games 2010
- Widening/strengthening of roads
- Improvement in education systems
- Improvement in disposal of solid waste
- Hundred percent achievement in power supply
- Development works in unauthorized colonies
- Delhi Metro Rail service
- Green Delhi
- Gardens and parks
- Medical facilities increased
- CWG Games a success
- RTI Act
- Water and power supply
- Streetlights
- International airports
- Facilities for senior citizens
- Good employment opportunities
- Increase in funds for all districts
- Plastic free Delhi
- Intrduction of CNG for all public transport
- Improvement in drainage system
- Increase in green area
- Introduction of midday meal in government schools
- Increase in electricity production
- Increase in per capita income
- Improvement in standard of living
- Night shelters for poor people
- Pension for handicapped poor
- Improvement in health services
- Introduction of Rajeev Ratna Yojana Awas
- Yamuna Action Plan
- Trifurcation of MCD
- Fifty percent reservation for woman in election for municipal corporation
- Plantation of trees
- Bhagidari
- Low-floor buses in DTC

- Network of flyovers
- Metro rail network
- Electricity supply has increased
- Laadli Scheme (Girls Education and Welfare Scheme)
- Midday Meal Scheme
- Development in unauthorized colonies
- Commonwealth Games successfully held
- Electric rickshaws
- RTI Act is a big achievement
- Above all Bhagidari Scheme
- Commonwealth Games
- Electricity improved
- Roads improved
- Computerized Ration Card
- Pension for old age, widows, handicapped
- Scholarships for students
- CNG in autos and taxis
- Cluster buses (AC buses)
- Good quality electricity in NDPL area
- Growth of Bhagidari is phenomenal
- Control of pollution in Delhi
- Education system has improved, better result achieved by government schools
- Traffic system has become better
- RTE (Right to Education) Act introduced
- Free education for the girl child
- Continuous power supply
- Regularization of unauthorized colonies
- Delhi Metro success story
- Increase in green area
- Signal-free traffic due to new flyovers
- Terminal-3 at IGI Airport
- New bus shelters
- Citizen's charter
- Implementation of Sarve Shiksha Abihyan (Education for All)
- Construction of new hospitals
- PPP (public private partnership)
- Development in colonies
- Implementation of pension scheme for widows and old
- Regular power supply
- E-stamping
- AIDS awareness programs

- Commonwealth Games 2010 successfully held
- DTC service better
- Use of CNG has made Delhi pollution free
- Best electricity service
- Bhagidari between public and government
- Malaria and dengue control in Delhi
- Health services
- Pulse polio program—polio eradicated
- Strength of police personnel has been increased
- Number of police stations has been increased substantially
- Introduction of scheme like senior citizen cell, child helpline
- Installation of CCTVs in many areas
- Improvement of the traffic system using GPRS, and so on
- Increase in wages of workers
- Metro rail service
- CNG Buses in DTC—AC and non-AC
- Government schools results improved
- Laadli Scheme (Girls Education and Welfare Scheme)
- E-tenders and E-billing
- Hospitals increased
- Legal Aid free for the poor
- E-banking
- Midday meal in government schools
- RTI Act 2005
- RTE Act
- E-SLA (96 time-bound services by government)
- E-ticket service in railways
- Adhaar Card
- E-driving license
- Radio taxis at ₹ 10 per km
- Environment is good with more gardens
- RTI Act introduced
- Online license for driving
- 5,500 MW of power consumption
- 850 MG of water (portable) available daily
- Monuments are well maintained
- Housing for EWS (Economically Weaker Sections)
- Right to Education for all
- Aahar schemes through mobile vans
- Development of industrial areas
- Bridges all over city smoothens traffic

- Development of infrastructure like flyovers, wide roads, FOBs, underpasses, rubs, and so on
- Upgradation of stadiums
- Proper maintenance/upkeeping of roads
- Pollution control
- Construction of hospitals in various parts of the city
- Flyovers and better roads
- Pollution under control with CNG transport
- Better electricity supply
- Education and literacy improvement
- Better planning for the National Capital Region
- Health improvement
- Bhagidari
- RTI Act
- E-governance
- Citizens Charters
- Laadli Yojana (Girls Education and Welfare Scheme)
- Old-age pension for the poor
- Old-age homes for the poor
- More employment opportunities
- Shifting of industrial estates
- Right to Education for all introduced
- Streetlights better
- Increased forest cover more city forests
- World-class stadiums provided
- Widened roads
- Administrative reforms
- World-class hospitals
- Gymnasiums
- Community centers
- Social security programs
- Citizens charters
- Industry outside city
- Solar power system
- Sewage treatment plants being added
- Recycling of waste
- Bhagidari—brainchild of CM
- Anti Child Labour Act
- Free computer education in government schools
- My Delhi I Care Fund increased
- Increase in literacy rate
- Introduction of Right to Information

- Improvement in infrastructure
- Regularization of unauthorized colonies taken up
- Potable water supply better
- E-governance facility
- Implementation of Citizens Charters for all departments
- Kerosene-free Delhi
- Solar water heaters introduced
- Rainwater harvesting
- Redevelopment of water bodies
- E-logistic, E-stamping introduction
- APL, BPL, Anna Shri Yojana introduced
- Yamuna Diversity Park
- Smooth supply of power/water
- My Delhi I Care Fund introduced
- Recycling of paper facility

Central + New Delhi District (July 6, 2012)

- Better public transport services
- Air pollution reduced
- Metro rail service—world class
- Administration reforms
- Old-age homes
- Pension for widows/senior citizens
- Green environment
- Water treatment plant
- Cultural programs for Delhiites
- Health facilities
- Education for all
- Laadli Yojana for girls education
- Bhagidari Yojana
- Welfare of senior citizens
- Metro rail service
- Power supply improved
- Government schools education system improved
- Streetlights improved
- Parks and greenery improved
- Beautification of city improving
- Leasehold to freehold conversion made easier
- Construction of pavements and side lanes improving
- Regularization of unauthorized colonies under process

- Public transport better
- Widow/old-age homes
- RTI facility
- Women welfare programs (for the poor)
- Facilities for senior citizens
- Industrial development (non-polluting)
- Regularization of unauthorized colonies
- New Police Stations
- Relocation of industrial units
- Footover bridges
- More underground water reservoirs for better water distribution
- Renovations of stadiums
- BRT corridors
- New hospitals
- Renovation of footpaths
- Tourism buses
- Renovation of Rajiv Chowk
- Celebration of 100 years of Delhi
- GGSIPU university
- Signature bridge being built
- ISBT renovation
- Commonwealth Games 2010 well organized
- IGI Airport—T-3 terminal
- Superior public transport system
- Improved health care system
- Improvement in the power system
- Quick response during exigencies
- Implementation of ESLA (96 time-bound government services)
- Successful completion of CWG 2010
- RTI and RTE
- Public participation in development of their locality
- Dust-free environment
- Successful introduction of CNG
- Improved streetlights
- Increase in per capita income
- Law and order situation improved
- Reduction in power cuts
- Transparency in government through e-governance
- Metro network
- Stadiums for CWG 2010
- Flyovers for smoother traffic
- CNG/ LPG stations increased

- New hospitals and dispensaries
- Old-age pension for the poor
- Night shelters for destitutes
- BRT corridors
- Rainwater harvesting scheme in government offices and public places
- Privatization of distribution of power supply
- Commonwealth Games 2010 well organized
- IGI Airport developed
- Flyovers for signal-free traffic
- Best electricity service
- Good administrative reforms
- Malaria and dengue control in Delhi
- Laadli Scheme (Girls Education and Welfare Scheme)
- Railway stations improvement
- Better public transportation
- Increase of green belt of the city
- Implementation of e-SLA and e-tendering
- Improved education system
- Better hospitals facilities
- CNG
- Super-speciality hospitals
- BPL Cards
- Senior citizen's pension (for the poor)
- Rajeev Ratan Awas Scheme
- Increase in RWAs projects through Bhagidari
- Infrastructure of school buildings becomes improved
- Supply of electricity is better
- Trifurcation of MCD
- Girl child incentives
- Incentive to SC/ST/OBC/minority classes
- LPG through pipeline in housing societies
- Implementation RTE 2009 (education for all)
- Escalators on footover bridges
- Express metro service
- Cluster buses
- Water reforms (three pilot projects)
- CNG for the entrire public transport system
- Huge increase in water supply networks and rehabilitation of sewer lines
- Hundred power supply
- Development works in unauthorized colonies

- Pollution reduced by use of CNG in transport
- Water supply improved
- World-class standard international airports
- Medical and hospital facilities improved
- Standard of education and result improved
- Mode of public transport improved
- Forestation and plantation—greenery improved
- World-class flyovers
- Signature Bridge under construction
- Introduction of multilevel parking
- Introduction of Bhagidari
- New district courts in Delhi
- New footover bridges
- Improvement in roads
- Polio-free Delhi
- Construction of more houses for the poor
- CWG Games were a huge success
- Increase in forest area
- Good employment opportunities
- Development of New Delhi Railway Station
- Good employment opportunities
- Increase in funds for all districts
- Super-speciality hospitals increased
- Good housing societies
- Quality buses and footover bridges
- Improvement in Jal Board water supply
- Universities and schools increased
- Trifurcation of MCD
- Scheme for girl child
- World-class hospitals
- EWS Ration Cards/housing facilities
- Job opportunities growing
- Better school results
- Insurance for weaker sections of society
- Regularization of unauthorized colonies being done
- Increase in schools/universities
- Improvement in quality of education
- Financial assistance to deserving students
- Increased number of hospitals
- Increase in city forest areas
- Increase in roads and parks
- Battery rickshaws

- Privatization of electricity
- Development of transportation (Multi-model)
- Removal of polluted industries from Delhi
- Implementation of CNG reduced air pollution
- Bhagidari between government and RWAs leading to the growth of Delhi
- Improvement in electricity supply
- Pension to poor senior citizens/widows/ handicapped
- Improvement in health care
- Polio-free Delhi
- Improvement in standard of living of citizens
- Highest minimum wages in India
- More hospitals and colleges
- Pedestrian crossing facility over main roads (increased)
- Airport upgradation—world class
- Railway station and ISBT upgradation
- Improvement in the electricity distribution system
- Improvement in the infrastructure
- Improvement in the public health system
- Improvement in civic amenities
- Strengthening of interdepartmental coordination
- Women empowerment schemes introduced
- Construction of new schools
- Scholarships for students
- Free health check-ups (in government schools)
- Free saplings to citizens
- MCD—50 percent reservation for women as councillors
- Public grievance commission set up
- Transparency in government work through RTI

Source: Reports on 8 One-day District level Consultation Meets held on June 26–29, 2012 and July 3–6, 2012.

Note: Since different table groups were working on same issue, many points are common, thus, indicating the common ground that emerges during the Bhagidari Workshops. They have been shared in its original form to give the flavor of democracy at work through this process.

Appendix 10
How to Improve
the Effectiveness of
Bhagidari: Feedback
and Suggestions from
Citizens' Associations
and Officials

West District (June 26, 2012)

- There should be more and more participation of RWAs.
- All RWAs should get registered with Bhagidari Cell of Delhi government.
- Problems raised by RWAs can be resolved if transfer policy of MCD engineers is made transparent so that responsibilities are fixed with the concerned officers.
- Bhagidari campaign should be conducted at group RWA level in each zone.
- A separate mechanism is needed to be created to implement the Bhagidari project as the present mechanism is not sufficient in MCD zone for doing the job effectively. This should be under DC.
- RWAs should submit weekly feedback to the concerned department about the works going on/taken up in the colony.
- Participation of RWAs in identification of unauthorized water connections, encroachments, and so on.

- The original system of seating officers and RWA members on the same table is a better idea. Grievance redressal up to some extent takes place automatically.
- More frequent exchange of ideas and experiences is required for improvement.
- Bhagidari meetings should be more frequent and in smaller groups—at least three to four times in a year.
- Development fund should be monitored by RWA committee/members.
- RWAs should participate in equal number of men and women members.
- Democratization in RWA and quasi-judicial powers should be given.
- There should be a fixed tenure for RWA members, not more than two years.
- Bhagidari meetings should be conducted three to four times in a year.
- Overall, we are satisfied with Bhagidari program.
- On behalf of MCD, I assure that all complaints will be resolved in a time-bound manner.
- Without waiting for the workshop, the RWAs should be able to write to Bhagidari Cell, if they have any suggestion/problem.
- A telephone directory of all departments under NCT, Delhi, including three Municipal Corporations may be provided to all the RWAs for better connectivity and cooperation.
- For carrying out any proposed development work in any colony, the councillor/MLA/MP should also be involved in discussion with the concerned RWA in advance/anticipation before approval and carrying out work.
- As discussed many times, some funds must be given to RWAs directly to carry out emergent works of colonies.
- Rainwater harvesting projects must be executed in every colony in collaboration with respective RWA.
- Department should call regular meetings and it should be an ongoing process.
- For a short time in-between the Bhagidari workshops, concerned officials should be introduced to the RWA.
- RWAs' complaints/suggestions may please be quickly resolved. Many times we don't get response.
- The RWAs/MTAs should be given due importance by the service providing departments like DJB, BSES, MCD, and so on, and

their representations should be considered on a different footing/priority.

- The representations/complaints sent by RWAs/MTAs should be monitored by Bhagidari Cell and the grievance should be redressed in a time-bound manner.
- Ensure that the promises made to RWAs are duly fulfilled.
- The problems of the members of RWAs attending Bhagidari should be heard and resolved as quickly as possible. This being a direct approach platform with CM/Delhi is considered the most powerful platform to solve the problem. But it is not done like that and I feel that is lessening the effectiveness of Bhagidari, which is a dream project of our CM. For example, so far no recreation center has been provided in Pragati Apartments Residents Welfare Association (PARWA), Paschim Vihar, New Delhi-63 for 100 senior citizens. All indoor facilities should be provided afterwards.
- Fulfillment of assurances given in monthly Bhagidari meetings.
- More power should be delegated to concerned DC, ADM, SDMs to execute the projects.
- Action Taken Report should be sent by all departments in response to RWAs letters/request.
- Greater participation and coordination between the citizens and the government is required.
- Effective and honest replies from the government to questions/problems raised by the people.
- Understanding the land of West Delhi since it is originally an agricultural rural area.
- My Delhi I Care Fund should be allotted to the concerned RWA.
- Display of the offices of the concerned authorities with phone numbers.
- West Delhi pays its taxes. Its development should be well planned.
- Wide publicity about Bhagidari may be given and all the registered RWAs should join Bhagidari.
- Bhagidari meetings/workshops should be conducted at the SDM-level and MLAs should also be involved.
- Last Bhagidari meeting Action Taken Report should be given in the next meeting. RWAs should be kept informed about the work done/expenditure.
- Bhagidari meeting conference should be conducted twice or thrice a year at least.
- Provide funds to RWAs for improvement of the blocks' works as per list per year.

- Provide mobile dispensaries in the areas where there is no facility. This must be done on a weekly basis.
- The time duration of this session should be reduced to three-five hours.
- Centralized meeting of Bhagidari should be conducted once in a year. Quarterly meeting should be conducted at district level to increase transparency.
- Shuttle bus service for senior citizens should be provided to make sure everyone reaches on time. It would reduce travel cost of RWA members.
- One-time request by any RWA for developmental projects under My Delhi I Care Fund should be considered, sanctioned, and executed by the DC's office with specification.
- Transparency in distribution/allocation of funds at the level of commissioners, DC, MLAs, and councillors, and it should be in the knowledge of RWAs to reach the benefits at the grassroots level.
- Concerned departments should, within timeframe, contact and inform the RWAs regarding the problems raised by them as the RWA is a constitutional body and has the same authority as the government.
- Field staff should contact the RWAs once in a fortnight to solve their problems.
- Good work by Bhagidari and government. The DC should have more powers to inspect from time to time with government officials to solve the problems of RWAs.
- Monthly meeting at district-level with competent authorities of civic agencies along with the representatives of RWAs.
- The problems in execution of any work should be intimated to the Bhagidari Cell.
- The Bhagidari spirit of citizen–government partnership, presently only at top, should be stressed upon and inculcated at department/executive level.
- More effective and involved meetings at district/departments nodal officer's level with the RWAs should be held and outcome should be monitored.
- First of all, there should be a monthly MCD ward-wise meeting with respective RWAs; thereafter, there should be a monthly interaction program of RWA with the concerned officers of the respective departments.
- Complaints/suggestions of respective RWA should be sent to one authority/designated channel.

- Channel (designated authority) should contact RWAs for suggestion or relevant problem faced by them.
- Collective participation of the representative of RWAs from various colonies/city for implementation of various projects assigned under Bhagidari.
- Assigning administrative power to the representative of various RWAs as described under the Panchayati Raj, which is the main principle of Bhagidari.
- Such Bhagidari meetings should be held at least twice in a year.
- DC/SDM should hold quarterly meetings with RWAs to discuss priority local issues and implementable suggestions coming out of such meeting.
- If there is no time-bound action taken by the department then responsibility should be fixed.
- There should be proper policy and its implementation.
- Execution of development works should be a continuous process as against only around election time.
- Why encroachments and unauthorized constructions are not checked-in at the initial stage? Demolition at a later stage results in public anger besides national loss.
- Why there is no workshop for the officers urging them to be more work-friendly.
- Time-bound response, progress, and reporting of all matters/ issues suggested by members in Bhagidari workshops.
- Members should take up the issues/matters of public interest and development.
- The spirit of Bhagidari Scheme is not being followed properly by all implementing servicing departments like MCD, DJB, discoms, PWD, Delhi Police, and so on. These departments should strictly follow Bhagidari guidelines in coordination with RWAs by creating minutes of each meeting and circulating them.
- The above minutes should be reviewed at DC level periodically with the concerned RWAs/senior officers of departments, if necessary, to ensure strict timely implementation.
- Bhagidari meetings should be held every three months in every assembly segment and concerned MLAs and councillors should also attend the meetings.
- Police, MCD staff, Jal Boards, and electricity authorities may be instructed to get in touch with the office-bearers of RWAs.
- Bhagidari representatives of RWA/senior citizens should be given due recognition by all government agencies.

- RWAs/MTAs should be involved in all decision-making bodies so as to increase their effectiveness and upgrade the quality of the partnership.
- Kindly provide at least ₹5 lakhs at the disposal of RWA and the work may be executed through DJB or MCD keeping in view the urgency of work; and the work may be completed within the stipulated period.
- All the development work in the colony should be done out of the allocated funds of councillors, in consultation with RWA. The resident ward committee of the area may be constituted urgently so that the RWAs may also be able to participate in the development of the area and also know the total expenditure incurred in the area.
- Suggestions may be sought from RWAs throughout the year.
- There should be joint, public and concerned officials, forum/blog on social-networking sites.
- Monthly meeting of RWAs with the concerned officials should happen on regular basis.
- Bhagidari website to be updated regularly with names, telephone numbers of Bhagidari office-bearers, as well as concerned authorities of civic agencies.
- New projects' preparation should be consulted with Bhagidari Association and shared at the Web site of Bhagidari (with specimen project online).
- Regular meeting of Bhagidar Association with departments of the concerned area.
- Space should be provided for organizing activities for senior citizens at community centers, and so on.
- Responsibilities of officers should be fixed.
- Joint meeting of RWA/MLA councillor of the concerned area should be held at least once in a month about the development of the area.
- Monthly meeting at the level of SDM/DC should be held and steps should be taken to make it more effective by fixing responsibility of the nodal officer, and the outcome should be conveyed to the RWAs in writing.
- Nodal officers from each department must come in the next meeting with data on timeframe for the completion of the work on issues raised in the preceding meeting.
- Accountability concept should be introduced to check absence of nodal officers and non-completion of work in the given timeframe.

- Frequent organization of workshops.
- Proper intimation/information should be given to the local RWAs and concerned departments about district-level meetings.
- Involve others: welfare societies, NGOs, trusts, and Senior Citizens Federation.
- Frequent meetings with—councillors, MLAs, respective MPs, departmental heads, and CM.
- Important: Minutes of the meetings to be recorded and circulated in respective areas.
- Bhagidari meetings should be held at regular intervals with MoM and Action Taken Report on previous MoM.
- The district level meeting should be decentralized in a smaller group for effective resolution.
- Bhagidari means partnership between government and public but public does not have any power and with no power, there is no Bhagidari, it is waste of time money and energy.
- Social scientists should be employed for long-term solutions.
- Interaction should be made possible in smaller groups for greater effectiveness of all system.
- Lack of effective coordination among the implementation agencies causes delay in successful works.
- The officers dealing with Bhagidari system should be fully involved and provide full guidance to RWAs, and so on.
- Registration process for Bhagidari should be uploaded on Delhi government's Web site and an exclusive Web site should be created for all members and government officers, this site should be more interactive and transparent like Facebook.
- All issues raised by RWAs and individuals must be resolved in a given time period like RTI 2005. Complaint center should be created with phone, fax, and email so that all complaints are comfortably lodged for action within maximum 15 days.
- Regular follow up action on the points made in the monthly Bhagidari meetings with the HoDs being made personally responsible.
- The concerned officials should be directed to have positive attitude in performance of their duties and to maintain cordial relation with the RWAs.
- Time-bound committee should be there for the completion of every job requested by RWAs.
- Such effective workshops may be held twice in a year so as to have interaction with government agencies.

- Mechanism of redressing grievances by RWAs. It may be given priority in the workshop and RWAs should be informed through Action Taken Reports by the concerned departments.
- The number of projects on which expenditure under My Delhi I Care Scheme can be incurred should be increased.
- In case any project submitted by any RWA under My Delhi I care Scheme is rejected, this should be by a written order giving valid reasons and with a provision for appeal.
- Members of the Bhagidari must be consulted at the time of upward revision of water and sewerage charges.
- Representatives of DDA must participate in such Bhagidari meetings.
- Officers of participating departments should meet in RWA meetings periodically.
- Actions Taken Report should be given by the concerned departments.
- Directory indicating location of the office and officer's name and telephone should be given to RWAs and display boards should be placed in each area on the pattern of NDMC.
- Bhagidari schemes should be displayed in each area boards, or literature should be sent to the RWAs.
- A mechanism to fix accountability on issues agreed should be evolved and feedback to Bhagidars through minutes of meetings (MoM) should be given.
- There should be proper monitoring or transparency regarding the funds sanctioned/spent on My Delhi I Care Scheme.
- Coordination committee to monitor this with members of RWAs also.
- In the meeting of current Bhagidari workshop, also discuss about the previous issues—whether they have been solved or not.

North-west District (June 27, 2012)

- For the effectiveness of Bhagidari please make RWAs aware about concerned officers of the departments for proper coordination, so that RWAs can take up the development work with the right authority.
- Regular interaction between the concerned authority and officers of the Bhagidari Cell with RWA should be arranged.

- Developmental fund should be allocated to the RWAs directly out of the MLA fund and councillor fund allocated for the development of the area.
- RWA office to be established in each block and considerable fund/ grant to be given to RWA, this will help department/MCD work.
- Councillor/MLA must listen to us. At present, they are working commercially, working against RWA by congesting road, illegal floor construction, and increasing pollution units in block.
- A community center in KP Block Pitampura.
- Pay and Use Toilet in DDA District Park, Pitampura.
- Removal of slum cluster from GP Block Pitampura.
- More and more participation should be encouraged may be through government and elected representatives.
- Public should be made aware of work done through Bhagidari.
- The RWAs are facing difficulty in running their offices without any office accommodation. There should be a provision of proper office accommodation as well as funds from the Bhagidari Fund so that RWAs can run their show effectively. Senior citizen RWA, CP Block, Pitampura, Delhi is facing this problem for the last four years, at least portable cabin should be provided to them.
- Whatever suggestions are given by the RWAs should be considered seriously by the concerned department. Follow-up action must be ensured and the concerned RWA should be intimated about the progress from time to time.
- Field work should be given more importance than the paper work.
- Maximum information should be displayed on the notice boards of the concerned offices.
- Office-bearers of the RWAs may be invited separately to discuss the problem.
- RWAs should be intimated about the works executed in the area.
- Meeting should be colony-wise with the officer or representatives of ministry.
- MLA or councillor should make a visit monthly to the colony.
- Police department should remain in touch with the RWA for security purpose.
- Minimum funds must be allotted to each every RWA of northwest district out of increased fund of ₹5 crores under My Delhi I Care Fund. It is observed that some influential RWAs are pocketing a lion's share of this fund.

- Monthly meetings with different departments of Delhi Government with the representative of RWAs.
- To involve representatives of RWAs in formulating proposals for development of the area.
- To strengthen RWAs to curb/check defacement of government properties—illegal garbage/malba dumping on the roads/drains, and so on, as well as encroachments.
- RWAs and Bhagidari officers should discuss solutions with each other.
- Resolve issues on ground level.
- RWA should put problems/solutions on the Web site of the Bhagidari.
- There should be bimonthly meetings of RWA at local level, and area-wise, at district level twice in a year.
- Action taken on the suggestion/problems should be intimated by the concerned department by mail to each RWA.
- Proper coordination between Bhagidari and local bodies along with RWA.
- RWAs should be allotted some funds for petty works to avoid delays.
- There should be some recreation place/programs for senior citizens and ladies.
- Quarterly meetings should be organized through Bhagidari along with local bodies for implementation of the activities.
- RWAs should be given some office place to have regular meetings.
- Meetings should be organized between the members of RWAs and representatives of all local bodies/departments in the societies/colonies premises. They should visit the site, work out problem solving plan and agree on the time-bound plan of action at least once a year.
- Provide regular feedback to all concerned on such agreed projects, including the local municipal councillor.
- RWAs should be involved in the plans/projects of government, MCD, and other departments in detail and these should be discussed with concerned RWAs; and regular meeting with MLA and ministers should be held with RWAs.
- Serious efforts required for implementations of the suggestions given by RWAs in the meetings of Bhagidari and by other mode, that is, letters/e-mail, and so on.
- There should be coordination among all departments.
- There should be incentive scheme for employees with 360° appraisal.

- Frequency of Bhagidari meetings should increase—at least quarterly, and a follow-up action on issues raised in such meetings should be taken.
- Most of the day to day problems are being faced by women, so participation of women should be increased.
- Regular meeting of RWAs with different government departments.
- Different welfare schemes should be widely publicized for outreach and increased participation of public.
- Government agencies, for example, DJB, MCD, police, and so on are not holding their meetings regularly, Bhagidari Cell of government should monitor it to make it more effective.
- Meetings with RWAs must be presided over by higher officers to make it more effective.
- Problems discussed in Bhagidari meetings and their solutions must be placed online for better results.
- Work report of the action taken by officials and discussion with local bodies individually time to time.
- Bhagidari meetings may be held quarterly on ward basis with local MLA, councillor, PWD, Jal Board, MCD, officials, and RWA, district-level Bhagidari workshop should be held annually.
- Participation of ladies and young team members should be encouraged.
- Mini Bhagidari should be planned quarterly in RWA area.
- One directory of concerned officers' phones, districts-wise, should be provided to RWAs and vice versa.
- Regular meeting should be conducted between RWAs and officers of all concerned department.
- RWAs should be involved at the stage of planning of development projects in their areas.
- All development projects in the colony should be planned with RWA (society). On completion No Objection Certificate to be obtained from RWA before making payments and contractors who shirk work after acceptance of tender should be blacklisted.
- Police and government authorities should first control and contain encroachments on government lands. Thereafter, remove all unauthorized encroachments at the earliest sincerely.
- Each Bhagidar should be issued the unique number and identity card and be accorded a protocol status whereby the office/officer that she/he approaches should be obliged to respond to him/her in proper manner to resolve the problem brought forward.
- All regional officers should have the list and contacts of Bhagidars in their area and they should invariably be called and involved

in all important meetings/workshops regarding the development activities in the area.

- Effective implementation of points suggested during Bhagidari meeting and result should be given by DC (revenue) of the district.
- Monthly meeting should be held with all civic agencies and RWAs representative.
- During meeting/review, the progress of previous meeting and problems faced to execute any work should be clarified in the meeting.
- There should be a computerized and centralized number for lodging any complaint with any authority.
- Time gap between complaint and job done by the authority should be tabulated by RWAs and be presented in Bhagidari meeting.
- Exclusive Bhagidari Cell in each department.
- High-level task force for implementation of suggestions/decisions as per merit.
- MCD, Delhi Police, and DDA, these three departments do not convene the monthly meeting of Bhagidari.
- MLA and councillors and concerned officers do not take remedial steps to solve grievances; Action Taken Report should be submitted invariably to DC office.
- ₹5,000 per month should be given to each registered RWA for small work of maintenance of park.
- MCD is not providing cleanliness in the area. This type of service may be started with the help of RWAs as Department of Environment has given its work of maintenance of parks to respective RWAs; all the occupied parks by RWA are green and having good arrangement of plants and grass.
- Senior citizens may kindly be provided recreation facilities and a place where they can get information.
- The contact numbers of various office-bearers and authorities involved with Bhagidari must be provided to all association members of Bhagidari.
- The elected representatives (MLA/councillor) should meet the Bhagidari associations of their areas regularly to identify the problems faced by them and to take up the same with various government agencies.
- Frequent meetings may be held for better communication with each other in a very positive manner.
- RWA should come forward with best possible suggestions along with the solution for rectification.

- Participation of all the interested groups including RWA should be ensured.
- Problems identified should be sorted out effectively.
- At least one workshop on monthly basis may be organized amongst all the Bhagidari members and local authorities, that is, MCD, PWD, DJB, Delhi Police, discoms, DTC, Education Department, Revenue Department of the concerned districts/zone. The contact numbers of the local authorities may also be provided to the RWA/Bhagidari members for making regular interactions.
- The grant/aid sanctioned by the government to the MLA and councillor of the concerned area for development of the same may be intimated to the RWAs/Bhagidari members for proper utilization of the same. RWAs may also be granted some funds to meet the exigencies.
- Action Taken Report by the departments for implementation of the suggestion by RWA to the DC.
- We senior citizens, more than 75 years old, are feeling very difficult to deposit house tax. MCD should make arrangements in our colony to collect the same.
- Some power should be delegated to RWAs to make it effective in Bhagidari.
- RWAs' consent should be taken by government officials regarding development work and other important issues.
- RWAs' complaints/suggestions should be taken up on priority basis.
- Regular meeting with RWA should take place at the district and subdivision level.
- Active participation of nodal agencies in the meeting with RWAs.
- Ensuring timely execution of work by district authority or MLA or councillor.
- The partnership of RWA should be strengthened in all decisions taken by authority.
- Bhagidari scheme is a welcome step but there is hardly any ownership by the various departments who do not care to keep contact with the associations. RWA suggestions should be honored.
- There should be a countercheck by the registrar of societies on progress of existing registered RWAs. Multiplicity of RWAs in the area is not helpful.
- Response of the concerned department on the suggestion made by RWAs should be intimated in writing or through the periodical meeting.

- Meetings between RWAs are not being held periodically and on regular basis particularly in Delhi Police and MCD. It is suggested that the meetings should be held on regular basis and periodically.
- All civil authorities should hold periodical meetings with office-bearers like the way NDPL is already doing.
- Agenda of Bhagidari workshop should be sent to RWA at least 15 days before the date of workshop to enable them to give a serious and considerate thought before coming.
- More and more RWAs and senior citizens groups should be associated with Bhagidari.
- These RWAs and senior citizens groups should be provided with facilities and regular quarterly meetings should be held by DCs and local administration with them.
- Various agencies like MCD, DJB, NDPL, DP, and so on should invite RWAs periodically with problems and suggestions to be incorporated and implemented.
- The departments should call two to three area RWAs at a time and not all, otherwise it makes the whole activity and its result negative.

East District (June 28, 2012)

- System should be evolved to ensure road repair work within timeframe.
- Regular Bhagidari meetings should be held.
- There should be regular Bhagidari meetings at district level which should by attended by senior officers of various departments who can take decisions in the meeting itself. Genuine demands from RWAs for My Delhi I Care Fund should be accepted.
- CCTVs should be installed at important points on the request of RWAs in order to check the incidence of thefts and unwanted activities in the area.
- In order to make Bhagidari more effective, any request/grievance received from RWA/MTA must be looked into through some coordinator to redress it in a time-bound manner, and Bhagidari schemes should be propagated widely.
- A copy of each work order should be given to RWAs and after completion of work the contractor should take NOC from RWAs.
- Every registered RWA/federation as per their strength of membership/area should be allocated funds from My Delhi I care or other sources.

- Monthly meetings should be held regularly by each department with RWAs viz. BSES, MCD, DJB, Police, DDA, Education, Transport, and DC (E) which are presently lacking.
- Issues discussed and agreed to must invariably be implemented.
- Leaves/twigs of bushes, trees, and overgrown grass when cut are burnt by *malis* (gardeners) of Horticulture Department of MCD contributing to further pollution of environment, instead of composting them in pits to produce manure. This bad practice should be stopped.
- New developments in the area should be brought to the knowledge of RWAs for more effectiveness/awareness.
- Bhagidari workshop should be organized more frequently.
- Transparency is needed in full system. More funds should be available for RWAs to improve the basic service in the area.
- Regular meetings with local authorities and reviews.
- Complaints of the citizens should be viewed seriously and Action Taken Report should be communicated.
- Regular meetings may be conducted by the respective department with RWAs.
- It has proved to be an effective instrument for taking people closer to the government.
- It has helped RWAs, federations, senior citizens/MTAs to participate in decision-making by the government and to give good recognition to the citizens of Delhi.
- Transparency in distribution of funds from the DC office to the RWAs/federation/MTAs, and group of senior citizens of east district.
- Most of the concerned offices and different departments are not attending the Bhagidari meeting.
- RWA and Bhagidari Cell should exchange good and bad experiences in the area.
- List of subjects covered under Bhagidari scheme should be enlisted and distributed among citizens.
- Regular meeting of Bhagidars every two months with all concerned by Deputy Commissioner office, where all nodal officers should be present.
- Suggestion of RWAs should be given priority in the works/projects to be undertaken in the area and the same should be informed.
- Meeting should be held with RWAs in jurisdiction of respective SDM concerned. Concerned officers must be present in the meeting to take necessary action.

- Action Taken Report should be prepared and sent to all RWAs of the jurisdiction. Wherever action has not been taken in any matter, the reason for not doing so should be communicated to the concerned RWAs.
- Bhagidari meeting should be held at various places with about 10 RWAs instead of DC office, and proceedings should be seriously followed up.
- List of employee of civic authorities with contact details, working in the colonies should be provided to RWAs for better and effective results.
- Provision of a functional office for RWAs should be included in My Delhi I Care Fund.
- Local ward development committee is formed to formulate norms for development/improvement and implementation of decisions taken for the area.
- Participation of MCD councillor be made mandatory who will be ex-officio chairperson of the said ward committee. This will help in effectiveness of Bhagidari meetings.
- Regular Bhagidari meeting at DC's office should be held, which should be represented by RWAs and representatives of departments; Action Taken Report should be circulated to all concerned.
- Computer with printer should be issued to all RWAs for office use under My Delhi I Care Funds.
- Delhi has been divided into wards. So ward-wise citizen–government partnership should be arranged for better results in improving Delhi as a whole.
- Regular interaction as mentioned below will definitely give better results: CM—twice in a year, MP—quarterly in a year, MLA—once in a month, and councillor—in two weeks.
- Meetings should be more regular.
- Better coordination among the government bodies/units.
- All the departments which come under Bhagidari should visit the respective areas of RWAs and should conduct meetings.
- There should be coordination among the executives and RWA for development works.
- The RWA should be consulted for expenditure and RWA should also certify the work done.
- Formulating and enabling the Bhagidari scheme on Facebook that may improve effectiveness by involving techo-friendly users of particular RWA.

- To widen the area of Bhagidari, elected representatives of each municipal ward and SHO (area) should be involved followed by monthly meetings at area police station.
- Updating of records of citizen groups/RWA every year as per their elections, audit of accounts, and replacement of names by new office-bearers.
- Officers to be responsive and regular meetings at nodal officer level in each department and district-level meetings on unresolved issues once in three months.
- Where there are small RWAs/citizen groups, these should be merged to form bigger groups.
- There should be coordination among the executive of government agency and RWA for development works.
- The RWA should be consulted for experience and RWA should also certify the work done.
- Time and again in the Bhagidari meetings at various levels, it has been suggested that RWA groups should be involved at the planning and implementation stage but this is not being done.
- Bhagidari meetings in DC office should be held in the pre-lunch period instead of 3:30 p.m.; meeting in post-lunch period during peak summer is nothing but punishment to senior citizens.
- All concerned officers should be present from all respective departments at Bhagidari meetings and Action Taken Reports should be communicated to all Bhagidar's within the specific periods.
- Bhagidari meetings should be held at regular interval on regular basis. Team Delhi member may be allowed to meet decision-making officials on priority basis to solve the problems.
- Meeting should be held with RWAs on monthly basis with different departments in a continuing way to solve and focus on the problem; this will increase the effectiveness of Bhagidari.
- There are many departments who do not treat RWA in proper way and also do not listen to the problem. It should be improved by making a complaint-redressal department.
- RWA meeting should be held two times in a year.
- RWA meeting should be assembly-wise with the department authority and two times in a year.
- Quantum of fund allocated under Bhagidari Scheme should be earmarked for respective RWAs.
- President/General Secretary under Bhagidari should be identified entity with all Delhi government departments.

- Regular meeting of Bhagidari should be held with every government department, senior officers, councillors, MLAs, and MPs, and also a special phone and address directory of Delhi government's Administration Department should be brought out.
- Give priority to active RWA president in core committee, like— community hall, schools, and hospitals, and so on.
- Time limit should be specified for each and every complaint and the Action Taken Report should also be provided at each and every level to respective complainant (RWA).
- There should be a meeting within a month with RWA at their locality.
- It must also be ensured that DDA also takes part in Bhagidari workshops.
- There must also be Bhagidari Workshops with individual government departments.
- The officers of the concerned department must visit the concerned area to sort out the problems at least once in 45 days.
- My Delhi I Care Fund should be provided on RWA's request for developing its area's small needs. Thanks for increasing the fund.
- Effective participation of RWAs in Bhagidari meetings with positive suggestion/contribution.
- More female participation is required in Bhagidari meetings.
- Encouragement of RWAs meetings at zonal level, and RWAs should be educated about the procedures of government department through short-term training.
- Financial power of government officers should be enhanced to execute emergency works for resolving the problems of residents.
- The ambit of Bhagidari scheme should be made crystal clear.
- The meeting should be issue specific and a mechanism should be devised for its assessment.
- Aggressive grassroots implementation of Bhagidari schemes.
- Majority of publicity should be in Hindi as Bhagidari is beneficial to all strata of society.

North-east District (June 29, 2012)

- There should be a meeting of Bhagidari Cell with SDM every month so that there is direct interaction between the government and the citizens.

- A senior officer of Bhagidari Cell, Delhi government should be posted in SDM's office for better relations between the government and RWA.
- Development works should be started in unauthorized colonies with the help of RWAs. RWAs should be given authority and fund for these development works in the colony.
- My Delhi I Care Fund should be executed in unauthorized colonies in order to address urgent problems, so that citizens through RWA get associated with the government.
- Regular, more and more meetings should be held at small intervals.
- All concerned officials should be present during the meeting.
- Members of RWAs should educate the area residents so as to not harm government property.
- A federation of RWAs should be made in which one or two representatives of different departments/government offices should be there, who will work towards finding solutions to the problems of the district.
- Generally, it is seen that the members of RWAs are mostly men and senior citizens who are unable to represent the society completely. Therefore, it is suggested that an RWA which has representation from all age, gender, and caste/religion should be given accreditation.
- Only one RWA in a colony should be registered and its responsibility should be ensured.
- From time to time, RWA members should be given short-term training about the departmental working system.
- The suggestions and problems given in Bhagidari workshops should be properly addressed and resolved.
- Special attention should be given to the facilities provided through Bhagidari by the government.
- Bhagidari should not be limited to meetings alone. Acute burning problems should be looked into and resolved by the officials of Bhagidari and the public on the spot.
- North-east district in Delhi is the most undeveloped area in regard to civic amenities. Bhagidari officials should take action in this direction and improve civic amenities.
- Each government department should hold a meeting with RWA in their office or in RWA office and inform RWA about the development work that has been done by them and invite suggestions from them.

- RWAs should also be kept informed about the benefits of the plans and work that Delhi government undertakes from time to time, for citizens' facilities (and not limited to the departments alone) in order to ensure citizen–government partnership.
- A joint help center should be made in each district, which will take forward the complaints to the concerned departments.
- RWAs should be given authority to use funds through Bhagidari.
- Meetings should be organized between RWAs and Delhi government or MCD, Delhi Police, and other departments.
- In order to achieve good coordination between RWA and the area SHO, Delhi government should consider making new policies and implement them.
- In order to properly conduct the Bhagidari meeting, all department officials should be called regularly in the monthly meeting in DC office, as was being done previously.
- All departments should organize monthly RWA meetings of their areas and send feedback report to SDM.
- SDM should also organize monthly meetings of the RWAs in which all departments should participate.
- The planning for development works of each colony should be done in collaboration with RWA representatives.
- Information about government's development plans and public interest works should be given to RWA from time to time.
- Area officials can make colony-level development work much easier by contacting colony members who are part of Bhagidari.
- Public interest works in the My Delhi I Care Fund, other than 14 works already given should be included. Partnership should be fixed for all RWAs of the area and a few special RWAs only should not be allocated funds.
- The response by the concerned department to problems raised by RWAs during the Bhagidari meeting should be given in writing.
- Each department, at its level, should hold monthly meeting with the RWA.
- All rules and regulations of Bhagidari should be such that they continue even after change of governments.
- All departments should listen to the complaints of RWA members and try to solve them immediately.
- Every month an RWA meeting should be held with SDM in which officials should be present.
- RWA should have constitutional authority so that officials are bound to listen to RWA representatives and find solutions to their problems.

- Once in a month one meeting of RWA representatives should be with the people's elected representatives (MLA and councillor).
- Government should introduce RWAs in all its departments.
- Monthly meeting of different government departments should be started again.
- We never know about the action taken on our suggestions. The completion of work should be time-bound and under intimation to RWA.
- Government should pass orders to the department officials that they should coordinate with the citizens who are working under Bhagidari scheme, so that government schemes reach people.
- The DC of the district should hold a meeting in the last week of the month with all RWAs and give them guidelines.
- Bhagidari Cell of Delhi government should give some rights to RWAs along with duties, so that the concerned departments increase their efficiency by respecting RWAs.
- All departments should first complete their correction-work and keep contact with RWA office-bearers before making/repairing lanes and roads, so that government money is saved and can be used in other development works. After completing the work, they should take satisfactory report from the RWA president/general secretary.
- The areas which are not developed should be given more budget by the government, and not those areas where all facilities are available. Government should provide equal facilities to all citizens.
- Government officials through Bhagidari, from time to time, should listen to RWAs suggestions/issues respectfully.
- Bhagidari Fund should be allocated impartially and later on government should audit it.
- Bhagidari meeting should be held at the district level once in every three months.
- RWAs permission should be made compulsory by Delhi government for incurring expenditure on that area's development work.
- Some funds should be given to each RWA to function properly.
- All work in the area should be done under the supervision of RWA.
- Any work of the area should be first endorsed by RWA so that it is done properly.
- Effective solutions to problems of RWAs should be brought about by holding a meeting of concerned departments and the RWA office-bearers.

- Problems of RWAs should be resolved by holding a meeting of local public servants like MLAs, MPs, and MCD councillors; RWAs should be provided with some funds to carry out developmental work.
- Each month a Bhagidari meet should be organized at the ward level/assembly level.
- Arrangement such as Aap Ki Sunwai should be made at the DC level.
- Each department of Delhi government should hold a meeting with RWA and resolve their problems.
- RWA members should have a say in all government offices such as hospitals, police station, DC office, schools, and so on.
- By regularizing unauthorized colonies and giving fundamental citizen's facilities, accelerate development of Delhi.
- Meeting of the Bhagidari Cell should be held on a holiday so that government employee associated with an RWA can also participate.
- Action taken/not taken on the applications of RWAs sent to the SDM or DC offices for the development of their area should be given in writing.
- SDM or DC should assess the development of the area from time to time and resolve the given problems.
- RWAs should be given constitutional rights.
- Forms for Ration Card, old-age pension, widow pension, handicapped pension, and identification card should be made available to RWAs so that they can help people of the area.
- Arrangements should be made to invite all office-bearers of the RWA to the workshop through telephone, post, or any other alternative.
- Every RWA should be given some primary rights.
- The top-team members of Bhagidari along with RWA president and general secretary take a zone-wise tour of the area once in six months and give an impartial summary of the Delhi government works to CM office.
- RWA office-bearer should be able to meet directly the officers at CM residence in the event of any complaint concerning Bhagidari.
- Bhagidari Cell should have an e-mail ID so that RWA can give information online about a problem or suggestion. Provide financial support to RWAs.
- It is necessary to respond to the problems/suggestions raised by RWAs/Bhagidars. Instructions should be given to all officials and employees to listen to RWAs and act upon them.

- A meeting with all RWAs in SDM office should be held every month, and a copy of decision taken duly signed by all RWA representatives should be sent to CM office regularly.
- The Action Taken Report on the decisions taken in the monthly meeting should be circulated in detail in the next meeting. Then only the decision on next issues should be taken.
- Important meetings of RWA are held from time to time which are attended by senior officials also. Therefore, to hold such meetings, RWAs should be provided with space, if available, in the nearest community center.
- A public help desk of the concerned government department should be arranged for people of each assembly area of north-east district.
- RWAs should be given some rights to get work done on their own in their colony just like village heads.
- Government officials should attend to the problems of RWAs immediately and if possible the area SDM should contact RWA and try to resolve their problems in the area itself.
- If a registered society with Bhagidari raises the area problem then the same should be resolved immediately. This will strengthen people's partnership with government.
- The meeting with the registered RWA should be held in the presence of their area officials so that problems could be resolved quickly and Bhagidari is strengthened.
- Advice of concerned RWA should be taken at the time of planning each development work of the colony, its implementation and completion.
- Online communication should be ensured between government and the RWA and the feedback of the same should be sent to RWA once in a week.
- RWA role in administration should be strengthened so that small schemes and works such as Ration Card, proof of caste, pension, and so on can be easily done and the public gets benefit of these schemes.
- RWA should be given fund to get small-level works done in the colony quickly, such as repair of hand-pump, dustbin, water tap, motor in the parks, and expenditure on RWA office.
- Citizen–government partnership should be increased so that all can avail of its benefits.
- An all inclusive committee of all RWAs in an assembly area should be formed and MLA should be its chairman.

- A meeting of the registered RWA members with the government officials should be held at the assembly level.
- The concerned department should provide a copy of the work order of the construction work to the RWA Samiti.
- All officials of the departments under Bhagidari should hold a meeting with RWA presidents or office-bearers about their problems once in three weeks.
- With establishment of coordination between RWA and government officials, decisions on very important development works should be taken.
- All RWAs should be provided with officers' names, designations, office addresses, and phone numbers of all departments like electricity, water, cleanliness, health, education, and transport. Immediate action should be taken on complaints of RWAs.
- Arrangements should be made for starting Bhagidari meeting (RWA) at the station level in which all concerned department officials are present. A meeting of all RWAs coming under one police station should be held once a month.
- A Bhagidari meeting with the departments of DC/Police Department/Power/Municipal Corporation and Jal Board should be held for taking appropriate action.
- For improvement, all government department officials should be directed to hold area-wise meeting with RWAs from time to time.
- RWAs of the area should sit together in a meeting and take action as per decision taken. North-east area should not be ignored and development plans should be made for the same.
- A compiled report should be circulated about the suggestions given in the meetings of the DC office.
- Bhagidari meetings with RWA office-bearers and members should be held once in a month in which solutions to all problems of the district can be found after consultation.
- In the next meeting, information on the action taken/solutions to problems should be given to RWA office-bearers.
- RWA meeting should be held with all officials of the district.
- The solutions to complaints and actions on suggestions should be done at the earliest and information on the same should be given to RWA and Bhagidari Cell.
- RWAs role should be ensured in the work done by the government for the benefit of people in the colony. The financial assistance that the Core Committee provides should be given to RWA directly and the same should be examined and audited by Delhi government.

- Effective plan for constructing roads, drains, and concerning encroachment should be made in consultation with all the departments and RWAs.
- Copy of action taken by RWA and department officials should be provided to RWA and department for their necessary action.
- DC should be invited in every meeting of the RWA.
- In order to undertake development/solutions of the area, presence of the top government officials, MLAs and councillors is necessary in the monthly meeting of the RWA office-bearers.
- In the Bhagidari, government officials should sit with members of RWA on one table and try to solve the problems of the area in consultation with each other and give information on the action taken to RWA office-bearers for their record.
- All RWAs should be given development fund under Bhagidari as is given to councillors and MLAs.
- In order to make citizen–government partnership more effective, all department officials should have coordination with RWA members so that each and every RWA can relate the problems of its area to the department officials and find solutions to them.
- Meeting of the SDM with department officials and the members of the RWA should be made regular and mandatory, in which time-bound solutions to problems should be found.
- All institutions of Delhi government should be associated with Bhagidari and all should be instructed that they have a meeting with RWA once a month and inform the RWAs about their future plans and schemes.
- Funds should be made available in time in order to make Bhagidari effective.
- Officers should be made answerable for implementing the schemes so that there is no laxity of any kind.
- RWAs' rights and budget should be increased.
- Regular meeting with local officials and response to complaints and suggestions should be ensured.

South District (July 3, 2012)

- There should be effective coordination in solving the day-to-day problems between civic agencies and RWAs/residents.
- Participation of youth in Bhagidari.
- Proper and effective representation of RWAs in district advisory committees.

- Funds utilized by coordinator and MLAs for development should be released in consultation with RWAs.
- The regular camps of Bhagidari are required in different colonies along with the responsible government officers so that collective or individual problems can be solved on the spot.
- My Delhi I Care Fund should be distributed quickly (within a month), so that the scheme can be started early.
- Number of gender resource centers should be increased with trained staff.
- District vigilance committee under the chairmanship of concerned MLA should have at least one member from RWA.
- In order to improve the effectiveness of Bhagidari, frequent review of functioning of acts and bylaws of the organizations should be done to meet the day-to-day challenges.
- Public awareness must be created at a large scale and transparency in organization's workings through frequent meetings with the members of RWAs and all government departments should be maintained.
- Consent of RWA members of VKS Government School should be taken for all the rules of government school regarding admissions, proper functioning, and other infrastructure problems of the schools.
- RWAs should have a say with the government in removal of encroachment, bad elements around the schools, and insist for good water supply and sanitation around the schools.
- Financial partnership with RWA for petty works of the colony.
- Any development work must be sanctioned in consultation with the RWA and after completion of work; NOC should be issued by RWA.
- Before implementation of various schemes like increasing water bills, electricity, and so on development schemes should be pre-consulted with the core committee of district Bhagidari like a participation in management.
- All the work/project sanctioned should be endorsed through concerned RWA of area to keep a watch.
- To nominate one person as a Bhagidari coordinator from each of the departments, for example, DDA, DJB, BSES, and so on for day-to-day work.
- The meeting should be conducted with these officials once in a month.
- Provide funds to RWAs for development work.

- All government official/staff must give respectful consideration to RWAs and solve their problem.
- Personal interest must be taken by all government officials.
- Complaints must be attended to immediately and reply, if possible, should be given on phone.
- Frequency of meeting should be increased between RWAs and government departments.
- Educate common man/students about Bhagidari.
- Regular interaction between RWA and government agencies.
- Issues raised by RWA should be resolved promptly.
- Efforts must be made to provide special facilities to senior citizens like recreation club or *barat ghar* (hall for marriage) or *chopal ghar* (hall for meeting of local bodies).
- RWA should share responsibilities for proper implementation of welfare schemes especially the broad schemes like Pension and Laadli Scheme by informing the department about needy poor persons of the community or about death of any pensioners, if any.
- A quarterly meeting with RWAs for mutual exchange of views.
- Schemes/suggestions submitted should be implemented.
- Main problems faced by residents are broken roads, broken pavements, clogged sewers, and storm water drains.
- Streetlights need replacement and repair.
- Community hall required for residents.
- Regularity in holding Bhagidari meetings.
- Divide south zone into smaller manageable groups of RWAs.
- Time-bound delivery of services and its notification by DC's office.
- Time-bound delivery—designate Bhagidari coordinator for better response, action, and continuity.
- Proper coordination and interaction with RWAs by concerned departments implementing Bhagidari schemes.
- Funds should be allowed in urban villages and unauthorized colonies under Bhagidari schemes.
- All RWAs should be involved in implementing the schemes.
- Most of the time there is no action on the complaints so it is requested that CM should personally look into some of the complaints to see what action has been taken by the department.
- There should be regular interaction with the DC/SDM and the police authorities (DCP).
- Presence of officials in Bhagidari meetings is very important. This should be improved.

- Parking facilities should be drastically improved.
- We suggest that to improve communication and accountability there should be a meeting at least every one month by way of visit of executive engineer of each service provider like MCD, horticulture, and DJB.
- Performance of each department should be uploaded on internet and should be supported by feedback from RWAs.
- Government should support RWA for organizing meetings in the office of the colony for empowering the citizens.
- The improvement of Bhagidari scheme can be effectively done by direct interaction with concerned officer/department about the complaint/grievances made by RWA representative.
- Discussion with local officer—MLA should be present during the discussion for solution of the problems. Remedies can be provided at the earliest with more meetings between officers and MLA.
- Bhagidari cells should be formed in each area.
- Bigger and better publicity of Bhagidari movement is required so as to reach the public more readily.
- To explain Bhagidari partnership to all RWAs, societies, senior citizen associations, and other associations.
- Funds sanctioned should be used in maximum for up-keeping of societies, RWA, and so on.
- Bhagidari Cell should visit colonies to find if the assigned projects have been executed. This review should take place along with RWA president/secretary for basic amenities, for example, water, power, and cleanliness, bridges, environment of the colony.
- There should be coordination between the officers of the area and the members of RWA; and the list of names, phone numbers, and designations of Bhagidari officers should be shared.
- There should be monthly meeting with RWA and officers of the areas.
- RWA to be taken into confidence and made aware of the work order for their area.
- RWA to be authorized to take sample of cement mix and bitumen mix for roads and send in sealed envelopes for testing in labs.
- Horticulture department to work with more efficiency, and prune trees within 15 days of request/complaint and report back under intimation to DC.
- Sewage lines (new) caving in—no action being taken.
- Dispensary required in SJ enclave area.
- Action Taken Report may kindly be given to local area RWAs.

- RWAs to be made aware of their duties. Government support should be only for those RWAs who are following rules and regulations related to RWA.
- The frequency of Bhagidari should be four times a year so the RWA will have maximum interaction.
- All the RWAs whether they are registered or not registered should be called.
- The senior citizens and ladies should be given more chance to attend the Bhagidari.
- CM may kindly chair Bhagidari video conference once in three months of our district for monitoring the action taken by various service providers.
- For any work undertaken by various departments in public interest, concerned RWA may please be given a copy of the order and be authorized to monitor the execution of work.
- Meetings of RWAs with the DC should be held at least once in a month to discuss the problems and their solution in the presence of the officials of DJB, PWD, MCD, DDA, Horticulture Department, and Police Department. The minutes of this should be provided to the RWAs and the Bhagidari Cell of Delhi government. Action Taken Report should also be provided to RWAs and Bhagidari Cell.
- The amount sanctioned for projects for any RWA should be utilized within a certain period. How much fund is utilized for the RWA should be reported regularly to the Bhagidari Cell.
- RWA should be recognized by the government.
- RWA should be given power to:
  - ◆ Stop overflowing of water tanks
  - ◆ Ensure disposal of waste after segregation
  - ◆ Report the defaulting members registration
  - ◆ Subscription
  - ◆ Illegal construction
- Prompt consideration/implementation of project proposals especially for basic amenities like water and electricity.
- Regular meetings/interactions with action taken reviewers on problems registered with RWAs.
- To have monthly meetings between RWAs/citizens groups and concerned department, respectively, to review the progress and the problem of developmental projects/programs.
- RWAs/citizens groups and schools to be consulted while formulating social welfare projects and programs.

- Mandatory guidelines are required so as to make the government machinery do all kinds of activities including development/ maintenance work in the area only in consultation with RWAs and under RWAs supervision as well.
- Government officials meet RWAs functionaries in the colony (at least once a month) and take on the spot decisions and ensure implementation to the satisfaction of all stakeholders.
- More financial and administrative powers to be given to RWAs.
- RWA members must be made part of governmental development committees for better coordination.
- Better coordination between civic bodies with RWAs is most essential.
- Continuous monthly meeting in concern district.
- Compulsory participation of local bodies such as DJB, BSES, DP, MCD, administration, and public representative.
- Bhagidari workshops shall be organized on a regular basis on a fixed interval at least quarterly to make it more effective.
- It should not be limited to RWAs, MTAs, or senior citizens but organizers along with the officers shall move to the colonies at least once in a month to know the problems of common mass so that it can be solved then and there if possible or at the earliest.
- Bhagidari participants/RWAs after pointing out the deficiencies should also extend their cooperation as and when required.
- Bhagidari meetings should also be at grassroots level and at short intervals and there should be required follow-ups till resolution.
- RWAs must participate in each and every activity of colonies from planning stage to execution. For example, RWAs must be aware of debris/malba generated from demolition of buildings and other structures, so that responsibility can be fixed for violation of rules/ policies. This will reduce quantum of malba that is being dumped on roads, footpaths, and adjoining parks.
- Bhagidari should make more effective awareness among the local people who know little about this program.
- Funds must be distributed to the RWAs and have rights for spending the funds.
- Schemes launched by Delhi government must be informed to RWAs from time to time in writing.
- Effectiveness of Bhagidari may be enhanced by promoting awareness of citizen charters of the each department.
- Effectiveness may also be increased by placing drop box at post offices/petrol pumps.
- RWAs should educate the residents to avoid wastage of water.

- There should be public interaction programs in different localities so that more and more residents may take part and may express their views for the improvement of Bhagidari.
- A monthly news letter of Bhagidari should please be circulated so that *aam admi* may come to know about the activities.
- My Delhi I Care Fund should be used for constructing water harvesting structures in all parks. No rain water should flow to the storm water drains.
- Bhagidari meetings with deputy commissioner (south) are not effective; since there is no space for the RWAs and officials to sit in the hall. All officials do not attend the meetings.
- All development work to be taken up should be discussed with the RWA.
- Office space should be provided by Delhi government/MCD to the RWAs.
- RWAs should be given power to collect contribution from members for carrying out work in their area, that is, collection of garbage/ security.
- Copies of tender documents of the work to be carried out in the area should be provided to the RWA.
- Effective coordination between government and RWAs before taking any major decisions effecting general public at large.
- New technology of e-mail, SMS should be used to communicate with RWAs.
- RWAs should be given administrative and financial powers to check work of small working agencies—cleaning, horticulture, sewage department, and so on.
- Multiplicity of authorities should be minimized and one nodal authority appointed so that frequent meetings at three months interval with RWAs are held to listen to routine problems.
- In very project, RWAs should be consulted before starting of project and it should be ensured to have completion certificate issued by respective RWAs.
- RWAs should be provided the status of Panchayat through Panchayati Raj Yojana.

South-west District (July 4, 2012)

- In school there should be one chapter on Bhagidari.
- Transparency in utilization of fund in RWAs.

- Sensitization of RWA about their roles and responsibilities.
- To mobilize youth for positive participation.
- By conducting district-level meetings in DC office for better communications/understandings at micro-level.
- Video conferencing should be more frequent to make it public-friendly.
- At every stage of planning and execution, RWAs must be involved.
- Any issue raised by the RWAs must be solved within timeframe.
- Quality of work must be checked by RWAs.
- Involvement of senior citizens and housewives in development works/activities in the area.
- Report of RWAs to be considered on satisfactory completion of work/projects before making payment to contractor.
- Bhagidari meetings should be held monthly and regularly with officers of all concerned government department and RWA and Senior Citizens' Associations in each colony.
- Social Welfare Department should be included in citizen's cluster.
- A joint committee of RWAs government officials and elected representatives to be constituted. To redefine processes to reduce cost and time of work inconveniences to people to improve the quality of life and services.
- Monthly meetings independently with each government department (DJB/MCD/DDA/DC [revenue]) for update.
- Reward must be given to the specific RWAs for the good job they have done.
- RWAs should be involved (including youth of the area) in coordination with the concerned offices of the local area.
- Maximum wide publicity should be given about objects of Bhagidari through newspapers and TV channels to create awareness in the general public.
- Frequency of its meetings should be increased to quarterly at district level and Action Taken Report from all concerned departments should be presented and discussed in the next Bhagidari meeting with clear transparency.
- Higher degree of cooperation as well as coordination by interacting more through Bhagidari workshop/meeting and video conferencing. Core committee meeting should be held at district level.
- Delegation of powers to core committee to use funds.
- Representatives of JJ clusters may also be included in Bhagidari workshop.

- There should be regular meetings of government officer/officers with the RWAs area residents after the workshop so as to solve the problems reported by the residents.
- Transparency and time-bound factor must be considered in solving problems reported during the workshop period.
- There should be regular meetings between DC and his staff and RWAs, with adequate follow-up on the discussion.
- Funds allocated to Bhagidari should be utilized for RWAs needs.
- Workshops under Bhagidari citizen–government partnership are really useful but they should be organized more frequently and more RWAs should be involved.
- Suggestions given at the workshop should be followed up with RWAs. This will improve effectiveness of Bhagidari and people will have more faith in the system.
- Officials should meet quarterly with RWAs to find out problems in locality and to resolve within commitment time.
- Bhagidari should also interfere in law and order situation—police and beat officers' meet with RWAs to improve law and order to minimize crimes.
- Communication/coordination/improvement is required in government agencies and RWAs.
- There should be a Bhagidari coordinator between the government and RWA to execute the desired project within the scope of Bhagidari Scheme and have the fund disbursed and also arrange other necessary clearances—making it a single window clearance like operation.
- Law and order is very poor in our area especially where school children go to school (in our area three schools are there) but no security measures has been taken by local police.
- In every development work RWA must be involved and NOC of work completion must be issued by RWA before making payment to concerned party.
- Bhagidari fund has been increased up to ₹5 crore but we are not able to get information under what heads fund may be utilized.
- Proper coordination with RWA for area development fund of MLA/councillor could be taken with their consent.
- Government official should hold monthly meeting with RWA (Delhi Police, DJB, electricity, transport, MCD, and so on).
- In-charge of Bhagidari local area should provide special time weekly/monthly to RWAs and should not ignore citizen problems

- They should be empowered to recommend action to the government against the erring department/authority.
- RWAs should share responsibility of constraints/problems of departments.
- RWAs should be made accountable and their achievement may also be monitored.
- Bhagidari meeting should be conducted on quarterly basis in SDM office of the area and on half yearly basis in DC office in the area.
- There should be advertising though TV channel of Bhagidari and its effective program.
- Coordination of RWA and Bhagidari should be very regular to improve its effectiveness.
- Mandatory membership of each (regards) RWA.
- Effective and reachable communication system development: Delhi Government–Bhagidari Cell–RWA–residents.
- Tenure of Bhagidari Cell core committee member should be restricted to two years only.
- Interaction between senior officials and RWAs for deciding projects and implementation, and no passing the buck.
- The project should be displayed giving information, that is, projects' name, contractor's name, cost, specification, and time frame for completion, thereafter maintenance.
- RWAs are ineffective since they have no jurisdiction over service providers. RWAs should be empowered.
- General public to be made more aware about Bhagidari through different sources.
- Participation of general public (other than RWA) should be more.
- Expansion of Bhagidari should be up to ward level/zonal level.
- Decisions taken during Bhagidari meetings should be implemented effectively with feedback.
- Multiple RWAs of same locality should be clubbed.
- Three best implementable suggestions from RWA should be rewarded.
- Monthly meeting of Bhagidari should be arranged in the office of the concerned DC/nodal officer with all the RWAs under his jurisdiction and the public representatives of the area.
- As my Delhi I Care Fund has been increased from 50 lakhs to 5 crores, scope of utilization of funds should be widened work-wise as well as fund-wise. There should be transparency in allocation of funds and it should not be restricted to the hands of DCs/nodal officers.

- A monthly meeting between RWA and concerned civic agencies including DJB and BSES should be conducted.
- Action Taken Report should be given to Bhagidari offices.

North District (July 5, 2012)

- The nodal official of various concerned departments must attend the monthly Bhagidari meeting.
- Any development in the area should be executed after taking into confidence the RWA regarding the scope of work.
- The payment to the executing agency should be made after due verification of the work, that is, work has been executed according to the requirement of the RWA.
- The citizens as well as public representatives can be made aware about the complete process/procedure involved in carrying out a work in the area.
- Bhagidari meetings should be held on monthly basis.
- Bhagidari programs should be decentralized up to colony/area level. For more effectiveness, feedback should be taken up in next meeting.
- Bhagidari Cell should have better coordination with the RWAs through which they will be able to know the problems faced by the RWAs.
- If Bhagidari Cell conducts frequent meetings with RWAs, they will be in position to sort out the problems.
- We should conduct the annual workshop as residential program to enable participants to interact with each other during evening on personal level and understanding.
- Bhagidari should be extended for resolving issues between utilities like power, MCD, metro, telephone, police, and so on to serve the citizens better.
- Nameplate of RWA on each table during Bhagidari meeting.
- Previous Bhagidari points: action taken to be shared and suggestions given.
- Issues to be captured in advance from RWA as well as from utilities.
- To hold meetings at regular intervals about feedbacks and suggestion/developments.
- Publicity about Bhagidari programs through display of hoardings/charts, handbills, as well as through visual media.

- Implementation on suggestions received from previous Bhagidari may be made public so that more and more people join Bhagidari.
- Drop boxes may be installed at prominent places.
- To make Bhagidari effective, the DC office is conducting RWAs meeting but the meeting is not regular—it should be conducted regularly at least once a month with participation from all area RWAs and the progress of the work be highlighted.
- The allocated funds from Bhagidari should be used for the development of the RWA and the fund's intimation and allocation should also be circulated to the RWAs.
- Bhagidari meetings will be more effective by regular meetings with RWAs and government department of Delhi.
- Funds given to all districts must be distributed properly to all the RWAs.
- Basic amenities provided by the government and problems raised by the RWA/MTS to the concerned department should be considered immediately. If not done its accountability be fixed under intimation to us.
- Let the district be divided into blocks. Each block should meet on monthly basis, and inter-block meetings should happen on quarterly basis, with districts meetings on yearly basis.
- Let monitoring mechanism be devised on inter-block levels and recognizing symbolically the most active groups.
- Maximum participation of the entire interested group including RWAs, self-help groups, and NGOs should be ensured.
- All suggestions received in the Bhagidari workshop should be noted very seriously and time-bound frame should be made for implementation of the suggestions. Also the respective officers should be made responsible for the same.
- Regular, good, senior participants in Bhagidari should be given a Senior Bhagidari Identity Card in accordance with their long experience and attendance. They should be allowed to participant in the working at the development of Delhi by being advisor in various developments. There by the government would take full advantage of the experience of the senior Bhagidars on the PPP basis.
- Departments participating in Bhagidari workshop should ensure copies of their Citizen Charter and name at least one coordinator/nodal officer.

- Efforts of the nodal officer/coordinator should be recognized and recorded in the ACRs.
- Role and importance of RWAs should be understood by government departments by empowering the RWAs properly.
- As per our experiences, we strongly feel there is very little implementation and redress of our complaints and suggestions in the Bhagidari meetings. Moreover, there is less participation of the officials of the concerned departments. They are mostly not present there.
- We request that it should be mandatory for the concerned departments to attend the meetings and their timely reply/work should be there. There should be disciplinary action taken if they do not adhere to this.
- Bhagidari Cell should be required at district level.
- Maximum participation required of general public.
- Monthly meeting with RWA and local bodies should be convened.
- Some essential items may be distributed among poor through Bhagidari.
- Bhagidari voice should be more effectively heard in all the Delhi government offices.
- A monthly sum should be provided to maintain the RWA office.
- Monthly meeting should be conducted between RWA and participating government official: MCD/Delhi Police/Jal Board, and MLA and MP.
- To assign some more tasks to Bhagidari, including transportation, repair works of hospitals, schools, and so on that are directly in public interest.
- Funds to RWAs should be increased, and by the way of conducting the elections of RWAs of Bhagidari, the working of RWAs should be monitored and funds should be utilized in an optimized manner.
- Projects recommended by RWAs should be implemented on a fast pace.
- Government officials should ensure full participation of the RWA before implementing the project in their respective areas.
- Each department's officers should have a meeting at least once in a month with all office-bearers of all RWAs of that particular area.
- Monthly meeting should be conducted with the MP, MLA, and councillor presiding.

Central + New Delhi District (July 6, 2012)

- Bhagidari meeting of a zonal area should be held at least once every month along with officials and local councillors.
- Senior Citizen Club should be started for central zone immediately and participation of senior citizen should be encouraged. Meetings of senior citizens of the area should be organized.
- There should be positive attitude between RWAs and departments.
- Time-bound program should be there for the work to be done.
- Problem-based Bhagidari workshop may be organized.
- Drop boxes may be installed at prominent places for larger effect/ impact.
- A monthly meeting of Bhagidari should be conducted at the district level comprising all concerned bodies and department to solve their problems/issues.
- Monitoring mechanism for evaluation of progress achieved is needed.
- Monthly meeting (Bhagidari) should be conducted at regular interval and with the participation of all stakeholders.
- Emphasis should be given on promoting intra- and inter-departmental cooperation/Bhagidari with public participation encouragement.
- Frequency of Bhagidari should be increased and every meeting should have Action Taken Report before the proceeding of next meeting.
- Officials having decision-making power should be called in the meeting.
- For effectiveness of Bhagidari government officers should be held responsible for the implementation of decisions taken in Bhagidari meetings very strictly.
- Local MLAs MPs, legislative councillors should also be invited in Bhagidari workshops as they are closely in touch with area RWA's residents.
- Genuine points of RWA/MTA need to be screened by Bhagidari Cell before meetings with the respective departments.
- Regular interaction of RWA/MTA with department may be initiated through Bhagidari Cell.
- RWA and NGOs activity role in Bhagidari.
- Prompt action by the concerned department.
- Frequent Bhagidari workshops/meetings should be held.

- Interdepartment cooperation needs to be strengthened and accountability be fixed.
- Nodal officers of all departments must attend each workshop/ meetings.
- Funds allocated to MPs, MLAs, councillors for the welfare of people should be utilized in consultation with the RWAs of the area.
- Delhi Police to interact with RWAs frequently.
- Bhagidari workshops frequency should be faster.
- Coordination between the government and public should be neat and clean and it should be time-bound.
- Bhagidari workshop should be held in the district instead of Talkatora Stadium.
- CM should take meetings of each district directly along with ministers and high official of different departments for implementing improvement suggestion under Bhagidari.
- There is less coordination between several departments, due to this the completion of work takes so much time.
- Every officer of different departments should visit physically in the area to take necessary steps.
- Area-wise Bhagidari meeting should be held with all departments officials once in a month.
- Specialists persons who are working in different fields should also be invited in Bhagidari meetings.
- Separate district-wise Bhagidari Cell should be established with sufficient staff, infrastructure, and other facilities for maintaining the implementation of decision taken in Bhagidari workshops and it should be made accountable and responsible for implementation.
- Frequent meetings in the RWAs to invite their suggestions and to analyze the work done.
- Government officials should be accessible to Bhagidari members/ RWA officials and give due weightage to our reasonable suggestions for implementation.
- Officials of participating departments to ensure completion of work in stipulated and agreed timeframe, and inform completion.
- MLAs and councillors should consult RWAs for disposal of funds allotted to them.
- Officers of Delhi government should oversee the action on letters by RWAs and should be advised the action taken.
- Right now the channel between the citizen and government agency is RWA or citizen groups. To make this channel more

effective, we should have monthly meeting or fixed date between the RWAs and its area Municipal Corporation (councillor).

- The area problem raised with DC office by the RWA is not addressed in time. It takes a long time to solve the problem. It should be a time-bound program.
- Single agency to be nominated by state government like (presently DC) should deal with RWAs without any interference by any third agency or authority. Periodical regular meetings with concerned departments followed by minutes/Action Taken Report.
- Election and participation of women representation should increase in RWAs.
- Bhagidari workshop needed once in three months.
- Permanent Bhagidari Board with powers should be in place to monitor regular interaction and action taken/implementation of Bhagidari decisions.
- Effective communication, transparency and time-bound action system, and management training to Bhagidari Cell and RWAs for effective implementation.
- RWAs/MTAs be strengthened financially and empowered to give satisfaction certificate after execution of projects.
- Monitoring teams at district level to fix responsibilities over delay in execution of projects.
- Implementation of decisions taken in Bhagidari program in a time-bound manner.
- Bhagidari concept should be enacted into a law by Delhi government.
- Officers and nodal officer of government departments should meet MTAs/RWAs at office once a month.
- Time-bound action should strictly be followed.
- Periodical interaction with RWAs and departments of the Delhi government, each help to identify key area that needs attention and long-term measurements.
- Delhi government officers to take serious action of the RWA representatives' suggestion.
- SDM of area should have meetings every month with RWA representatives, listen to their problems, and take action immediately.
- Bhagidari should be a two-way communication with regular feedback and meetings.

The office of the CM would be analyzing and giving serious consideration to these suggestions and creating a plan on how to improve the effectiveness of Bhagidari (that is, citizens' partnership with government in the metropolis of Delhi) as an example of urban democracy at work across a whole city of 16 million people.

Source: RWA and MTA participants in eight one-day Bhagidari workshops conducted by ACORD, 2012, for Government of NCT of Delhi.

Appendix 11

Office of the Chief Minister, Delhi Government: The Bhagidari Teams of Civil Service Officers

S. No.	Name	Designation
		(January 2000–June 2001)
1	Shri S. Regunathan	Principal Secretary to CM
2	Ms Renu Sharma	Secretary to CM
3	Shri Ravinder Kumar	Superintendent
		Also associated were:
	Shri G.D. Badgaiyan	Secretary to CM (January–June 2000)
	Ms Rita Kumar	Additional Secretary to CM (June–October 2000)
	Shri Sanjiv Pandey	Deputy Secretary to CM (January–October 2000)
	Shri Rajesh Bhatia	Superintendent (January 2000–June 2001)
		(July 2001–October 2002)
1	Shri S. Regunathan	Principal Secretary to CM
2	Ms Renu Sharma	Secretary to CM
3	Shri Arun Mishra	Deputy Secretary
4	Shri Ravinder Kumar	Superintendent

Appendix 11 continued

Appendix 11 continued

S. No.	Name	Designation
(November 2002–December 2003)		
1	Shri S. Regunathan	Principal Secretary to CM
2	Ms Renu Sharma	Secretary to CM
3	Shri Arun Mishra	Deputy Secretary
4	Shri Ravinder Kumar	Superintendent
(January 2004–March 2005)		
1	Shri S. Regunathan	Principal Secretary to CM
2	Ms Renu Sharma	Secretary to CM
3	Shri Arun Mishra	Deputy Secretary
4	Shri Ravinder Kumar	Superintendent
(April 2005–March 2006)		
1	Ms Renu Sharma	Secretary to CM
2	Shri Kulanand Joshi	Deputy Secretary
3	Shri Surinder Sharma	Superintendent
(April 2006–March 2008)		
1	Shri P. K. Tripathi	Principal Secretary to CM
2	Shri S. S. Yadav	Special Secretary to CM (April 1, 2006–June 27, 2007)
3	Shri Keshav Chandra	Special Secretary to CM (June 28, 2007–March 3, 2008)
4	Shri Kulanand Joshi	Joint Secretary to CM
5	Shri Surinder Sharma	Superintendent
6	Shri Manoj Jain	Superintendent
(April 2008–March 2010)		
1	Shri P. K. Tripathi	Principal Secretary to CM
2	Shri Keshav Chandra	Special Secretary to CM
3	Shri Kulanand Joshi	Joint/Additional Secretary to CM
4	Shri Manoj Jain	Superintendent
5	Shri Muzaffar Imtiaz	Superintendent ("Bhagidari")
(April 2010–March 2012)		
1	Shri P. K. Tripathi	Principal Secretary to CM (up to March 2011)

S. No.	Name	Designation
2	Dr M. M. Kutty	Principal Secretary to CM (from April 2011)
3	Shri Keshav Chandra	Special Secretary to CM
4	Shri Santosh Vaidya	Special Secretary to CM
5	Shri Kulanand Joshi	Additional Secretary to CM
6	Shri Manoj Jain	Deputy Secretary
7	Shri Muzaffar Imtiaz	Superintendent (Bhagidari)

Source: Working reports on Bhagidari by the Bhagidari Cell, Government of NCT of Delhi.

Bibliography

Ackoff, Russell. 1974. *Redesigning the Future: The Systems Approach to Societal Problems.* NY: Wiley.

ACORD. 2012. *Suggestions and Inputs by the Citizens* (ACORD's Reports on 8 Bhagidari Workshops). Submitted to Government of NCT of Delhi.

Agazarian, Yvonne M. & Janoff Sandra. 1993. "Systems Theory in Small Groups." In H. Kaplan and B. Sadock (eds), *Comprehensive Textbook of Group Psychotherapy.* Baltimore: Williams & Wilkins.

Antonakis, J., Cianciolo, A. T., & R. J. Sternberg (eds). 2004. *The Nature Of Leadership.* Thousand Oaks, CA: Sage.

Argyris, C. 1977. "Double Loop Learning in Organisations." *Harvard Business Review,* 55 (September–October): 115–125. Boston: President and Fellows of Harvard College.

Asch, Solomon. 1952. *Social Psychology.* New York: Prentice-Hall.

Banfield, Edward C. 1961. *Political Influence.* New York: The Free Press.

Bass, B.M. 1990a. *Bass & Stogdill's Handbook of Leadership: Theory, Research, and Managerial Applications* (3rd edn). New York: Macmillan.

Bass, B.M. 1990b. "From transactional to transformational leadership: Learning to share the vision." *Organizational Dynamics,* 18(3): 19–31.

Bertalanffy, Ludwig von. 1952. *General Systems Theory.* New York: Wiley.

Bion, Wilfred. 1961. *Experiences in Groups.* London: Tavistock.

Blau, Peter M. 1964. *Exchange and Power in Social Life.* New York: John Wiley and Sons, Inc.

Bunker, B.B., & B. T. Alban. 1992. What Makes Large Group Effective Interventions? *Journal of Applied Behavioral Science,* 28 (4, Special Issue: *Large Group Interventions*): 579–591.

———. 1997. *Large Group Interventions: Engaging the Whole System for Rapid Change.* San Francisco: Jossey-Bass.

Burns, J.M. 1978. *Leadership.* New York: Harper & Row.

Buzan, Tony. 1976. *Use Both Sides of Your Brain.* New York: Dutton.

Choi, S. 2007. "Democratic Leadership: the Lessons of Exemplary Models for Democratic Governance." *International Journal of Leadership Studies,* 2(3): 243–262.

Dahl, Robert A. 1961. *Who Governs?* New Haven: Yale University Press.

Delhi Government Brochure "Bhagidari": Citizen-Government Partnership, Delhi Smiles—"Awards and Citations".

Department of Education. *Analysis of CBSE Results 2012 Class X* (p. 6). Available at: http://edudel.nic.in/Result_Analysis/2012/ResultCBSE10th2012.pdf

———. *Analysis of CBSE Results 2012 Class XII* (p. 4). Available at: http://edudel. nic.in/Result_Analysis/2012/ResultCBSE12th2012.pdf

———. Government of Delhi. *A Quick Report 2008—Results of Class X and XII At a Glance over the Last 10 Years* (Table 7). Available at: http://edudel.nic.in/ quick_report_2008/6-20.pdf

Department of Environment. Available at: http://www.delhi.gov.in/wps/wcm/connect/environment/Environment/Home/Campaign.

Dewey, J. 1926. *The Public And Its Problems*. New York: Henry Holt.

Diamond, L.J. 1999. *Developing Democracy: Toward Consolidation*. Baltimore: Johns Hopkins University Press.

Diamond, L.J. 2008. *The Spirit of Democracy: The Struggle to Build Free Societies Throughout the World*. New York: Times Books.

Diamond, L.J., & M.E. Piattsner (eds). 2001. *The Global Divergence of Democracies*. Baltimore: Johns Hopkins University Press.

Economist Intelligence Unit. *Delhi most competitive city in India*. EIU report, *Times of India*, June 24, 2012.

Emery, Fred E. 1989. *Toward Real Democracy*. Toronto: Ontario Quality of Working Life Centre.

Emery, Fred E. & Eric L. Trist. 1973. *Toward a Social Ecology*. New York: Plenum.

Emery, Merrelyn (ed.). 1993. *Participative Design for Participative Democracy* (revised). Canberra: Centre for Continuing Education, Australian National University.

Fiedler, Fred E. 1967. *A Theory of Leadership Effectiveness*, New York: McGraw-Hill.

Forest Survey of India. 2009. *India State of Forest Report 2009*. Ministry of Environment & Forests, Government of India.

Fritz, Robert. 1989. *The Path of Least Resistance*. New York: Fawcett Columbine.

Gouldner, A.W. (ed.). 1950. *Studies in Leadership: Leadership and Democratic Action*. New York: Russell & Russell.

Government of NCT. 2000/2001. *"Bhagidari"—The Citizen-Government Partnership (Phase I): January 2000 to June 2001*. Working Report. Department of Administrative Reforms, Ministry of Personnel, Pension & Public Grievances, Government of India.

———. 2001/2002. *"Bhagidari"—The Citizen-Government Partnership (Phase II): July 2001 to October 2002*. Working Report. Department of Administrative Reforms, Ministry of Personnel, Pension & Public Grievances, Government of India.

———. 2002/2003. *"Bhagidari"—The Citizen-Government Partnership (Phase III): November 2002 to December 2003*. Working Report. Department of Administrative Reforms, Ministry of Personnel, Pension & Public Grievances, Government of India.

Government of NCT. 2004/2005. *"Bhagidari"—The Citizen-Government Partnership (Phase IV): January 2004 to March 2005.* Working Report. Department of Administrative Reforms, Ministry of Personnel, Pension & Public Grievances, Government of India.

————. 2005/2006. *"Bhagidari"—The Citizen-Government Partnership (Phase V): April 2005 to March 2006.* Working Report. Department of Administrative Reforms, Ministry of Personnel, Pension & Public Grievances, Government of India.

————. 2006/2008. *"Bhagidari"—The Citizen-Government Partnership (Phase VI): April 2006 to March 2008.* Working Report. Department of Administrative Reforms, Ministry of Personnel, Pension & Public Grievances, Government of India.

————. 2011. "Working Report 2011." Directorate of Information and Publicity, Government of NCT, Delhi. Available at: www.publicity.delhigovt.nic.in

Grint, K. (ed.). 1997. *Leadership: Classical, Contemporary, and Critical Approaches.* New York: Oxford University Press.

Jacobs, Robert J. 1994. *Real Time Strategic Change.* San Francisco: Berrett Koehler.

Kanter, Rosabeth. 1984. *The Change Masters.* New York: Simon and Schuster.

Kotter, John P. & Paul Lawrence. 1974. *Mayors in Action.* New York: John Wiley.

Kreeger, L. 1975. *The Large Group: Dynamics & Therapy.* London: Constable.

Lewin, K. 1950. *The Consequences of an Authoritarian and Democratic Leadership.* In A.W. Gouldner (ed.), *Studies in Leadership: Leadership and Democratic Action* (pp. 409–417). New York: Russell & Russell.

Lewin, Kurt. 1948. *Resolving Social Conflicts* (edited by Gertude W. Lewin). New York: Harper & Row.

Lewin, Kurt. 1951. *Field Theory in Social Science.* New York: Harper Collins.

Lijphart, A. 1999. *Patterns of Democracy: Government Forms and Performance in Thirty-six Countries.* New Haven, CT: Yale University Press.

Lippitt, R. 1983. "Future Before You Plan." In R.A. Ritvo and A.G. Sargent (eds), *The NTL Managers' Handbook* (p. 7). Arlington, VA: NTL Institute.

Lorsch, Jay and Steven A. Allen. 1973. *Managing Diversity and Inter-dependence.* Cambridge, MA: Harvard University Press.

Luke, J.S. 1998. *Catalytic leadership: Strategies for an Interconnected World.* San Francisco: Jossey-Bass.

Marrow, A.J. 1969. *The Practical Theorist.* New York: Basic Books.

McClelland, David C. 1970. "The Two Faces of Power." *Journal of International Affairs,* 24 (1): 29–47.

McClelland, David C. 1975. *Power: The Inner Experience.* New York: Irvington Publishers.

Ministry of Home Affairs. *Census 2011—Delhi Per Capita Income.* Government of India.

Morley, D., Proud foot, S., & T. Burns. 1980. *Making Cities Work.* London: Croom Helm Ltd.

Mughan, A., & S.C. Patterson. 1992. *Political Leadership in Democratic Societies.* Chicago: Nelson-Hall.

Planning Department. Available at: http://delhi.gov.in/wps/wcm/connect/ DoIT_
Planning/Planning/our+services/budget+of+delhi

Population India, Map of Delhi. Available at: http://populationindia.files.
wordpress.com/2011/05/population-of-delhi-2011-map.jpg

Salancik, G. and J. Pfeffer. 1977. "Who Gets Power and How They Hold On To
It: A Strategic Contingency Model of Power." *Organisational Dynamics*, Winter
5 (3): 3–21.

Schindler-Rainman, Eva and Ronald Lippitt. 1980. *Building the Collaborative
Community: Mobilizing Citizens for Action* Irvine: University of California.

Singh, Mahendra Kumar. 2012. "With 13.1% Growth, Bihar Tops States; Delhi
Second." *Times of India*, June 2.

Waterman, R.H., Jr. 1987. *The Renewal Factor*. New York: Bantam.

Weisbord, Marvin R. 1987. "Productive Workplaces: Organising and Managing
for Dignity, Meaning and Community" (Chapter 14). In *Future Search*. San
Francisco: Jossey-Bass.

Weisbord, Marvin R. & 35 coauthors. 1992. *Discovering Common Ground*. San
Francisco: Berrett-Koehler.

Weisbord, Marvin R. & Sandra Janoff. 1995. *Future Search: An Action Guide to
Finding Common Ground in Organisations and Communities*. San Francisco:
Berrett-Koehler.

Wheatley, Margaret J. 1992. *Leadership and the New Science*. San Francisco:
Berrett-Koehler.

Wilber, Ken. 1985. *No Boundary: Eastern and Western Approaches to Personal
Growth*. Boston & London: Shambhala.

Wright, Susan and David Morely (eds). 1989. *Learning Works: Searching for
Organisational Futures: A Tribute to Eric Trist*. M3JIP3, Faculty of Environmental
Studies, York University, Toronto, Ontario, Canada.

Index

About the Authors

George Koreth has been interested in valid and reliable measurement in the social sciences and behavioral sciences, in order to improve organization effectiveness and results. During his career in management of industry, he explored the measurement of responsibility based on the methods developed at the Tavistock Institute, UK. Subsequently, he went deep into reliable instruments and methods of measuring and enhancing human motivation (achievement, power, affiliation, and security motivation) based on Dr David McClelland's work at Harvard University. Midway through his industry career, he moved to teaching and research in management as a professor at the Shri Ram Centre for Human Resources, New Delhi, and was, subsequently, a visiting faculty at Faculty of Management Studies (FMS), Delhi University. He has been the University Grants Commission's visiting professor in the social sciences faculty of a central university in New Delhi (2009–2010). On returning to industry, he held senior responsibilities in the HCL Group, including that of HR director and CEO, and was senior vice president (global HR & OD) in Ranbaxy Laboratories Ltd. Since 1997, he is a consultant to companies on performance improvement through measurable results and an adviser to government organizations on rapid and sustainable change, through multistakeholder participatory processes.

He is currently advising the Government of Delhi, India, on building and sustaining "a citywide citizens' partnership in good governance."

His authored books include *Developing Effective Organizations* (with Nitish De, Abad Ahmad, and B.M. Kapur, 1980), *We: The People of India* (coauthored by Kiron Wadhera, 2003), and *Empowering Rural Women: Micro-enterprise through Achievement Motivation*, published by SAGE (coauthored by Kiron Wadhera, 2012).

Kiron Wadhera has held various senior responsibilities with the Asian Centre for Organization Research and Development (ACORD), New Delhi, including that of president and CEO. She was a member of the program faculty at the International Youth Centre (Vishwa Yuvak Kendra), New Delhi. She was a visiting faculty for two years for the post-graduate course in communication at Jamia Millia Islamia, New Delhi. She was also a member of the NGO Prerna and chairperson of Prerna-CEDPA for two years. She has been a member of the Fulbright Alumni Association and a fellow of the UN.

Dr Wadhera has extensive experience in organization development, experiential training, survey research, communication, and management of socioeconomic field projects. Her areas of expertise include motivation and leadership training; designing, organizing; and conducting research studies and surveys, both quantitative and qualitative; mass communication; counseling and guidance; personal growth and personality development.

She is currently a consultant to the Government of Delhi, India, on developing citizens' partnership with the government on "a citywide" basis.

The published works of Dr Wadhera include *The New Bread Winners: A Study on the Situations of Young Working Women* (1976), *Case Study—A Method of Training* (1977), *Training Manual in Helping Professions* (1982), *We: The People of India* (coauthored by George Koreth, 2003), and *Empowering Rural Women: Micro-enterprise through Achievement Motivation*, published by SAGE (coauthored by George Koreth, 2012).